ANNUALS
AND BIENNIALS

ANNUALS AND BIENNIALS

ROGER PHILLIPS & MARTYN RIX

Assisted by James Compton & Alison Rix
Layout by Jill Bryan

MACMILLAN

Acknowledgements

We would like to thank James Compton for writing the *Labiatae*, Chris Grey-Wilson for his help with *Impatiens* and Michael and Lois Warren (Photos Horticultural Picture Library) for the photograph of *Primula sinensis*.

Most of the specimens were photographed in the studio, and the photographs of cultivated plants came from the following gardens; we should like to acknowledge the generous help we have had from their staff:
The Crown Estate Commissioners at the Savill Gardens, Windsor Great Park; The Royal Horticultural Society's Gardens, Wisley; The Royal Horticultural Society's Gardens, Rosemoor; The Theodore Payne Foundation, Sun Valley, California; The Royal Botanic Gardens, Kew; The Royal Botanic Garden, Edinburgh; Ventnor Botanic Garden, Isle of Wight; Hanshow Botanical Garden, China; the University Botanic Garden, Cambridge; the Chelsea Physic Garden, London; The National Botanic Gardens, Kirstenbosch; the Karroo Botanical Garden, Worcester; Glenlyon, Nieuwoudtville; Padstal Farm, Nieuwoudtville; Longwood Gardens, Pennsylvania; Huntington Gardens, San Merino, California; Santa Barbara Botanic Garden; Monet's garden at Giverny; Leiden Botanical Garden; Berkeley Botanical Garden, California; Chateau de Hex, Belgium; Eccleston Square Garden, London; The Dower House, Boughton House, Northamptonshire; Cockermouth Castle, Cumbria; Levens Hall, Cumbria; Glenbervie, Grampian; Cluny, Perthshire; Littlewood Park, Aberdeenshire; Le Clos du Peyronnet, Menton; Tresco Abbey Gardens, Isles of Scilly; Cothay Manor, Somerset; and Tapely Park, Devon.

Photos were also taken at the trial grounds of the following seed suppliers: Colegrave Seeds, Kees Sahin, Suttons, Thompson and Morgan, Unwins.

Among others who have helped in one way or another we would like to thank:
Lieve Adriaensens, Igor Belolipov, Alan Bloom, John Bond, Chris Brickell, Sheila Bryan, John Coke, Tania Compton, Brandy Cravens, Debby Curry; John d'Arcy, Ghislain and Stephanie d'Ursel, Pamela Egremont, Valerie Finnis, Nicky Foy, Candida Frith-Macdonald, George Fuller, Jim Gardiner, Geoffrey and Katie Goatcher, François Goffinet, Tony Hall, Harry and Yvonne Hay, Tinge Horsfall, Barbara and Peter Knox-Shaw; Jonathan Lloyd, George and Loveday Llewellyn, Roger Macfarlane, Neil and Neva MacGregor; Deborah Maclean, Richard Manson, Mike Nelhams, Mikinori Ogisu, Terrence Read, Anthony Rix, Richard Rix, Alastair and Mary-Anne Robb, Lesley Sleigh, Jimmy and Margaret Smart, Gill Stokoe, Elizabeth Strangman, Leigh Walker, William Waterfield and Derry Watkins.

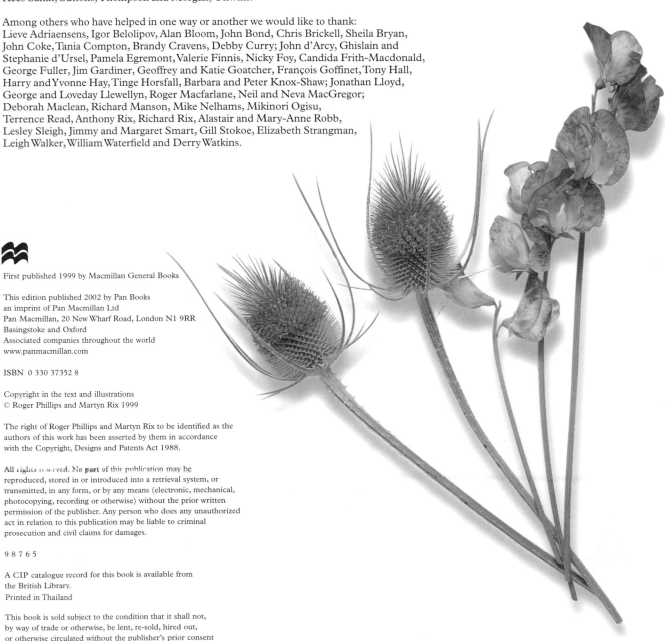

First published 1999 by Macmillan General Books

This edition published 2002 by Pan Books
an imprint of Pan Macmillan Ltd
Pan Macmillan, 20 New Wharf Road, London N1 9RR
Basingstoke and Oxford
Associated companies throughout the world
www.panmacmillan.com

ISBN 0 330 37352 8

Copyright in the text and illustrations
© Roger Phillips and Martyn Rix 1999

The right of Roger Phillips and Martyn Rix to be identified as the authors of this work has been asserted by them in accordance with the Copyright, Designs and Patents Act 1988.

9 8 7 6 5

A CIP catalogue record for this book is available from the British Library.
Printed in Thailand

Contents

Introduction

In this book we illustrate over one thousand annuals, biennials and short-lived perennials suitable for gardens in temperate climates. Many will also do well in the hills in the tropics. Annuals are plants which germinate, flower, set seed and die, all within a single year. Biennials germinate one year and usually flower the following year, after spending a dormant winter. We have also included some plants which, although perennial, are nearly always treated as annuals.

As all the energy of an annual is put into seed production for following generations, the removal of faded flowers before they set seed will promote a much longer flowering period. This is well-known in the case of sweet peas or pansies, but it holds for most other annuals as well. Biennials may also persist for a second flowering if dead-headed regularly.

Depending on the climate where they are found in the wild, some annuals germinate in cool temperatures and grow through the winter to flower in spring; others wait for the warmth and wet of summer before they germinate, and then grow quickly to flower in late summer. Most, however, are easy, and germinate as soon as they are sown. Their original habitats, their countries of origin and their needs in the garden are covered in the following pages.

The Photographs

The majority of pictures in this book were taken by the authors on Ektachrome 64 professional film, that used for the field shots being pushed one stop in development. Several different exposures are taken of each shot, one as indicated by the camera's exposure meter, the others half or one stop above or below those indicated. On an automatic camera the same effect may be achieved by altering the film speed indicator.

Californian annuals in the wild near Oak Grove, Palomar, including lupins, *Eschscholzia*, *Oenothera*, and the white, forget-me-not-like *Cryptantha*

The studio shots are taken on a Hasselblad 500 C/M with a normal lens and a studio flash as a light source. The field shots are taken with a Nikon FM and a variety of lenses, using natural light.

When shooting flowers in the garden or in the wild, it is preferable to work with a tripod, so that you can take advantage of the opportunity to use a slow shutter speed and therefore a smaller aperture, giving a greater depth of focus. In practice, the best speed to use is 1/15th sec., although if there is a wind you may have to go to 1/30th or even 1/60th. In bright light conditions, the camera can be hand-held with the speed set at 1/60th sec.

The Order

The plants are arranged in families and the families in a traditional botanical order, beginning with the *Ranunculaceae* and ending with the daisy family and the monocotyledons, i.e. the grasses. This is generally the same order that was used in Perennials, though in that case the plants were also divided by flowering time. The order follows a handy little book by Davis and Cullen, *The Identification of Flowering Plant Families* (1965).

The Names

The Latin names generally follow those used in the most recent floras, as *The RHS Plant Finder,* which has established itself as the most accurate and up-to-date list of names of cultivated plants readily available, does not cover annuals. The Latin name is put in bold italics, and is followed by the name of its author, usually abbreviated, e.g. L. for Carolus Linnaeus, the names of whose *Species Plantarum*, published in 1753, form the starting point of botanical names.

The English name follows the author, and is in bold type, without inverted commas, when it refers to the whole species. When the English name is a cultivar, rather than a common name, it is also in bold, but is within single inverted commas.

Cultivar names of annuals are difficult to use with any degree of certainty. There are several sources of difficulty.

Old cultivars may continue to be grown for many years under the same name, though selection during this time may cause the plant grown to change. This genetic drift has been studied in wild annuals, notably by A. Strid using *Nigella arvensis* in the Greek islands. This is the reason why, in trials, different sources of seed of the same cultivar may perform differently.

New names may be attached to plants that are very like old cultivars; it is difficult to check this without comparison of old and new dried specimens, or specimens grown from old seed taken from a seed bank.

Echium lusitanicum subsp. *polycaulon* and other annuals by a ruined adobe dovecote, near Salamanca in western Spain

A curved mixed border of annuals, edged with box

Cultivar names are also sometimes attached to seed that is identical to the wild form, possibly because the seed may sell better with a cultivar name attached. However, over many generations of cultivation, the wild plant may change, so that a cultivar name is justified. Many current cultivars with different names are so similar to one another as to be virtually indistinguishable, and so the accurate identification of an unknown specimen is almost impossible.

F_1 hybrid seed should be the most reliable as to name, since it is produced by the crossing, often by hand, of two self-fertile strains.

The Text

The text begins with a brief description of each plant and its most important characteristics, followed by the country of origin, habitat and flowering time in the wild. This is intended to help travellers who may want to see the flowers in the wild, and gardeners who can use the information to grow a relatively unknown plant better in their own climate. Remember that in the southern hemisphere the seasons are reversed, so spring flowering is in July–September, and we have put the actual months of flowering in the text in almost all cases. The text continues with brief measurements of the important parts of the plant, and finally a sentence on cultivation, possible use in the garden or any other point of general interest. Closely related species are often covered here. Measurements are given in metres, centimetres and millimetres; as a guide 1m equals around 3 feet, and 2.5cm equals an inch.

Hardiness

As annuals are not generally grown over winter, their hardiness is not significant. The four main groups are winter, spring and summer annuals, and biennials. Those which germinate in autumn and grow through the winter are considered winter annuals; they mostly come from Mediterranean climates and will survive around −5°C, if they are not too wet at the root. They flower in spring. Spring annuals germinate as the soil warms in spring; they grow and flower quickly, usually in the early summer. Summer annuals germinate in hot, moist conditions and flower in late summer and autumn. They usually originate in summer rainfall, subtropical areas, such as Mexico, and are often called "half-hardy", though they are killed by the first significant frost.

Biennials germinate in spring or summer, and grow through one summer before flowering the next. Sometimes several years of growth are needed to build the plant up to flowering strength, and then the plants are called monocarpic or once-flowering perennials. Their hardiness varies greatly depending on the climate in their country of origin, and the conditions in which they are grown. Good drainage and a rather dry winter aid the survival of most that are on the borderline of hardiness.

Orange cosmos and wild sunflowers in full flower in mid-October along a roadside near Volcan Tequila, Mexico, with the blue fields of agaves, grown for the production of tequila, in the background

The Main Wild Localities of Annuals and Biennials

Annuals, like bulbs, are especially well-developed in semi-desert climates, where they survive a hot or warm, dry season as seed. The five main areas of winter-rainfall climate mentioned below have floras exceptionally rich in species, and are the homes of most annuals. Winter and spring annuals growing in these Mediterranean-type climates spend the hot, dry summers as dormant seed.

Summer-rainfall areas are also rich, especially where they are adjacent to deserts or Mediterranean-type climates, as in Mexico or parts of South America, but these do not have the exceptional diversity of the winter-rainfall areas. Most are summer annuals, and spend the dry winter and spring as dormant seeds.

Biennials are commonest in areas with a preponderance of perennials; they often grow in open woods and need an extra growing season to reach sufficient size to flower.

WINTER RAINFALL AREAS

1. **California and Baja California** The western Californian landscape consists of dry, rolling hills between the sea and the Sierra Nevada mountains. This is a Mediterranean-type climate, in some places covered with evergreen scrub, in others with grassland and annuals, sometimes beneath widely spaced oak trees. The coastal hills are cooled in summer by fog from the sea. Inland of the Sierra are the deserts of Arizona and eastern California. Sheets of annuals in spring are a feature throughout the area, and especially after fires or in the lower parts of the deserts after sufficient winter and spring rain. Miniature purple monkeyflowers, white evening primroses and magenta sand verbenas often carpet the ground for a few weeks. Important garden annuals originating in California include *Clarkia*, *Phacelia*, *Eschscholzia*, *Limnanthes*, *Nemophila* and many others.

2. **Chile and South America** The Mediterranean-type climate in Chile is confined to quite a small area between Santiago and the Atacama desert, as that in California is confined to quite a narrow coastal strip between the mountains and the sea. The Valparaiso area has chaparral-like scrub gradually turning to desert. Some of the best sites are oases in the desert, with almost no real rainfall, but fed by winter mists and fog from the sea. Areas suitable for annuals are found elsewhere in South America, but in nothing like the concentrations found in Chile. South America is the home of familiar annuals such as *Calceolaria*, *Mimulus*, *Salpiglossis*, *Schizanthus* and *Nicotiana*.

Trachymene, after a fire, in the poor sandy soils of Western Australia, in December

3. **Mediterranean basin**   The whole coastline of the Mediterranean sea has the typical summer-dry climate, mainly between the sea and the mountains, as in the south of France and Turkey, but between the sea and the desert in much of North Africa. Typical scenery consists of rolling hills covered in low scrub, here called maquis or garrigue, of *Cistus*, rosemary, lavender, oleander and evergreen oaks. Annuals originating in this area spread northwards and eastwards with early agriculture, and are now found as weeds throughout Europe and much of Asia, and in other wheat-growing areas of the world. Poppies, corncockles and cornflowers are among the arable weeds which have become common garden plants. Other familiar annuals from the Mediterranean basin include sweet peas, marigolds, annual *Convolvulus*, *Limonium sinuatum*, and larkspur.

4. **South Africa**   The winter-rainfall area of Cape Province is one of the richest areas for plants in the whole world, and is famous for its displays of spring annuals. Whole valleys filled with orange, red, yellow and blue daisies are a feature of the area. The winter-rainfall area stretches from the mouth of the Orange River in the north-west to the Cape Peninsula and from there along the coast eastwards to Port Elizabeth. Annuals are most prolific in the semi-desert area known as Namaqualand, which extends roughly from Vanrhynsdorp to the Orange River, and there is a remarkable concentration of annuals and bulbs around the small town of Nieuwoudtville on the edge of the Bokkeveld plateau.

    The most familiar garden annuals which originate in the Cape are *Osteospermum*, *Gazania*, *Heliophila*, *Lobelia erinus* and various species of mesembryanthemum.

5. **Southern and Western Australia**   Though Australia has a very rich flora, comparable with that of South Africa, most of the large genera are of shrubs, and there are comparatively few annuals or bulbs. Annuals that have become popular in cultivation include *Trachymene coerulea*, *Lobelia rhytidosperma*, and *Brachyscome*, *Rhodanthe*, *Bracteantha*, and other *Helichrysum*-like daisies.

SUMMER RAINFALL AREAS

6. **Texas, and the Gulf coast**   The southeastern states of the USA have frequent cold spells in winter and hot, humid summers. Of the annuals that come from this area, *Phlox drummondii* is probably the most commonly cultivated, *Eustoma* originated here and the blue lupins, *Lupinus subcarnosus* and *L. texensis* can produce a good show of colour in the wild. Many of these germinate in spring.

7. **Mexico and Central America**   The great diversity of climate and topography in this area means that the flora is very rich and annuals are well represented. The flora contains both temperate and tropical elements. Most of Mexico has rather dry, cold winters and warm, dry springs, followed by hot, wet summers. Numerous familiar garden plants originated in Mexico, not least because the pre-Columbian inhabitants were themselves great gardeners. *Cosmos*, *Zinnia*, *Cuphea*, *Salvia*, *Verbena* and *Tagetes* are common annuals originating in Mexico, as well as dahlias, poinsettias, and numerous vegetables like maize, runner beans and pumpkins, which came to Europe from here.

8. **China and Himalayan foothills**   The monsoon climate of Asia reaches from Taiwan across China into northern India and Kashmir. Winters are dry, and minimum temperature depends mainly on altitude. Summers are wet; in the mountains they are cool too, because of the cloud and, in places, almost continuous rain brought by the monsoon. Numerous garden annuals have originated in this area, some of them developed by the Chinese in ancient times; aster (*Callistephus chinensis*), *Dianthus chinensis*, several *Impatiens*, and *Primula obconica*, *P. malacoides* and *P. sinensis* are all native of this area.

Osteospermum pinnatum in the bush near Springbok, Western Cape

Impatiens delavayi in mossy mountain woods near Lijiang, in September

Annual bedding at Wisley, with *Nicotiana*, *Cleome*, zonal pelargoniums and *Cineraria maritima*

The Uses of Annuals in the Garden

Annuals tend to be looked down on by many gardeners as being shapeless, lacking in form, and brash in colour. In short, they are thought of as not suitable for the refined garden, as well as being a lot of trouble. There is some truth in this, and there are several reasons for it, but there are also many beautiful annuals, with elegance and subtle colours which will satisfy the most discerning gardener.

Modern annual cultivars tend to be lower, stockier and brighter than their wild relatives, the flowers rounder or double, the colours more garish, the plants all uniform in height. Part of the reason for this is that annuals are tested in patches in open fields, which bear little resemblance to normal garden conditions; in trials fields, those with taller, more graceful stems tend to blow over, and the more subtle colours look dull beside their neighbours.

Thus the modern cultivars have all the characteristics *not* wanted by the gardener who is looking for a more natural effect. Another factor is that the breeders are looking not to the amateur market, but to local authorities and corporations who will buy large numbers of seeds for municipal plantings. This is the market for the brightest, most uniform orange French marigolds, the largest petunias, the stockiest flowering tobaccos. In the amateur's garden these make a splash of colour, but tend to get mildew in wet summers and in the sheltered, partly shady confines of dense planting.

In the wild, annuals are found mostly in cornfields planted with wheat, rye or barley, in open valleys and on gentle slopes in semi-desert areas, which, if too dry to cultivate, may be a wonderful sight with sheets and splashes of different colours for a short season. Most are plants of open habitats, and few are found closely packed in with shrubs or other plants, even in dry climates. In Mediterranean areas, they may grow between scattered shrubs such as *Cistus* and low oaks, and in California among grasses between widely spaced oaks, so by their very nature they prefer an open, airy position, with little or no rain while they are in flower.

There are many ways of using annuals in the garden, and below are some ideas of their possibilities and their suitability for a particular type of garden.

1. **Formal Bedding**   This is seen best in public parks and other municipal plantings, though I know one or two cottage gardens which are planted out in this way every summer. The plants are put in a carefully designed pattern, often with contrasting shapes or colours, and fill the whole bed producing, as it were, a colourful carpet. This requires planning, a good standard of cultivation and the planting out of young plants raised in pots or as plugs. Often a spring planting includes pansies, wallflowers or forget-me-nots combined with tulips, and a summer planting some bright flowers offset by silver foliage. This is the large market that the seed companies aim to satisfy.

2. **Annual Bedding**   In this type of scheme, annuals are either sown direct or put out as young plants. The beds are completely filled with annuals, planted informally in blocks.

A scheme for double annual borders along a grass or gravel walk is shown in Gertrude Jekyll's 'Annuals and Biennials', first published by *Country Life* in 1916. The borders were 42m long, 3.6m wide, with elongated lozenges of each species. The taller plants, such as hollyhocks, foxgloves, sweet peas, opium poppies and *Impatiens glandulifera*, are at the back, low plants along the front. She described the colour scheme as "progressive harmonies –harmonies throughout being the guiding principle, contrasts the occasional exception". White recurs almost throughout the border, while at one end pale blue is dominant, with a little pink and yellow; the red-purples, reds and oranges without white are confined to the other end on one side, with purples, pinks and deep blues on the other.

It would be interesting to recreate a border of this type, and both practical and useful where old herbaceous borders are being completely replanted or ridded of ground elder or other perennial weeds. Perennial plantings of this type can usually be seen at The Royal Horticultural Society garden at Wisley in the summer.

3. **Annuals as Fillers**   This is how most annuals and biennials are used, and where they can be most effective in filling gaps at one season or another. Those which flower early, such as forget-me-nots, can accompany bulbs, or fill empty areas between late-flowering perennials. Those that flower late,

Meconopsis paniculata with other Himalayan plants in Devon

A few of Kees Sahin's experimental beds of annuals, in Holland

such as cosmos, can replace early-flowering perennials such as *Papaver orientale*, or aquilegias, which flower only once or become semi-dormant during late summer. The shade given by tall-growing annuals will be beneficial to many of these perennials which grow wild in open woods. In newly-planted areas of shrubs and perennials, annuals are useful to provide vitality and fill the ground in the first couple of years.

Many biennials are excellent for use as uprights among low shrubs, such as shrub roses; foxgloves are ideal for this, as are the forms of *Campanula pyramidalis*. Cleomes are another group of annuals that are good for giving height and interest in a late-summer border. *Meconopsis*, shown on pages 32–35, are ideal for planting between rhododendrons and azaleas

4. **Natural Planting** In a natural scheme, the intention is to create a planting that will appear natural and uncontrived, though it may in fact be carefully planned. One colour may be dominant, but is generally interspersed with another colour or several different colours, and the boundaries between one colour and another are never hard. I have tried to recreate this natural effect in the garden, and to do this have planted the varieties that are closest to the wild species or have a natural look to them, and to mix the plants as they might occur in nature.

Poppies, cornflowers, corn-cockle and *Nigella*, combined with some grasses, umbelliferae and white daisies, will make a fine scheme to recreate a neolithic Mediterranean cornfield.

White and pale orange *Osteospermum*, combined with blue *Heliophila* and *Felicia*, yellow *Nemesia* and yellow and white *Dorotheanthus* will recreate the sunny valleys of Namaqualand.

Californian annuals include the wonderful blue and purple *Phacelia* and the pale blue *Nemophila*, as well as the different colours of Californian poppies. Lupins, clarkias and white *Oenothera* complete a grouping which could occur in California.

Show beds of *Tagetes*, *Salvia* and *Pelargonium* at Colegrave Seeds

A mixed planting of easy annuals at Suttons Seeds, Torquay

Quick-flowering South African annuals, *Dimorphotheca*, blue *Nemesia* and *Heliophila*, sown together and flowering together

An informal mixed planting from plugs, at Quince House

Seedlings of Californian annuals in plug trays;
some are ready to be planted out

Seed Raising and Cultivation

Most annuals are very easy to raise from seed, and most seed packets show the optimum temperature for germination. Not many annuals require chilling (as do many hardy trees, shrubs and perennials). In general, the longer an annual has been in cultivation, the more regular and prompt will be its germination. Wild annuals depend on irregular germination, with a percentage of seeds surviving for several years in the ground until suitable conditions come again.

Temperatures In general, winter and spring annuals germinate while temperatures are low, and may become dormant at very high temperatures. They germinate best between 10°C and 15°C, temperatures which may be found in the open in autumn or spring.

Summer annuals and most of the so-called half-hardy annuals require higher temperatures, between 20°C and 27°C. Except in the tropics, therefore, these are best planted indoors in a heated greenhouse or propagator, and only put outside when the weather has warmed up.

Composts For most annuals, a peat-based compost is adequate, provided that care is taken that it becomes neither dry nor waterlogged. Composts containing both peat (or coir) and some sand are slightly easier to use. They soon lose all their nutrients, and after a few weeks any seedlings will need regular feeding. Loam-based seed composts hold nutrients better, and generally contain 2 parts loam, 1 part peat or sterilised leafmould, and 1 part sand. Annuals from South Africa and California, especially those which are most frequent after fires, benefit from 1 part burnt soil from a bonfire in the mix, in place of 1 part loam.

Annuals are rich feeders when young, and it is important to build up a strong plant before buds and flowers appear. A good, strong, young plant will have many more flowers and flower for much longer than one that is starved and springs up quickly to flowering.

Direct sowing Many annuals will do well if sown directly where they are to flower in early spring, or in autumn in Mediterranean climates. In these circumstances, however, they will have to compete on an equal footing with any weed seeds that may happen to be in the ground, and the weeds may well grow as fast as the desired annuals, if not faster. Any direct sowing should therefore be done only in very clean ground.

Sowing in modules By sowing seed into trays of modules one can easily control their spacing, and the young plants have a better chance of survival. Root disturbance when planting out is at a minimum. I have found this method very easy and effective, using trays 50cm × 30cm, containing 84 modules. Having so many modules to fill ensures that the seed is well-distributed. The young plants should be planted out before the leaves begin to overlap, but many smaller annuals will make good plants if allowed to root through into the ground or into a sand plunge.

Seed Saving With most annuals it is possible to save your own seed. Most annuals are self-pollinated and will come true from seed. The main limitations are the weather, which in wet, cool, northern summers may not be warm enough for seed to ripen properly. F_1 seed will not come true, and will be F_2 and therefore likely to produce variable offspring with the characters of the F_1 parents combined in different ways. Many F_1 hybrids may be triploid, or sterile for some other reason, so they flower longer, and do not set seed.

Seed should be collected and dried as soon as it is ripe, and then kept as cool and dry as possible. Long-lived seeds can be dried and stored for many years in a special container in the freezer. The drier the seeds and the colder they are stored, the longer they will survive. Air-dry seed has a moisture content of around 30%; 5% is the dryness to be aimed at. Drying can be either by artificial heat (for a day near the radiator, range, or on a storage heater, at a temperature not exceeding 35°C), or by the use of silica gel (putting the seed into a sealed container with the gel for a few days or more at room temperature) before storing the seed in a sealed box in the freezer.

Summer-flowering petunias planted out in the great parterre at Pitmedden, near Aberdeen

Put the dry seed into a warm, waterproof packet before cooling it. A little folder of foil is suitable to hold the dry seed in a box in the freezer. The box should also contain silica gel to maintain its dryness, and should be opened for as short a time as possible when seed is removed or added.

Even if long-term storage is not needed, it is beneficial to keep seed in paper packets in a fridge; the combination of drying and cold will keep them alive longer.

Seed can last many years under suitable conditions; e.g. at −18°C, with a 5% moisture content, half of a sample of barley seed should last for 13,000 years. Even under natural conditions, some *Magnolia kobus* seed in Japan is thought to have survived in wet peat for a few thousand years; seed of herbarium specimens of hare's foot clover were germinated after 65 years. In an experiment with buried seeds, 83% of black nightshade germinated after 39 years; this longevity is the source of the saying "one year's seeds, seven years weeds".

European cornfield annuals (and a stray cosmos), from a direct sowing

Bibliography

A handbook of Annuals and Bedding Plants by Graham Rice, Croom Helm and Timber Press 1986.

An Encyclopedia of Annual and Biennial Garden Plants by C.O. Booth, Faber & Faber 1958.

Annuals and Biennials by Gertrude Jekyll, Country Life 1916.

B & T World Seeds Sub-List -53 Bedding Plant Seed List B & T World Seeds, Paguignan, France 1998.

Garden Flowers from Seed by Christopher Lloyd and Graham Rice, Viking 1991.

The Ladies' Flower-Garden of Ornamental Annuals by Mrs Loudon, London 1840.

A page from *The Ladies' Flower-Garden of Ornamental Annuals* by Mrs Loudon. Jane Webb, (1807–1858), married John Claudius Loudon in 1830. He was 47; she was 23, and met him after he wrote a review of her clever novel, 'The Mummy', describing England in the 20thC., which he thought was written by a man. They worked together on botanical encyclopedias and other books on gardening, and both before and after his death she published many books under her own name, including a series on 'The Ladies' Flower-Garden'. The annuals volume is a very valuable source of illustrations of many familiar annuals in unimproved forms, and of many others now seldom or never seen in gardens.

Southern Africa

The Botany of the Southern Natal Drakensberg by O. M. Hilliard & B. L. Burtt, National Botanic Garden 1987.

Wild Flowers of Malawi by Audrey Moriarty, Purnell 1975.

Plants of the Cape Flora. A Descriptive Catalogue by Pauline Bond & Peter Goldblatt, Journ. of South African Botany suppl. vol. 13 (1984).

South African Wild Flower Guides Botanical Society of South Africa, in association with the the National Botanical Institute.

1. *Namaqualand* by Annelise Le Roux & Ted Schelpe; photography by Zelda Wahl, 1994.

5. *Hottentots Holland to Hermanus* by Lee Burman and Anne Bean; photography by Jose Burman, 1985.

7. *West Coast* by John Manning and Peter Goldblatt; photography by John Manning, 1996.

9. *Nieuwoudtville, Bokkeveld Plateau & Hantam* by John Manning and Peter Goldblatt 1997.

Australia

Encyclopaedia of Australian Plants by W. Rodger Elliott and David L. Jones, vols. 1–5, The Lothian Publishing Co. Pty. Ltd 1980–1990.

Flora of New South Wales ed. Gwen J. Harden, New South Wales University Press, 4 vols. 1990–93.

Wild Flowers of southern Western Australia by Margaret G. Corrick, Bruce A. Fuhrer ed. by Alexander S. George, Five Mile Press Pty Ltd. in association with Monash University 1997.

Europe, south-west Asia and Central Asia

New Flora of the British Isles by C. A. Stace, Cambridge University Press 2nd ed. 1997.

Flora Iberica vols. I–VIII Real Jardin Botanico, Madrid 1986- 97.

Flora Europaea by V. H. Heywood et al., Cambridge University Press 1964–80.

Flora of Turkey by P.H. Davis et al., Edinburgh University Press 1965–1987.

Pictorial Flora of Israel by Uzi Piltmann, Clara Heyn, Avinoam Danin and Avishai Shmida, Massada Ltd 1983.

Conspectus Florae Asiae Mediae by A.I.Vvedensky (ed.), Tashkent 1971 onwards.

Flowers of Greece and the Balkans by Oleg Polunin, Oxford University Press 1980.

Flowers of Southwest Europe by Oleg Polunin, Oxford University Press 1973.

Flore de la France by H. Coste, Paris 1901.

India, China and the Himalayas

Flowers of the Himalaya by Oleg Polunin & Adam Stainton, Oxford 984; and Supplement, Dehli 1990.

Flora of Bhutan by A. J. C. Grierson and D. G. Long, Royal Botanic Garden, Edinburgh 1983–94.

Travels in China by Roy Lancaster, Antique Collectors Club 1989.

Flora of Japan by J. Ohwi, Smithsonian, Washington 1965.

North America

Flora of North America north of Mexico ed. Flora of North America editorial committee Vols. 1–3, Oxford University Press 1993 onwards.

A California Flora and Supplement by Philip A. Munz, University of California Press 1973.

Arizona Flora by Thomas H. Kearney, Robert H. Peebles and collaborators, University of California Press 1951.

The Audubon Society Field Guide to Northern American Wild Flowers, western region by R. Spellenberg, Knopf, 1979.

Mexico

Flora of the Valley of Mexico by J. and G. Rzedowski 1985.

South America

Plant Hunters in the Andes by J. Harper Goodspeed, Robert Hale undated (around 1941).

References for Particular Genera

Cosmos, see Sherff in *Publications of the Field Museum of Natural History Botanical Series* VIII, 401–447 (1932).

Cuphea, see Engler, *Das Pflanzenreich*, IV, 216: 80–179 (1903).

Campanulas by Peter Lewis and Margaret Lynch.

Nigella arvensis, 'Biosystematics of the *Nigella arvensis* complex, with special reference to the problem of non-adaptive radiation' by Arne Strid, *Opera Botanica* no. 28 Lund 1970.

Phlox, 'The genus *Phlox*' by Edgar T. Wherry, Morris Arboretum Monograph, III, Philadelphia 1955.

Hardy geraniums by Peter Yeo, Croom Helm, Timber Press 1985.

Meconopsis by James S. L. Cobb, Christopher Helm 1989.

Saxifrages of Europe by D. A. Webb and R.J. Gornall, Christopher Helm 1989.

Seed Suppliers

Source Books

Andersen Horticultural Library's Source List of Plants and Seeds
University of Minnesota 1996. A source list of all seeds for
North America.

The Seed Search compiled, edited and published by Karen Platt
A source list of all seeds worldwide; over 43,000 seed entries
and addresses of over 100 suppliers.

Suppliers

B & T World Seeds, Rue des Marchands, Paguignan, 34210
Olonzac, France. Tel : (33) 4 68 91 29 63. Fax. 33 4 68 91 30 39
An excellent source of all seeds including many rare and new
annuals.

Chiltern Seeds Bortree Stile, Ulverston, Cumbria LA12 7PB
A long list of seeds of all kinds; many good annuals.

Colegrave Seeds Ltd., West Adderbury, Babury, Oxon. OX17
3EY. Tel. 01295 810632

Mr Fothergill's Seeds Kentford, Newmarket, Suffolk CB8 7QB

Plants of Distinction Abacus House, Station Yard, Needham
Market, Suffolk

K Sahin Zaden bv Loevestein 48, 2403 JB Alphen aan den Rijn,
Holland

Silene Bosstraat 128, 9255 Buggenhout, Belgium (32) 52 336404
Supplies many unusual annuals as small plants.

Silverhill Seeds P.O. Box 53108, Kenilworth, 7745 Cape Town,
South Africa. Tel. (27) 21 762 4245 fax (27) 21 797 6609
Specialises in seeds of South African plants of all kinds.

Southwestern Native Seeds Box 50503, Tucson, Arizona 85703
USA

Suttons Woodview Road, Paignton, Devon Tel 01803 696363

Thompson and Morgan, Poplar Lane, Ipswich, Suffolk IP8 3BU
Tel. 01473 680199

Theodore Payne Foundation, 10459 Tuxford Street, Sun Valley,
California 91352 Tel. (1) 818-768--1802

Unwins Seeds Ltd., Histon, Cambridge CB4 4ZZ
Tel. 01945 588 522

Glossary

Achene a small, dry, single-seeded fruit
Acuminate gradually tapering to an elongated point
Amplexicaul with the base of the leaf encircling the stem
Anther the part of the stamen that contains the pollen
Auricle, Auriculate small, ear-like projections at the leaf base
Axil the angle between the leaf stalk and the stem
Bract a modified leaf below a flower
Calyx the outer parts of a flower, usually green , formed by the often
fused sepals
Capitate head-like
Capsule a dry fruit containing seeds
Carpel the part of the flower that produces the seeds
Clavate shaped like a club, narrow at the base, swelling towards the
apex
Cleistogamous flowers that never open and are self-pollinated
Clone the vegetatively propagated progeny of a single plant
Corolla the inner parts of the flower, comprising the petals, usually
used when the petals are united into a tube
Crenate with shallow, rounded teeth
Cultivar a cultivated variety, denoted by a fancy name in inverted
commas, e.g. *Zinnia* 'Envy'
Cuneate wedge-shaped
Dehiscent opening to shed its seeds
Dentate with sharp, regular teeth
Diploid containing twice the basic number of chromosomes (the usual
complement)
Erose appearing as if gnawed
Exserted sticking out, usually of the style or stamens from the flower
Falcate sickle-shaped
-fid split, **bifid** or **2-fid** split in two, **trifid** or **3-fid** split in three
Filament that part of the stamen which supports the anther
Filiform thread-like
Floccose, Flocculose woolly

Forma, f. a minor variant, less different from the basic species than a
variety. Abbreviated to f.
Fynbos the South African name for the scrub found on hillsides in the
Cape region, a rich community of heathers, pelargoniums, proteas,
bulbs etc., subject to renewal by fire
Genome a group of genes, generally a group of chromosomes ·
belonging to an ancestral species
Genus a grouping of species, such as *Hibiscus*, *Fuchsia* or *Pelargonium*
Glabrous without hairs or glands
Glandular with glands, which are usually stalked, like hairs with a
sticky blob on the apex
Glaucous with a greyish colour or bloom, especially on the leaves
Globose more or less spherical
Glomerule small, crowded, rounded heads of flowers
Hispid coarsely and stiffly hairy
Hyaline transparent, often soft or papery
Hybrid the progeny of two different species
Inflorescence the flowers and flower stalks, especially when grouped
Keeled with a ridge along the lower side, like the keel of a boat
Laciniate deeply and irregularly toothed and divided into narrow lobes
Lanceolate shaped like a lance blade, widest below the middle, with a
tapering point
Lyrate leaf with a broad, but pointed apex and lobes becoming smaller
towards the leaf base
Meiosis cell division producing the halving of the number of
chromosomes during reproduction
-merous e.g. **5-merous** or **five-merous**, having parts in fives
Monocarpic usually dying after flowering and fruiting
Mucronate with a short sharp point
Nectary the part of the flower that produces nectar
Palmate with lobes or leaflets, spreading like the fingers of a hand
Panicle a branched raceme
Papillose with small, elongated projections
Pappus ring of fine hairs (parachute-like)
Pedicel the stalk of a flower
Peduncle the stalk of an inflorescence
Peloric regularity in a normally irregular flower
Peltate shaped like a round shield, with the stalk in the centre
Perfoliate a leaf joined right round the stem, thus looking as if pierced
by the stem
Phyllary an incurved, usually narrow bract, on the base of a daisy
flowerhead
Pilose hairy with long soft hairs
Puberulent with a fine but rather sparse covering of hairs
Pubescent with a fine coating of hairs, denser than **puberulent**
Raceme an inflorescence with the flowers on a central stem, oldest at
the base
Reticulate marked with a network, usually of veins
Rugose wrinkled
Saccate with a baggy pouch
Scarious dry and papery, usually also transparent
Seta, Setose bristle, bristly
Sinus, Sinuate a deep notch between two lobes, towards the centre of
a leaf
Species group of individuals, having common characteristics, distinct
from other groups; the basic unit of plant classification. Abbreviated to
sp. or **spp.** if plural
Spicate like a spike
Spinose with weak spines
Stigma the sticky part of the flower which receives the pollen
Stipule leafy lobes along or near the base of a leaf stalk, found
especially in roses
Style that part of the flower which carries the stigma
Suborbicular almost round, but usually slightly narrower
Subspecies a division of a species, with minor and not complete
differences from other subspecies, usually distinct either ecologically or
geographically. Abbreviated to **subsp.** or **subspp.** if plural
Succulent fleshy, storing water in the stems or leaves
Terete not ridged or grooved
Ternate in a group of three
Tetraploid with four times the basic number of chromosomes
Triploid with three times the basic number of chromosomes: these
plants are usually sterile, but robust growers and good garden plants
Tuberculate warty
Umbel an inflorescence in which the branches arise from a single
point, usually forming a flat or gently rounded top
Variety a group of plants within a species, usually differing in one or
two minor characters. Generally referring to natural variations, the term
cultivar is used for man-made or chosen varieties. Adjective varietal,
abbreviated to **var.** or **vars.** if plural

Nigella damascena, wild form

Nigella papillosa

Love-in-a-Mist The genus *Nigella*, in the family *Ranunculaceae*, consists of around 20 species of annuals, found mostly in S Europe and SW Asia. Apart from the ornamental species, *Nigella sativa* or black cumin is grown in India, Turkey and SE Europe for its black aromatic seeds, which are used to decorate bread or flavour curries; they also yield an antibacterial oil, the use of which is described by Gerard. The flowers of *Nigella* have 5 petal-like sepals, and 5–10 petals, which contain the nectar and are very small, often curiously marked, and forked and hidden beneath the stamens. Only in *N. nigellastrum* and *N. unguicularis*, which are often put in *Garidella*, are the petals longer than the sepals.

Nigella papillosa (*N. hispanica*) in Eccleston Square

Nigella damascena 'Miss Jekyll', sown into long grass at Wilton Cottage, Wiltshire

Nigella damascena L. **Love-in-a-Mist**
A hardy winter annual, with greenish or blue flowers surrounded by curved, feathery bracts, native of S Europe and Turkey to North Africa, growing in cornfields and open ground, flowering in May–August. Stems to 50cm. Leaves deeply divided, with narrow lobes. Flowers 2–4cm across. Sepals 5, with an ovate blade and narrow stalk. Petals small, deeply divided, with rounded lobes. Seed pods usually 5, around 2cm long, fully joined to form an inflated capsule. Cultivars have larger flowers, often with extra rows of sepals, and vary from white to pink, purple and blue.

'Miss Jekyll' Flowers semi-double, blue or white with stems around 45cm. As Gertrude Jekyll wrote in her own book *Annuals and Biennials* in 1916, "The variety Miss Jekyll is the result of many years' careful selection, and may be said to be the best garden *Nigella*. The colour is a pure, soft blue of a quality distinctively its own. As it does not remain very long in bloom it should be sown in September, in March, and again in May."
The 'Persian Jewel' series flowers double, including a number of rose, pink, deep blue or white; stems around 45cm; 'Mulberry Rose' is a deeper pink selection; 'Oxford Blue' a tall variety, to 75cm, with dark seed pods and double deep blue flowers; and 'Shorty Blue' and 'Dwarf Moody Blues' shorter cultivars, 15–20cm tall, with deeper blue flowers. 'Albion Black and Green' has seed pods either purple or green. Sow in spring, or in autumn in mild areas.

Nigella papillosa G. Lopez, syn. *N. hispanica* auct. A hardy winter annual, with large, deep purplish-blue flowers, native of Spain and Portugal, with the smaller-flowered subsp. *atlantica* in S Spain and NW Africa, growing in fields and open ground, flowering in May–August. Stems to 45cm. Leaves deeply divided with narrow lobes. Flowers 4–5cm across. Five sepals, with a heart-shaped blade and very short stalk. Petals 6mm long, with divergent lobes, hidden by masses of dark reddish stamens. Seed pods usually 10, densely glandular, 2–3cm long, joined for most of their length, papillose on the ridges, the long styles divergent. The name *N. hispanica* L., under which this species is usually listed, has been found to belong to another species, now called *N. gallica* Jord. Sometimes sold with the name 'Curiosity'.

Nigella damascena 'Miss Jekyll'

Nigella bucharica, with *Iberis*, *Linaria* and *Saponaria calabrica* at Quince House

Nigella sativa

Nigella arvensis var. *caudata* near Göreme, Cappadocia

Nigella bucharica at Kew

Nigella arvensis at Kew

Nigella orientalis

Nigella arvensis L. (*Ranunculaceae*)
A hardy winter annual, with pale blue or greenish flowers, native of S Europe and Turkey to North Africa, growing in fields and open ground, at up to 1700m, flowering in May–September. Stems to 55cm. Leaves deeply divided or simple, with narrow lobes. Flowers 2–3cm across. Sepals 5, with a heart-shaped blade and narrow stalk. Petals small, deeply divided, with blackish bands. Usually 5 seed pods, 7–17mm long, joined for half to two-thirds of their length. This is a very variable species; plants with stiffer and more glaucous leaves, subsp. *glauca*, are found in Turkey. Shown here also is var. ***caudata*** Boiss., from Cappadocia, which has widely divergent styles, oblanceolate petal lobes, and no bract leaves.

Nigella bucharica Schipcz., syn. *Komaroffia bucharica* Kem.-Nat. A hardy winter annual with feathery leaves and small blue flowers with upright petals like a coronet, native of Central Asia, in the Pamir-Alai, flowering in May–June. Stems to 30cm, often sprawling. Leaves in entire, linear, flattened segments, with a fine point. Flowers 3cm across, with 5 lanceolate, partly spreading sepals, and an upright ring of linear petal-lobes around the stamens and styles. Seed pods 3, 1–1.2cm long, joined for around half their length, upright or slightly spreading. Seeds 2mm long. Quick to flower from a spring or summer sowing. *N. integrifolia* Regel, is similar, but has smaller flowers almost hidden by the broader bracts. It is widespread in Central Asia.

Nigella bucharica is often sold with the name 'Summer Stars', and erroneously under the name *Garidella nigellastrum* L., syn. *Nigella nigellastrum* (L.) Willk., *Nigella garidella* Spenner, a very different species which has compound leaves and forked, pinkish or pale blue petals twice as long as the sepals.

Nigella orientalis L. A hardy winter annual, with greenish-yellow flowers, native of SE Europe and Turkey to Central Asia, growing in fields and open ground, at up to 900m, flowering in April–May. Stems to 90cm, stiffly upright. Leaves deeply divided, with linear lobes. Flowers 2–3cm across. Sepals 5, with an ovate blade tapering into a short stalk. Petals small, ovate, shortly lobed. Seed pods 2–14, smooth, flattened, joined for half their length. Sometimes sold with the name 'Transformer', because the dry seed pods can be turned inside out to form a brownish star.

Nigella sativa L. **Black Cumin, Roman Coriander** A winter annual, with hairy leaves and whitish or pale blue flowers, probably native of SW Asia, but cultivated since ancient times, and now growing wild in fields and open ground in much of SE Europe to North Africa at up to 900m, flowering in April–July. Stems to 90cm. Leaves deeply divided with flat lobes. Flowers 2–3cm across. Sepals 5, with an ovate blade tapering into a short stalk. Petals small, ovate, shortly lobed. Seed pods 2–14, smooth, flattened, joined throughout their length, forming a hard tuberculate capsule, with erect styles.

Nigella papillosa
(text page 17)

Nigella bucharica

Nigella orientalis

Nigella sativa

Specimens from Quince House, July 1st, ½ life-size

Consolida ambigua 'Giant Imperial'

Consolida ambigua in Eccleston Square

Consolida ambigua 'Sublime'

Larkspur The genus *Consolida* in the family *Ranunculaceae*, which includes all the annual cultivated larkspurs, differs from *Delphinium* in having a single seed pod per flower, and in having the inner petals joined together. In *Delphinium* there are 3–5 seed pods per flower, and the petals are not joined. Delphiniums are usually perennial, but there are several annuals and biennials in the Mediterranean and the Middle East. *Consolida* reaches its greatest complexity in Turkey, where 23 species are recognised.

Consolida ambigua (L.) Ball & Heywood **Larkspur** A hardy winter annual, with tall spikes of bright blue flowers, native of the Mediterranean region, growing in cornfields and open ground at up to 1000m, flowering in May–August. Stems to 1m. Leaves deeply divided with narrow lobes. Bracteoles not reaching the base of the flowers. Flowers 2–2.8cm across. Spur 1.3–1.8cm, longer than the sepals. Seed pods pubescent, gradually narrowed to apex.

This Larkspur has provided most of the cultivars. Indeed, Linnaeus' original of the species from North Africa had double flowers.

Modern cultivars of *C. ambigua* include: **'Frosted Skies'** with pale flowers deepening to a blue edge, a very beautiful combination; 'Hyacinth-flowered' series with double flowers in dense spikes, sold both as Dwarf (30–40cm) and Giant (to 1m), in both mixed and white; **'Giant Imperial'** very similar but taller, reaching 150cm; **'Sublime'**, double-flowered, in slender spikes to 120cm, available blue or mixed; the 'Exquisite' series, with more branching stems 90–130cm tall, available from Chiltern seeds in 8 separate colours, and especially recommended for drying, and 'Earl Grey', an unusual dusky mauve-pink.

Consolida regalis 'Snow Cloud' at Suttons Seeds trial grounds, near Torquay

Consolida ambigua 'Frosted Skies' at Thompson and Morgan's trial grounds

Consolida orientalis (Gay) Schröd., syn. *Delphinium ajacis* L., *Consolida ajacis* (L.) Schröd.   A hardy winter annual, with tall spikes of purplish-blue flowers, native of Spain, Portugal and NW Africa eastwards to Central Asia and Iran, growing in cornfields and open ground at up to 1900m, flowering in May–August. Stems to 1m. Leaves deeply divided with narrow lobes. Bracteoles attached to the upper part of the pedicels, reaching the base of the flowers. Flowers 1.5cm across; spur 1–1.2cm, a little shorter than the sepals. Seed pods pubescent, gibbous above. *C. ambigua* differs by having the bracteoles not reaching the base of the bright blue flowers, and a longer, 1.3–1.8cm, spur.

Consolida regalis S.F. Gray subsp. **paniculata** (Host) Soo   A winter or spring annual, with repeatedly branched, wiry stems and solitary or paired, deep-blue flowers, native of SE Europe, eastwards to Iran and Turkmenia, growing in cornfields, steppe and waste ground, at up to 1000m, flowering in June–September. Plant to 40cm high and wide. Flowers 2–2.6cm across; spur 1.5cm long, longer than the sepals. Seed pods small, glabrous or pubescent in var. *divaricata* (Ledeb.) Davis. **'Snow Cloud'** is a white-flowered cultivar. The normal blue-flowered form is sometimes listed under the name 'Blue Cloud'. Var. *divaricata*, which I have grown since 1969, has the habit of *Gypsophila paniculata*; the seeds germinate in autumn or spring and grow quickly in early summer. Once they start flowering they resist any drought, and should be watered very little.

Consolida orientalis, growing wild near Isparta, Turkey

Adonis flammea

Delphinium requienii

Delphinium grandiflorum near Lijiang, Yunnan

Adonis aestivalis

Circeaster agrestis near Zhongdian in NW Yunnan

Adonis aleppica, wild near Gaziantep, Turkey

Pheasant's Eye The genus *Adonis* in the family *Ranunculaceae* consists of around 20 species, half annuals, half perennials. The perennials usually flower in spring, and have many-petalled yellow flowers, though usually white with a blue reverse in the lovely *A. brevistyla* Franch. from Bhutan and SW China. The annual species mostly have small red flowers, and differ mainly in details of the achenes, single-seeded fruits crowded in an elongated head.

Adonis aestivalis An annual with widely branching stems and small, bright red flowers, native of Europe from France and Spain eastwards to the Caucasus, Syria and Iran, growing in cornfields and waste ground, flowering in May–July. Stems to 50cm; flowers 1.5–3cm across, the petals narrowly obovate, 2–3 times as long as wide. Achenes crowded in an elongated head, around 5mm long, with a short, outward-pointing beak and a wavy ridge. This is the commonly cultivated species. *A. annua* L., which is now very rare in chalky cornfields in England, has smaller achenes with a small curved beak, and no ridge.

Adonis aleppica Boiss. An annual with widely branching stems and large, bright red flowers, native of SE Turkey, from Maras to

Delphinium grandiflorum with a white *Caryopteris* at low altitude near Dali, Yunnan in October

Mardin, of Syria and N Iraq, growing in cornfields, vineyards and fallow fields, flowering in April May in the wild, though later from a spring sowing. Stems to 40cm; flowers 4–5cm across, without a black centre; the petals obovate, twice as long as wide, shining scarlet. Achenes crowded in an elongated head, 5–7mm long, with a long outward pointing beak and a wide, wavy ridge. A beautiful plant which deserves to be cultivated more often. We saw bunches of it decorating the fat tails of sheep in a butcher's shop in Maraş. In the same area, and extending to N Africa and Iran, the yellow-flowered annual *A. dentata* Del can be found. Both species likely to be somewhat tender, surviving –5°C, perhaps.

Adonis flammea Jacq.   An annual with sparsely branched stems and small, bright red flowers with narrow petals, native of NW Africa and Europe from France and Spain eastwards to the Caucasus, Syria and W Iran, growing in cornfields and waste ground, flowering in April–June. Very similar to *Adonis aestivalis*, but forms a less bushy plant with narrower petals up to 4 times as long as wide, and a more elongated seed head. The achenes have a rounded hump just behind the short, upward-pointing beak.

Circeaster agrestis Maxim. (*Circeasteraceae*) A minute annual, with a rosette of obovate leaves at the top of a sort stem, native of Sikkim, Bhutan and SW China, growing on mossy banks in *Rhododendron* scrub at over 3000m, flowering in July–August. Stems to 8cm, though generally around 2cm. Leaf rosette 2–4cm across, with the leaf veins dichotomously branched. Flowers minute, about 0.5mm at flowering. Achenes around 3mm, covered with hooked hairs. A curious plant, the only species in its family, and closely allied to *Ranunculaceae*.

Delphinium (*Ranunculaceae*) This familiar genus contains over 100 species, mostly herbaceous perennials; there are also several tuberous species, which become dormant in summer, and some annuals and biennials. Some of the species grown as annuals, such as *Delphinium grandiflorum*, are really short-lived perennials that will flower in a few months from seed.

Delphinium grandiflorum L., syn. *D. chinense* Fisch., *D. tatsienense* Franch. An annual, biennial or short-lived perennial, with deep blue flowers on branching stems, native from Siberia to SW and NC China, growing in open ground and on rock ledges, flowering in June–October. Stems to 1m, but usually 20–50cm, with curled, downward-pointing hairs. Leaves deeply divided into linear segments. Flower stalks more than 1cm; flowers 2.8–5cm across. Sepals to 1.1cm wide.

Spur 1.7cm or more. 'Blue Butterfly' is an annual selection, usually found under *D. chinense*, and other named white and pale blue strains were grown in the past. 'Blauer Zwerg', syn. 'Blue Dwarf' is also listed. *D. tatsienense* is now considered part of the variable *D. grandiflorum*; it has shorter, less leafy stems and longer spurs; a white form is available. All are easily grown in well-drained, limy soil, but the plants often die after seeding, especially in mild, wet winters.

Delphinium requienii DC   An autumn annual or biennial, with a rosette of long-stalked, deeply lobed, pale-veined leaves, and spikes of small bluish flowers, native of Corsica, Sardinia, the Balearic islands and les Isles d'Hyères, growing in rocky places, flowering in June. Stems very hairy, to 1m. Basal leaves shining, with 5–9 lobes. Lower and middle pedicels longer than the flowers. Flowers 2.5–4cm across, usually rather pale blue. Spur at least ⅖ the length of the sepals. A somewhat tender plant, the evergreen rosettes surviving around –5°C. In cold, exposed areas the seedlings should be overwintered under cover. *D. staphisagria* L., an ancient medicinal plant, is now found throughout the Mediterranean region, often growing among classical ruins and near villages. It is also biennial, and has taller stems, shorter pedicels, and flowers of a dull purplish-blue with a very short spur.

Eschscholzia caespitosa 'Sundew'

Eschscholzia caespitosa

Eschscholzia californica (orange inland form)

Hunnemannia fumariifolia, near Saltillo, NE Mexico

Platystemon californicus

Eschscholzia caespitosa Benth. (*Papaveraceae*) An annual with a tuft of basal leaves and many short stems with yellow flowers, native of California in the central valley southwards to Orange Co. and of Baja California, growing in grassland and chaparral at up to 1500m, flowering in March–June. Leaves 3 times divided, into very narrow but blunt lobes. Flowers without a wide rim around the base, with petals 1–2.5cm long. Capsule 5–8cm long. An attractive plant with smaller flowers than *E. californica*; the variety **'Sundew'** with pale, lemon-yellow flowers is often cultivated. Easily grown as a spring annual, or in warm-winter climates planted in autumn to flower in spring.

Eschscholzia californica Cham. **California Poppy** A usually robust annual or perennial with leafy stems and orange or yellow flowers in the wild, native of NW America from Washington to S California, growing in grassland, chaparral and desert at up to 2000m, flowering over a long period in February–September. Leaves several times divided, into very narrow lobes. Flowers with petals 2–6cm long and a wide rim around the base, which is conspicuous at the base of the capsule. A very common and variable species in California, and frequently naturalised in other parts of the world. In California, plants on coastal bluffs and dunes have large, rich yellow flowers; further inland the flowers are mostly large and orange in spring, smaller and yellow in summer. The numerous lovely cultivars are shown on the following page.

Eschscholzia parishii Greene A delicate desert annual with almost leafless stems and yellow flowers, native of California from the south Mojave to the Colorado desert, and NW Mexico, growing in dry, rocky places at up to 1200m, flowering in March–April. Stems to 35cm. Leaves 4 times divided, into very short, pointed lobes. Flowers without a wide rim around the base, with petals 1.5–3cm long. Capsule 5–7cm long.

Hunnemannia fumariifolia Sweet (*Papaveraceae*) An *Eschscholzia*-like perennial, often grown as an annual, with grey, dissected leaves and yellow flowers, native of Mexico, in the Sierra Madre Orientale, growing in dry, rocky places, flowering in May–November. Leaves with flattened segments to 5mm wide. Stems around 20cm. Two separate sepals, forming an ovoid bud. Petals 2.5–3cm long. Capsule linear, around 10cm. Easily grown in the same conditions as *Eschscholzia*.

Platystemon californicus Benth. (*Papaveraceae*) **Cream Cups** A dwarf, hairy annual with linear leaves and small yellow or white flowers with many conspicuous stamens, native of California, where it is common in open grassland below 1500m, and eastwards to S Utah and Arizona, where it is usually found along streams, flowering in March–May. Stems to 30cm. Leaves undivided, usually opposite or all basal, 2–5cm long. Flowers with 6 petals 8–16mm long. Seed head of 6–25 carpels, which eventually break up into single-seeded joints. A pretty, dwarf annual, easily cultivated. The genus *Meconella*, with 3 species from British Columbia to California, is similar, but has a 3-valved, dehiscent capsule with minute black, shining seeds.

Eschscholzia californica and *Platystemon californicus* near Russian River on the coast of NW California

Eschscholzia parishii, with *Phacelia* and *Opuntia*, in the San Andreas Canyon, Anza-Borrego Desert

Eschscholzia californica 'Alba' at Cockermouth Castle, Cumbria

Eschscholzia californica 'Single Carmine'

California Poppy Numerous varieties and cultivars of *Eschscholzia californica* have been grown since the 19th century. Named varieties differ in colour, and several are semi-double with fluted petals. Seed suppliers now offer around 10 varieties; a selection is shown here. All may be sown in early autumn and kept through the winter free from too much frost or wet, or sown in spring where they are to flower. March is generally a suitable month in NW Europe, or with the onset of spring in E North America, as young plants will tolerate a few degrees of frost.

'Alba' Flowers rather small, opening creamy, becoming white; probably the same as 'Milky White' and 'Single White'; 'Ivory Castle' is a new variety, said to be pure white.
'Apricot Flambeau' Flowers medium size, semi-double with fluted and ruffled orange petals streaked with red.
'Ballerina' A mixture with flowers double or semi-double of different colours, including pink and cerise, in which the petals are frilled and fluted. Plants rather short, around 40cm high.
'Cherry Ripe' Flowers crimson at the edge, gradually fading to a pale centre.
'Inferno' Flowers deep orange, with some extra petals.

Eschscholzia 'Cherry Ripe'

Eschscholzia 'Single Red'

Eschscholzia 'Ballerina'

Eschscholzia 'Apricot Flambeau'

Eschscholzia 'Thai Silk Rose Chiffon'

'Mission Bells'   A mixture with flowers mostly semi-double, some single, in all shades from white to pink, orange and yellow.
'Single Carmine'   Flowers single, deep pinkish-carmine. 'Purple Gleam' and 'Purple-Violet' seem to be the same colour.
'Single Red'   Flowers single, bright scarlet on opening, becoming orange-red. 'Red Chief' seems to be very similar.
'Thai Silk Rose Chiffon'   A lovely double flower in pale pink. The 'Thai Silk' series can have similar flowers of different shades from red and purple to white.

Eschscholzia 'Mission Bells'

Eschscholzia 'Inferno'

Glaucium flavum at Dungeness, Kent

Stylomecon heterophylla

Glaucium corniculatum at Quince House

Glaucium squamigerum in cold desert near Urumuchi, Sinjiang

Horned Poppy   The genus *Glaucium* in the family *Papaveraceae* contains around 20 species, mainly originating around the Mediterranean and the near East, extending to N China. They are easily recognised by their 4-petalled flowers, narrow capsules 10–25cm long, and pinnately divided, greyish leaves.

Glaucium corniculatum (L.) Rud.
A many-stemmed annual or biennial with bluish-grey leaves and orange flowers, native of the Mediterranean area and eastwards to the Caucasus (and often found as a casual in other areas), growing on loose slopes, roadsides and waste places, at up to 2000m in SE Turkey, flowering in May–July. Plants to 50cm, and as much across. Leaves usually hairy. Petals 2.5–4cm, usually orange-red, with or without black spots at the base. Stalks of the capsules shorter than the subtending leaf. Easily grown in a warm, dry summer. In subsp. *refractum* (Nab.) Cullen, from Turkey eastwards, the stalks of the capsules are bent back and the capsules curved.

Glaucium grandiflorum Boiss. & Huet, from the drier parts of Turkey, Iran and southwards to Sinai, is sometimes perennial with larger, dark orange to crimson petals 4–6cm long, usually with a black spot at the base, and hairy capsules.

Glaucium flavum Crantz   A few-stemmed biennial or short-lived perennial with bluish-green leaves and yellow flowers, native of the Mediterranean and the Black Sea and the coasts of Europe as far north as Norway, growing on sand dunes, shingle and waste places, near the sea and as an escapee inland, flowering in May–July. Plants to 50cm, and as much across. Leaves usually hairy. Petals 3–4cm, usually yellow, rarely orange or with a purple spot at the base. This makes a very attractive plant for a gravel garden.

Glaucium squamigerum Kar. & Kiril.
An annual with a rosette of greyish pinnate basal leaves and small yellow-orange flowers, native of Central Asia east to Xinjiang, growing in cold alpine deserts and on river gravels, flowering in May–August. Leaf rosette to 20cm across. Stems around 30cm. Petals 3cm. Capsule covered with scaly warts. We found this delicate-looking plant in an exceedingly hostile environment in the Borohorashan in NW China, flowering in early spring, at the end of May.

Roemeria refracta DC. (*Papaveraceae*)
An upright annual with finely divided leaves, black-centred, red flowers and a long, narrow capsule, native of Asia from NE Turkey and Iran to NW China and W Pakistan, growing in cornfields, deserts and waste places, flowering in May to July. Plants to 50cm, bristly hairy. Four petals, 2.5–4cm long. Capsule glabrous except for four setae projecting between the stigmas. *Roemeria hybrida* (L.) DC. from S Europe and SW Asia to NW China, has purple flowers and capsules setose near their apex.

Stylomecon heterophylla (Benth.)
G. Taylor (*Papaveraceae*) **Wind Poppy**
A delicate winter annual with pale orange flowers and a short, smooth capsule, native of California and NW Mexico from Lake Co. southwards, growing in dry grassy places and chaparral below 1200m, flowering in April–May, especially after fires. Stems 10–60cm. Leaf deeply pinnatifid, to 12cm long. Flowers on stalks 5–20cm long, in the leaf axils. Petals 1–2cm long, with a dark brown spot at the base. Capsule flat-topped, with a prominent stigma, 8–15mm long. From a late spring sowing, I managed to grow only a very feeble specimen of this; it is better sown in autumn, and overwintered away from frost. The only species in the genus.

Glaucium corniculatum growing wild near Isparta in May

Glaucium grandiflorum in the Amankutan valley near Tashkent

Roemeria refracta in cornfields near Ining, Sinjiang

Argemone pleiacantha subsp. *pleiacantha*, or 'White Lustre', at Quince House

Argemone squarrosa var. *glabrata* in the order beds at Kew

Argemone polyanthemos wild in Montana in August

Argemone mexicana in the Chelsea Physic Garden

Argemone ochroleuca in Oaxaca, Mexico in April

Prickly Poppy The genus *Argemone* in the family *Papaveraceae* has around 30 species of spiny-leaved poppies and is found mostly in semi-desert areas of North and Central America, from Montana to Mexico and the Carribean. Some are annuals, some biennials and many are short-lived perennials. Most have white flowers. All are easily raised from seed, but likely to die in wet winters with alternating freeze and thaw. Sow seed at 15–20°C in spring and plant out in a dry, sunny position in early summer. In wet areas protect any surviving plants over winter.

Argemone mexicana L.   An annual with grey, spiny leaves and bright yellow flowers, native of Central America and Mexico, northwards into the SE USA as far as Florida, but widely naturalised in the tropics and further north, growing in dry, open ground. Stems to 2.5m. Leaves few-lobed, the upper clasping the stem. Buds nearly spherical, with long horns on the sepals. Flowers 4–7cm across, usually bright yellow, but sometimes paler; petals often obovate and not overlapping. Capsule usually spiny. In the cultivar 'Yellow Lustre' the flowers are small and bright yellow. The closely related *A. ochroleuca* Sweet has pale yellow flowers.

Argemone pleiacantha Greene subsp. *pleiacantha*   An annual or short-lived perennial with grey, prickly leaves and white flowers with a mass of crimson stamens, native from Arizona and New Mexico to N Mexico, growing on dry hills and plains, flowering in June–September. Stems prickly, to 1.2m. Leaves many-lobed, the upper clasping the stem. Buds nearly spherical, with short, flattened horns on the sepals. Flowers 8–15cm across. Capsule ovoid to narrowly ellipsoid, densely spiny. An abundance of this species is often a sign of overgrazing. Sometimes sold as 'White Lustre' and 'Silver Charm'.
    Argemone grandiflora Sweet, from Mexico, differs in having flowers 6–10cm across, with the horns on the buds not flattened, and the spines on the capsule more scattered.

Argemone polyanthemos (Fedde) Ownby An annual with grey, spiny leaves and white or rarely mauve flowers, native of Montana, Wyoming and South Dakota to Texas and New Mexico, growing in dry, open ground, flowering in spring–summer. Stems to 80cm. Leaves few-lobed, the upper clasping the stem. Buds elongated, with spine-tipped horns on the sepals. Flowers 7–10cm across. Capsule strongly spiny, with widely spaced prickles.

Argemone squarrosa Greene var. *glabrata* Ownby   An annual or short-lived perennial with grey, prickly leaves and lovely white flowers with a mass of crimson stamens, native of Texas and New Mexico, growing on dry hills, flowering in July–September. Stems to 1.2m. Leaves many-lobed, the upper scarcely clasping the stem. Buds slightly elongated, with short horns on the sepals. Flowers 6–10cm across. Capsule spiny, the lower spines themselves spiny or hairy. Very close to 'White Lustre'.

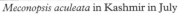
Meconopsis aculeata in Kashmir in July

Meconopsis wallichii at Quince House

Meconopsis (*Papaveraceae*)   A genus of around 50 species of biennials or perennials, with 1 species, the Welsh poppy, *Meconopsis cambrica*, in SW Europe, and the remainder in the Himalayas and China. Most of the biennials form a large and decorative evergreen rosette in the first year or two, then flower and die the following summer. Sow seed at 15–18°C in early spring, and prick out the seedlings when they have two good leaves. Young plants are best put out as soon as they are large enough, or can be kept in a cold frame until the next spring. All need well-drained, leafy or peaty soil, moist and cool in summer, with some shade around midday, and drier in winter; in wet areas the hairy rosettes are less likely to rot if covered with a sheet of glass in the winter.
See C. Grey-Wilson, "A survey of the genus *Meconopsis* in cultivation", *The Plantsman*, vol. 14: pt.1 June 1992.

Meconopsis wallichii, evergreen rosette of young leaves in the frost

Meconopsis aculeata Royle   A biennial with deeply lobed leaves and delicate, pale blue flowers, native of the W Himalayas from Ladak and Hazara to Kumaon in Uttar Pradesh, growing on rocky slopes by streams and among damp rocks, at 2500–4375m, flowering in June–August. Rosettes to 60cm across, the leaves irregularly pinnatifid or pinnatisect, usually with well-spaced, rounded and toothed lobes, with bristly hairs. Stems to 60cm. Flowers single from the main stem, 4–6cm across, usually sky-blue, but sometimes reddish or purplish. Capsule bristly. An attractive species, common in Kashmir.

Meconopsis latifolia Prain   A tall biennial with toothed but not lobed leaves and pale

blue flowers, native of Kashmir, growing on cliffs and among large rocks, at 3500–4000m, flowering in July–September. Plant completely dormant in winter. Rosettes to 40cm across, the leaves long-stalked. Stems to 1m. Flowers in a spike-like cluster at the top of the main stem, with four petals, each 3.5–4cm long, usually sky-blue, but sometimes white. Capsule bristly. A very beautiful species, found only in Kashmir, rare in cultivation.

Meconopsis wallichii Hook.   A tall biennial or monocarpic perennial with deeply toothed leaves and pale blue or purplish flowers, native of the Himalayas from E Nepal to Bhutan, growing in scrub, openings in forest and sheltered gulleys, at 2800–3700m, flowering in

July–September. Plants evergreen. Rosettes to 60cm across, the leaves with yellowish, bristly hairs. Stems to 2.5m. Flowers with 4 petals, each 2–3cm long, in a compound inflorescence with many-flowered side branches. Stamen filaments purplish. Capsule with stiff hairs. I have found this one of the easier species to grow as it is more tolerant of winter wet and summer shade than the more woolly species. Other evergreen monocarpic species are: *M. dhwojii* with leaves with paired toothed lobes with purple swollen spine bases, and pale yellow flowers; *M. gracilipes* with slightly broader leaf-lobes, no purple colour and yellow flowers; *M. regia* with untoothed leaves and yellow flowers; and *M. superba* with broad, shallowly toothed leaves and white flowers.

Meconopsis latifolia at Rasbal, Kashmir in July

Meconopsis nepaulensis

Meconopsis punicea at Cluny, Perthshire

Meconopsis nepaulensis

Meconopsis integrifolia from above Wolong

Meconopsis integrifolia (Maxim.) Franch. (*Papaveraceae*)   A low-growing annual or biennial, with a few large, yellow flowers, native of NE Tibet eastwards to NW Yunnan, Sichuan and Gansu, growing in alpine meadows, scrub, screes and rocky places, at 2800–5300m, flowering in May–July and sometimes, as an annual, into autumn. Stems 15–90cm; flowers 2–10, usually 4–5, nodding or horizontal, usually with 6–8 petals forming a globe, but sometimes opening rather flat, and then 13–28cm across. Capsules around 2.5cm long. Easily grown in moist, stony soil, but prone to die in warm, wet winters. *M. pseudointegrifolia* Prain, the name given originally to forms with several stems from the base and a long style, is now considered to fall within *M. integrifolia*.

Meconopsis nepaulensis DC   A tall biennial or monocarpic perennial with deeply toothed or lobed leaves and red, purple, blue or white flowers, native of the Himalayas from W Nepal to SW China, in Yunnan and Sichuan, growing on open slopes and in clearings in *Abies* forest, as well as on the rocky banks of mountain streams, at 3000–5000m, flowering in June–August. Plants evergreen. Rosettes to 1m across, the leaves stalked and hairy, the hairs not stellate at the base. Stems to 2.5m. Flowers with 4 petals, each 4–5cm long, in a compound inflorescence with many-flowered side branches. Stigma green. Capsule with stiff hairs. One of the easier of the monocarpic species, thriving in deep, moist but well-drained soil, with shade at mid-day.

Meconopsis paniculata Prain   A tall biennial or monocarpic perennial with deeply toothed leaves and yellow or white flowers (sometimes pink in cultivated specimens); it is native of the Himalayas from Uttar Pradesh in N India to SE Tibet, growing on open slopes, meadows and in clearings in *Abies* forest and in scrub, at 3000–4100m, flowering in June–August. Plants evergreen. Rosettes to 1m across, the leaves with yellowish or reddish hairs, the hairs stellate at the base. Stems to 2.5m. Flowers with 4 petals, each 3–5cm long, in a compound inflorescence with many-flowered side branches. Stigma purple. Capsule with stiff hairs. Most of the *M. paniculata* in cultivation in England at present are probably of hybrid origin with *M. nepaulensis* or the yellow-flowered *M. regia*. The cultivated hybrids commonly have yellow or pinkish flowers and a green stigma.

Meconopsis punicea Maxim.   A biennial or short-lived perennial, with a rosette of simple basal leaves and nodding, blood-red, rarely white, flowers, native of NE Tibet, NW Sichuan and S Gansu, growing in grassy alpine meadows. and dwarf *Rhododendron* scrub, at 2600–4500m, flowering in June–September. Stems 15–60cm; flowers with 4–6 hanging petals 6–10cm long. Capsules around 2.5cm long. I have found this a difficult plant to grow: the seed needs cold to germinate, unlike most *Meconopsis*; the seedlings are adored by slugs; the young plants need cool, airy conditions and moisture, and tend to rot in hot summer weather, but I have seen it flowering well at Kew, as well as in Scotland.

Meconopsis paniculata with Himalayan perennials at Quince House

Meconopsis integrifolia from Yunnan

Meconopsis paniculata in a natural setting at Cluny, Perthshire

Poppy The genus *Papaver* in the family *Papaveraceae* contains around 80 species of annuals, biennials and perennials, with one species, *Papaver aculeatum,* in S Africa and Australia, one, *P. californicum* Gray in the Coast Ranges in California and the rest in Eurasia.

Plants from 6 sections of the genus are commonly cultivated. Sect. *Macrantha* contains the largest flowers, in *P. bracteatum* and its allies, perennials commonly grown in herbaceous borders. Sect. *Pilosa* contains perennials for walls and rocky places, including *P. spicatum* and *P. pilosum*. Sect. *Miltantha* contains several biennials from SW Asia, including *P. triniifolium*, with very finely divided leaves, found wild on screes in C Anatolia. Sect. *Mecones* contains the opium poppy and the red-flowered *P. glaucum*. Sect. *Papaver* contains mostly annual species, including the field poppy. Sect. *Argemonorhoeades* contains the bristly-headed poppy, *P. argemone*, and other annual species with bristly capsules. Sect. *Scapiflora* contains dwarf alpines and the cultivated Iceland poppies.

Most annual poppies are winter or spring annuals, and can be sown in autumn in warm winter climates, or in spring where winters are either very cold or wet. They are best sown directly into position and will flower in early summer from an early spring sowing. Thin them ruthlessly to about 15cm apart and they will make much larger plants; dead-heading will greatly prolong their flowering season.

Papaver argemone L. A winter or spring annual with narrow leaf segments, small, orange flowers and narrow, bristly seed capsules, native of Europe, including the British Isles, and North Africa, eastwards to SW Asia, growing in arable fields and waste places, flowering in spring and summer. Stems to 50cm; flowers with the petals not overlapping, with a blackish-purple blotch at the base, about 2cm long. Capsule 1–2cm long.

Papaver commutatum Fisch. & Mey. **Lady Bird Poppy** A robust winter or spring annual with greyish, narrow leaf segments and bright red flowers with a rectangular black blotch around the centre of each petal, native of Turkey, N Iran and the Caucasus area including the Crimaea, growing on gravelly slopes and hills, flowering in May–June. Stems to 50cm; flowers with the petals overlapping, about 4cm long. Capsule 1–2cm long, similar to *P. rhoeas*. An easily grown and very striking annual, doing well from a spring sowing.

Papaver dubium L. **Long-headed Poppy**
A winter or spring annual with flat leaf segments, pale scarlet flowers and long, smooth seed capsules, native of Europe, including England, and North Africa, eastwards to SW Asia, growing in arable fields and waste places, flowering in spring and summer. Stems to 60cm; flowers with the petals barely overlapping, unspotted, about 2cm long. Capsule 1.5–2cm long, tapering from near the apex.

Papaver glaucum Boiss. & Held. **Tulip Poppy** A robust winter annual with bluish-grey, toothed leaves, and crimson flowers with the inner petals cupped and blotched, the outer spreading and overlapping each other, native of Turkey, Syria, N Iraq and W Iran, growing in chalky vineyards and waste places, flowering in May–June. Stems to 50cm; leaves clasping the stem; flowers about 8cm across. Capsule 1.5–2cm, with a short stipe. A relative of *P. somniferum*, but forming a much more delicate plant.

Papaver gracile Boiss., from SW Turkey, is an even more delicate plant, with small, pale pink flowers. I grew it for a year from seed collected in Turkey, but then lost it.

Stylomecon heterophylla (Benth.) G. Taylor (*Papaveraceae*) **Wind Poppy** A relative of *Meconopsis*, native of California and NW Mexico. For text see page 28.

Three species of wild poppy in a strawberry field in Hampshire

Papaver commutatum

Papaver argemone

Papaver dubium

Papaver glaucum

Stylomecon heterophylla

Papaver glaucum

Papaver dubium

Papaver commutatum

Specimens from Quince House, August 16th, ½ life-size

Papaver rhoeas in Spain

Papaver rhoeas in Provence

Papaver rhoeas 'The Shirley Poppy'

Papaver rhoeas 'Mother of Pearl'

Papaver rhoeas L. (*Papaveraceae*)
Field Poppy A bristly-hairy winter or spring annual with deeply lobed leaves, red flowers, and short, smooth capsules, native of Europe and North Africa, east across Asia to NW China, and naturalised elsewhere throughout the temperate world, growing in cornfields and disturbed ground, flowering in spring and summer. Stems branching, to 1m; leaves with narrow toothed segments. Flowers 6–10cm across, the four petals usually with a black blotch at the base, and sometimes with a black blotch edged with white. Capsule 1–2cm long, the stigmatic disc rather flat. This poppy has long been associated with cultivation, and its seeds have been found together with barley in Egyptian deposits over 4500 years old, as well as in Bronze Age deposits in Britain. It is also well-known to have seed which survives burying for at least 100 years.

'The Shirley Poppy' Near his vicarage in Shirley, Kent in around 1880, the Reverend William Wilks spotted a field poppy with petals that had a narrow white edge. By marking this flower, collecting its seed and selecting the progeny for several generations, he acheived a strain with single flowers in clear shades of white, rose-pink, salmon, and white-edged pink, without any black spot, and with yellow or white stamens (he did not approve of those with double flowers or the greys that are now so popular). Pale-flowered poppies had been grown in the 17th century, but had since died out in gardens until he recreated them. Wilks' other great service to horticulture was his tenure of the secretaryship of the Royal Horticultural Society from 1888 to 1920, during which time the society changed from a small social gardening club to a thriving, learned and scientific society; his

rather severe portrait hangs on the stairs of the New Hall.

'Fairy Wings' A selection with very pale colours and single flowers, very similar to 'Mother of Pearl', and sometimes listed as a synonym of it.

'Mother of Pearl' A modern strain with a large number of flowers very pale or greyish-pink or even lavender. Raised by Sir Cedric Morris, in his garden at Benton End, Suffolk. Similar colour forms in the 1920s were known as 'Celeste' and Carter's 'Raynes Park Hybrids'.

'Reverend Wilks' A mixture with pale single and semi-double flowers. This type of mixture has had many names including 'Shirley Improved'. 'Angel Choir' is a newer selection with a large number of soft colours.

Papaver rhoeas 'Fairy Wings'

Specimens from Eccleston Square, July 15th, ⅔ life-size

Papaver rhoeas 'Reverend Wilks'

Specimens from Eccleston Square, July 15th, ½ life-size

PAPAVER

Papaver somniferum L. (*Papaveracea*)
Opium Poppy   A large annual with fleshy, greyish leaves and large flowers and seed heads, cultivated since ancient times, but probably native of SW Europe, where the wild subsp. *setigerum* (DC) Corb. is found. Stems to 120cm. Upper leaves clasping the stem. Flowers 10–15cm across. Capsules 5–7cm long. The opium poppy is grown both for the narcotics contained in its latex and for its seeds, which can be pressed to produce oil or used as a flavouring for bread. This poppy has a long history of cultivation, having been found in Bronze Age deposits in Sussex. It was also known in early settlements in the Mediterranean area, nearer to its probable native range. The flowers were originally whitish or lilac, but now cover the full range

from white through pinks, reds (some with a white centre), and purples, to almost black. In form they may be single, double, or paeony-flowered, some with laciniate or fringed petals, var. *laciniatum*. There is also a strange form called 'Hen and Chickens' in which some of the stamens proliferate into small capsules. The form used for the production of opium has extra-large capsules, around 10cm tall.

'Black Paeony'   Flowers dark purplish-black, fully double. A fringed form of this was called 'Nubian Prince'.
'Danebrog Laced'   Flowers single, red with a white centre, the petals laciniate. In 'Danebrog' or 'The Admiral', the colour is similar, but the petals have smooth edges.

'Paeoniflorum' or 'Paeony-flowered'
A mixture with double flowers of white, lilac, scarlet, purple or pink, to 12.5cm across.
'Pink Beauty'   Flowers pale pink, fully double; a selection of 'Paeoniflorum'.
Single mixed   The single garden varieties contain a mixture of colours, including white, purples and red, some with fringed or laciniate petals. A few have been selected, including a large white, 'The Bride', with flowers 17cm across, a good black with flowers 10–12cm across, which has been called 'Charles Darwin' or 'Black Prince', and red with a black blotch.
'Swansdown' or 'White Swan'   Double white with the petals finely fringed. A white var. *laciniatum*, also available in other colours.
'White Cloud'   A very good, pure white with fully double flowers.

Papaver somniferum 'White Cloud'

Papaver somniferum 'Swansdown'

Papaver somniferum single mixed

Papaver somniferum 'Pink Beauty'

Papaver somniferum 'Black Paeony'

'Pink Beauty'

'Danebrog
Laced'

*Papaver
somniferum*

Specimens from Eccleston Square, August 8th, ⅜ life-size

'Constance Finnis' strain at Boughton House

'Garden Gnome'

'Scarlet Bubbles'

Iceland Poppy (*Papaveraceae*) The cultivated Iceland poppy is generally known as *Papaver nudicaule*, but was developed from a distinct but related central Asian species, *P. croceum* Ledeb. The wild Icelandic poppy is *P. radicatum* Rottb., a smaller Arctic species which is found also in the Faeroes, Norway and N Sweden.

P. croceum is native of Central Asia and NW China, in the Tarbagatau, Dzungarian Alatau, Tien Shan and Pamir-Alai mountains, where it grows on stony alpine slopes, flowering in June–August. It is also naturalised on shingle beaches near Ushaia in Tierra del Fuego.

Modern Iceland poppies are annuals, biennials or short-lived perennials with a rosette of hairy basal leaves and single-flowered stems arising from among the leaves; flower colours range from red and orange to yellow and white, and the flowers may be as much as 20cm across. Sow the seed in spring and plant out in a frame or bed to grow on through the summer before planting out in flowering position in autumn or the following spring. The plants rarely flower well for a second year and need very well-drained soil to survive the winter. Modern strains include:

'Constance Finnis' strain A large-flowered strain with a high percentage of soft colours originated by Constance Finnis, and continued by her daughter Valerie Finnis, Lady Scott at Boughton House, Northamptonshire.

'Garden Gnome' A sturdy strain with a wide range of colours on stems around 30cm tall.

'Scarlet Bubbles' A selection with bright scarlet flowers. 'Matador' is another scarlet.

'Constance Finnis'
strain

Specimens from Boughton House, May 15th, ½ life-size

Fumaria capreolata in France

Adlumia fungosa at Quince House

Hypecoum procumbens at the ruins of Cnidos, SE Turkey in April

Adlumia fungosa (Ait.) Britton, Sterns & Pogg. (*Fumariaceae*) A smothering biennial climber with ferny leaves and masses of small, pale pink flowers, native of eastern North America from Ontario and New Brunswick southwards to North Carolina and Tennessee, growing in moist woods and scrub, flowering in June–October. Stems to 3m or more; leaves 2–3 pinnate. Flowers in branching cymes in the leaf axils, 1–1.5cm long, the two outer petals opposite, equal and swollen, the inner narrower. Dead petals cover the capsule.

Corydalis aurea Willd. (*Fumariaceae*) A winter annual or biennial with ferny, very glaucous leaves and short spikes of small yellow flowers, native of North America from Nova Scotia to Alaska and southwards to Texas, Arizona and California in the mountains, growing in woods and scrub, flowering in March–August. Stems much branched, to 40cm. Leaves with the segments 3–8mm long. Flowers 1–1.2cm long, with a short, blunt spur. Capsules constricted between the seeds, recurved. Attractive for its grey foliage.

Corydalis incisa (Thunb.) Pers. A striking, upright biennial with tall spikes of purple or rarely pale pink or white flowers above finely cut, bright green leaves, native of Japan, Korea and E China, growing in scrub and bamboo forest, flowering in April–June. Plant forming a rosette of leaves in the first spring, then dying back to a thick, radish-like root in summer, before emerging in autumn to flower the following spring. Stems 20–50cm; leaf segments laciniate, 1–2cm long. Racemes 4–12cm; flowers 1.2–1.8cm long, with round, spreading lips and a blunt slightly down-curved spur. Capsules nodding, 15cm long.

Corydalis linstowiana Fedde A spreading or creeping annual or biennial with spikes of pale blue or purplish flowers, native of China in W Sichuan, growing in gravelly limestone soil by streams in dry valleys in the mountains, at about 1200m, flowering in April–November. Plants flowering late in their first year or in their second, rarely persisting for a third. Stems 10–20cm. Leaves bluish,

Corydalis incisa at the Botanical Garden, Hangschow

Corydalis linstowiana from Luding, Sichuan

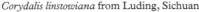

Corydalis aurea

with blunt lobed segments about 1cm long. Flowers 1.5cm long, the spur curved at the tip. A modest species, which will seed itself in suitable conditions. Shown here are plants from C.D.& R. 605, collected 15km N of Luding.

Fumaria capreolata L. (*Fumariaceae*)
A sprawling annual with spikes of magenta and white flowers, native of Europe, W Turkey and the Caucasus, growing in gardens, cornfields, scrub and rocky places, flowering in April–August. Leaves finely divided with broad, deeply lobed segments. Flowers white or pink, tipped with dark magenta, 1–1.4cm long, the upper petal with a short, rounded spur. Capsule rounded, single-seeded, not opening when dry. There are around 30 species of *Fumaria* in Europe, reaching their greatest diversity in the west. *F. occidentalis* Pugsley, one of the finest, is endemic to Cornwall; some others are confined to the British Isles, and a few are found from Ireland eastwards to China.

Hypecoum procumbens L. (*Fumariaceae*)
A winter annual with prostrate or spreading stems and upright, lemon-yellow flowers, native of the Mediterranean coast, N Iraq and the Syrian desert, growing in stony and sandy places near the sea, flowering in March–June. Stems around 20cm. Leaves finely divided. Flowers with the outer pair of petals shallowly 3-lobed, the inner pair smaller, deeply trifid, with ciliate middle lobes that enfold the anthers and hold the pollen until pushed aside by a visiting insect. Fruits curved, jointed. The similar *H. imberbe* Sibth. & Sm. has orange-yellow flowers with the middle lobe of the outer petals slightly narrower and more pointed than the side lobes. The genus *Hypecoum* has around 15 species of annuals from Spain to NW China.

Iberis umbellata 'Flash'

Iberis umbellata 'Flash Red'

Iberis umbellata 'Flash' mixed

Iberis umbellata 'Mixed' at Littlewood Park, Aberdeenshire

Candytuft The genus *Iberis* in the family *Cruciferae* contains around 40 species of annuals, perennials and subshrubs, found mainly around the Mediterranean. Most have a flat-topped inflorescence, in which the outer 2 petals of the flowers enlarge as they develop, while the inner 2 remain small.

Iberis amara L. A spring annual with white or purplish flowers in a flat-topped inflorescence which elongates during fruiting, native of W Europe from SE England and Spain to Germany and Italy, growing on chalky hills, and in cornfields, flowering in May–October. Stems 10–40cm. Leaves fleshy, spathulate, pinnatifid or with few broad teeth or lobes. Outer petals about 10mm long. Fruits suborbicular, about 7mm across, with a narrow notch in the apex, formed by 2 upright teeth. Most of the white-flowered cultivars belong to this species.

'Hyacinth-flowered' or **'Hyacinthiflora'** A large variety with stems to 45cm, and an elongated inflorescence. Very easy to grow, with a long flowering season, into November in wet summers. 'Mount Hood' and 'White Pinnacle' belong to this group.

'Iceberg' A small variety, with stems to 30cm, and pure white flowers.

'Snowbird' A dwarf variety, said to be a hybrid, with spreading stems to 30cm, leaves with several small teeth, and a long flowering season.

Iberis stricta Jordan A tall and elegant winter annual with linear leaves, only the lowest sometimes toothed, and small heads of pink to lilac flowers, native of SE France and NW Italy, growing in limestone screes, quarries and rocky hills, flowering in July–October. Stems to 60cm, much branched. Fruit 3–5mm long, almost round, the divergent teeth forming a shallow notch. A very attractive species, common in the hills above Vence. *I. pectinata* Boiss. & Reut., syn. *I. crenata* auct. is a small (10–30cm) upright, hairy annual with toothed leaves, flat umbels of white flowers with purplish buds and fruits with obtuse, spreading teeth. It is wild in SE Spain and S Portugal, in chalky places at low altitudes.

Iberis umbellata L. An upright and branching annual with linear-lanceolate, acuminate leaves, pink or purplish flowers, remaining umbellate in fruit, native of the Mediterranean region from S France to Italy and Greece, growing in rocky places on limestone and serpentine, flowering in May–August. Stems 20–70cm. Leaves linear-lanceolate, usually not toothed. Outer petals about 8mm long. Fruits suborbicular, about 1cm across, with a deep notch in the apex, formed by 2 upright, acuminate teeth. Most of the pink-, red- or purple-flowered cultivars belong to this species; the strain sold as **'Mixed'** has stems around 30cm tall.

'Fairy', **'Fairyland'** or **'Dwarf Fairy'** A short-stemmed strain with stems 15–25cm tall, in shades of purplish pink, crimson and reddish purple.

'Flash' series Tall plants with 25–35cm stems and flowers of particularly bright colours. Available as a mixture or in separate colours of cream, red, rose and white.

Iberis stricta

Iberis amara at Kew

Iberis stricta in an old limestone quarry near Gorges du Loup, Alpes Maritimes

Iberis amara 'Hyacinth-flowered'

Iberis amara 'Snowbird'

Iberis umbellata 'Fairy' in the trial fields of Kees Sahin in Holland

Iberis amara 'Iceberg' in late October

Cochlearia danica in Cornwall

Lobularia maritima 'Easter Bonnet' in the trial grounds of Suttons Seeds

Lobularia maritima 'Wonderland Red' at Wisley

Cochlearia danica L. (*Cruciferae*) **Danish Scurvy-grass** A winter annual with small, triangular leaves and mauve or white flowers, native of W Europe from Finland to Portugal, growing on sandy and rocky coasts and shingle, flowering in January–June. Stems usually prostrate, to 20cm long. Leaves with stalks about 2cm long, the blades cordate, 5–10mm wide. Flowers 4–5mm across, with 4 petals. Fruits ovoid, about 4mm across. This dwarf was originally found only around the coast, but is now widespread along the central reservations of motorways inland in Britain, forming sheets of pale purple and white.

Cochlearia officinalis L. **Scurvy-grass** A biennial or short-lived perennial with rounded basal leaves and masses of white or pale lilac flowers, native of NW and C Europe, growing on rocky coasts, shady banks and salt marshes, and occasionally in damp places in the mountains, flowering in April–August. Stems spreading or upright to 50cm. Basal leaves around 2cm across, round or kidney-shaped. Flowers 8–10mm across. Fruit ovoid to globose, 4–7mm across. The annual form shown here is a conspicuous feature of roadside banks in parts of North Devon.

Iopsidium acaule (Desf.) Reichenb. (*Cruciferae*) A dwarf, bushy winter annual with rounded or 3-lobed leaves, and small, 4-petalled lilac flowers, native of the coast of S Portugal, growing in damp, sandy places by the sea, flowering in November–April. Stems 1.5–6cm. Leaves 2–6mm across. Flowers 4–5mm across. Fruits obovoid-orbicular, 2–4.5mm across. A miniature, easily grown if protected from slugs, frost and drought.

Lobularia maritima (L.) Desf. (*Cruciferae*) **Sweet Alison, Sweet Alyssum** A spreading perennial, usually grown as an annual, with narrow leaves and honey-scented, white to purple flowers, native of the Mediterranean area, and widely naturalised in other parts of the world, growing in sandy places near the sea, flowering most of the year. Stems usually less than 8cm tall, spreading to 40cm. Flowers to 6mm across. Fruits 2–3.5mm, obovate or rounded. In addition to the cultivated varieties shown here are 'Apricot Shades' and 'New Apricot' in cream and buff to apricot orange, 'Creamery' in cream, and 'Trailing Rosy Red' for hanging baskets and walls.
'**Easter Bonnet**' A mixture from white and red to purple. 'Easter Basket' is probably the same. Available mixed or in separate shades of deep pink, deep rose, lavender and violet. Height to 12cm.
'**Wonderland Red**' Still rather a dirty red. The 'Wonderland' series is also available in purple and white. Height to 10cm.

Thysanocarpus curvipes Hook. var *elegans* (F. & M.) Rob. (*Cruciferae*) **Lace Pod** A delicate winter annual with minute white flowers and pretty hanging fruits, with perforations between the ribs, native of California, growing in grassy places below 1500m, flowering in March–May. Stems 15–30cm. Rosette leaves usually hairy; stem leaves lanceolate, amplexicaul, with long, narrow basal lobes. Fruits 5–6mm wide; style about 1mm long. Other varieties of *T. curvipes* have smaller fruit without perforations; *T. radians* Benth., from Oregon to the Sacramento valley, has larger fruit, 8–10mm wide, with dark, narrow, radiating nerves, on ascending pedicels with only the tips recurved.

Cochlearia officinalis on a bank near Bishop's Nympton, N Devon

Iopsidium acaule, a very poor specimen

Thysanocarpus curvipes var. *elegans* in the trial fields of Kees Sahin

Thysanocarpus curvipes var. *elegans*, showing the unusual seed pods

Erysimum capitatum

Wallflower 'Harpur Crewe' at Cedar Tree Cottage, Sussex

Wallflower 'Golden Bedder'

Wallflower 'Primrose Dame'

Wallflower, a self-sown seedling

Bedding wallflowers and forget-me-nots

Wallflower, a self-sown seedling

Wallflowers with white tulips at Hever Castle, Kent

Wallflower The genus *Erysimum* in the family *Cruciferae* contains about 200 species of annuals, biennials and perennials, found throughout the northern hemisphere; *Cheiranthus* on the other hand has 1 species, *C. cheiri*, the main ancestor of the cultivated wallflowers, which is now usually included in *Erysimum*. *Cheiranthus* differs from *Erysimum* in the absence of median nectaries on the petal.

Erysimum capitatum (Dougl.) Greene
A tall, slender biennial with narrow leaves and orange, yellow, brick-red, orange-brown or sometimes purplish-maroon flowers, native of western North America from California to British Columbia and Idaho, growing in dry, stony places in the foothills up to 1800m, flowering in March–July. Stems 20–80cm. Lower leaves 4–15cm long, 4–10mm wide, usually with small teeth. Petals 1.5–2cm long. Fruits 5–10cm long, 4-angled. A very widespread and variable plant. The commonly cultivated *E.* × *allionii* is said to be a hybrid between the *E. capitatum* and *E. hieraciifolium* L. from N Europe. It has bright orange flowers, or pale yellow in 'Lemon Delight', and is usually grown as a biennial.

Erysimum cheiri (L.) Crantz, syn.
Cheiranthus cheiri L. **Wallflower** A shrubby perennial, with leafy stems and orange-yellow, scented flowers, native of Rhodes, Ikaria, some of the S Aegean islands and possibly the coast of Antakya, but commonly naturalised elsewhere in Europe from Ireland to Hungary, growing on cliffs, rocks and old walls, flowering in March–June. Stems usually to

50cm. Leaves entire or weakly toothed, narrowly elliptic to lanceolate. Petals 1.5–2.5cm long. Fruits flattened, greyish, 4.5–6.5cm long.

Though perennial, most wallflowers are treated as biennials; the seed should be sown in May or June in a sheltered position and the young plants set out in autumn where they are to flower. Winter losses are usually caused by heavy, waterlogged soil or hard frost on sappy growth, and they prefer chalky soil with excellent drainage. In suitably poor soil, and with dead-heading before they seed, the plants will survive for around 5 years. Over 30 varieties, differing mainly in height and colour, are now available as seed, of which most were grown in a trial at Wisley in 1923–24. Single-colour varieties include 'Blood Red', a velvety crimson; 'Fire King' a bright orange; 'Primrose Monarch' pale yellow; and 'Ruby Gem', a deep reddish-purple. The 'Tom Thumb' series has stems 15–23cm; the 'Monarch' and 'Vulcan' series reach 40cm. Numerous other named perennial varieties, including the popular 'Bowles' Mauve', are hybrids with species of *Erysimum*, and are propagated by cuttings.

'Golden Bedder' A good variety of *E. cheiri*, with deep golden-yellow flowers. Stems to 30cm. The 'Bedder' series is also available in orange, primrose and scarlet, or as a mixture.

'Harpur Crewe' A double-flowered variety of the wild wallflower. To keep it going, take cuttings every other year. A very old clone, named after the Rev Henry Harpur Crewe

(1830–83), a keen collector and grower of plants, who distributed it from his garden. Crocuses were one of his specialities, and *Crocus crewii* Hook. is named after him.

'Primrose Dame' Flowers opening creamy-yellow, fading to white. Stems to 30cm. 'White Dame' is also still grown.

Wild wallflowers on an old wall

Matthiola tricuspidata in the Peloponnese in April

Matthiola sinuata

Matthiola incana, single white

Matthiola longipetala subsp. bicornis

Matthiola longipetala subsp. bicornis

Stocks The genus *Matthiola* in the family *Cruciferae* contains around 50 species, from tall seaside annuals to tufted alpine perennials, found mainly around the Mediterranean and in the Atlantic islands. Most have purple or greenish flowers, scented at night, and long, narrow fruit with short horns at the apex. Double-flowered varieties of *M. incana* are commonly cultivated.

Matthiola incana (L.) R. Br. **Stock**
An annual, biennial or short-lived, shrubby perennial with grey, untoothed leaves and scented purple, pink or white flowers, native of W Europe from S England to the Mediterranean and Arabian peninsula, growing on rocks and cliffs near the sea, flowering most of the year. Stems to 80cm, or 1m in tall cultivated varieties. Petals 2–3cm long. Fruits 5–12cm, flattened, greyish, not glandular, with 2 horns about 1mm long.

Garden Stocks The double garden stocks are derived from *M. incana*. The two main groups are the biennial Brompton stocks and the annual 10-week stocks, which flower the same year from an early sowing. Most modern varieties are annuals; many have been selected for growing under glass as cut flowers. They include both double- and single-flowered types; in many the double-flowered plants can be recognised as seedlings by a lobe in one of the cotyledons. Most are available as single colours or as mixtures. The tallest, 'Sentinel Columnar', has stems to 1m, and 'Mammoth Excelsior' has stems to 90cm. Dwarf or branched varieties are usually preferred for garden use.
'Cinderella' Stems around 25cm, very compact. Flowers red, pink, lavender or dark blue, with a good scent. Double-flowered plants with notched cotyledons.
'Heaven Scent' Stems to 15cm. Flowers double; a feeble plant.
'Legacy' Stems to 30cm, well-branched. Around 80% of plants with double flowers; available in an attractive mixture of colours.

Matthiola longipetala (Vent.) DC. subsp. **bicornis** (Sibth. & Sm.) P.W. Ball
Night-scented Stock A branching winter

Matthiola 'Legacy' mixed with *Diascia*

Matthiola 'Cinderella' mixed

annual with divided lower leaves and purplish, pinkish or greenish petals, which curl up in the sun and open on dull days or at night, native of S Greece and Turkey to Arabia and Cyrenaica, growing on sand dunes, dry fields and hills, at up to 1300m in Turkey, flowering in March–September. Stems to 50cm, usually about 20cm. Petals 3–7mm wide. Fruits with horns curved upwards. Very easily grown, and quick to flower from seed. Sow in spring in cold areas.

Matthiola sinuata (L.) R. Br.   A biennial, rarely an annual, with branching stems, deeply toothed or lobed lower leaves, pale purple flowers, and fruits with conspicuous glands, native of W Europe from England (N Devon) to NW Africa and the Mediterranean, growing on rocky and sandy coasts, flowering in May–July. Stems 8–60cm. Petals to 2.5cm long. Fruits 6–12cm long, without horns.

Matthiola tricuspidata (Vent.) DC. An annual with rounded leaf lobes, light purple flowers and terete fruits with 3 divergent horns at the apex, native on sandy shores around the W and S Mediterranean, except the former Yugoslavia and Albania, flowering in March–June. Stems 7–40cm. Leaves with rounded lobes. Petals 1.5–2.2cm long. Fruits 3–5.5cm, terete, with 3 triangular, divergent horns 2–6mm long. A very lovely species not often cultivated. *M. lunata* DC, which grows in rough places and scrub in S and E Spain and western North Africa, has toothed leaves, purple petals to 2.5cm long and fruit 5–8cm, with 2 incurving horns.

Matthiola 'Heaven Scent'

Matthiola 'Legacy'

Ricotia carnulosa on Symi

Hesperis steveniana at Sissinghurst

Ricotia carnulosa, showing fruit

Ricotia carnulosa on roadside cliffs south of Anatalya, towards Phaselis, in March

Hesperis steveniana DC. (*Cruciferae*)
A biennial with branching stems, semi-amplexicaul stem-leaves and large, pale purplish to whitish flowers, native of C Turkey, the W Caucasus and the Crimaea, growing in wood edges and scrub, flowering in April–June. Stems to 60cm, bristly below, with long unbranched hairs. Lower leaves stalked, with backwardly directed lobes. Petals 2.4–2.8cm long. Fruits erect, densely hairy. An attractive, early-flowering plant for a partially shaded position. *H. matronalis* L., the Dame's Violet, is a familiar garden plant; it is a short-lived perennial with scented flowers varying from white to mauve. It stem leaves are not amplexicaul, and usually short-stalked.

Malcomia maritima

Malcomia maritima (L.) R.Br. (*Cruciferae*)
Virginia Stock   A fast-growing, dwarf
annual with small, bright purple flowers and
slender fruit, native of S and W Greece and
S Albania, and naturalised elsewhere, growing
in sandy places near the sea, flowering in
March–June. Stems 10–35cm; leaves obovate
to oblong. Petals 1.2–2.5cm, pink or purple.
Fruits 3.5–8cm, with a narrow stalk. The
Virginia Stock is one of the most easily-grown
annuals, with charming, brightly-coloured but
scentless flowers. If the night-scented stock is
sown with it, each provides something the
other lacks.

Ricotia carnulosa Boiss. & Held.
(*Cruciferae*)   A dwarf winter annual with
narrow, divided leaves, white or lilac flowers
and flattened, hanging fruit, native of SW
Turkey from the Amanus westwards, and of
Symi, growing in rocky places at up to 700m,
flowering in March–April. Stems to 15cm.
Petals 1.1–1.2cm long. Fruits linear-oblong,
about 2cm long. A very attractive, dwarf
annual, not often cultivated. *Ricotia lunaria*
(L.) DC. from Syria, N Israel and Egypt, is an
attractive annual with deeply lobed leaves,
lilac, white-centred flowers with the petals
rounded and deeply emarginate, and
honesty-like fruit.

Tchihatchewia isatidea Boiss. (*Cruciferae*)
A biennial with a large, dense inflorescence of
scented, pinkish-lilac or reddish-purple
flowers and broadly winged fruit, native of
NE and C Turkey from Gümüsane to Kayseri,
growing on limestone screes and roadside
banks, at 1000–2000m, flowering in
May–June. Plant with long whitish hairs.
Stems to 25cm in fruit. Leaves narrowly
elliptic. Petals about 2cm long. Fruit hanging
down, 4.5cm long. A beautiful plant, and very
hardy, but difficult to grow in a climate with
mild, damp winters. I found that it rotted off
in the winter.
   The only species in the genus, named after
Count Pierre de Tchihatchef (1808–90),
author and traveller, who discovered it by the
headwaters of the Euphrates near Erzinçan.

Tschihatchewia isatidea near Kayseri in May

Heliophila species and other annuals at Padstal Farm near Nieuwoudtville in September

Heliophila coronopifolia

Heliophila pinnata

Schizopetalon walkeri

Heliophila patens near Kamieskroom

Heliophila The genus *Heliophila* contains around 71 species of annuals, perennials and shrubs, found throughout southern Africa. They have blue, white or pink flowers and a variety of fruit shapes, from thread-like to beaded, flattened or pendulous.

Heliophila africana (L.) Marais (*Cruciferae*) A winter annual with roughly hairy stems, and bright blue flowers, native of South Africa in the Western Cape, from Swellendam and the Peninsula northwards to Namaqualand, growing in sandy fields, wet in winter, flowering in August–October. Stems to 1.3m, usually about 40cm. Leaves flat, linear-lanceolate to oblanceolate, simple or the lower lobed, often hairy. Flowers around 1cm across, blue or mauve. Fruits thread-like, with straight margins, not beaded. One of the most robust of the annual species.

Heliophila coronopifolia L. A winter or spring annual with smooth stems, thread-like leaves and bright blue flowers, native of South Africa in the Western Cape, from the Peninsula northwards to S Namaqualand, growing in sandy places, flowering in August–October. Stems to 60cm, usually about 30cm. Lower leaves deeply lobed into narrow, fleshy segments. Flowers around 1–1.2cm across, blue with a pale centre. Fruits narrow, beaded. This is the most commonly grown of the species, and is very quick and reliable from seed at almost any time of year in mild, moist weather. It is often sold under the name *H. longifolia*.
  'Mediterranean Blue' appears to be a good strain of this species. *H. refracta* Sond.,

Heliophila thunbergii

Heliophila africana in the Tinie Versfeld reserve near Ceres

from the W Cape, is similar but has thread-like pendulous fruit. *H. arenaria* Sond. has hairy pedicels and sepals, and flowers to 1.5cm across with a small, pale centre.

Heliophila thunbergii Steud. A winter annual with slender stems and mauve, pink, white or blue flowers on long, slender pedicels, native of South Africa in the N Western Cape, from the Pakhuis mountains northwards to S Namaqualand, growing in sandy or clay soils, flowering in July–September. Stems to 25cm, usually about 10cm. Lower leaves roughly hairy, deeply lobed into narrow, fleshy segments. Flowers 8–10mm across, with pale centres. Fruits oblong, flat, drooping.

Heliophila patens Oliver A winter annual with spreading stems and white flowers, native of South Africa in the N Western Cape, from the Piketberg northwards to S Namaqualand, growing in sandy or clay soils, flowering in July–September. Stems to 20cm. Lower leaves pinnate, roughly hairy. Flowers around 8mm across.

Heliophila pinnata L. fil. A winter annual with slender, wiry stems and blue, mauve or pink flowers, native of South Africa in the N Western Cape, from Worcester northwards to S Namaqualand, growing in sandy soils, flowering in August–September. Stems to 15cm. Lower leaves finely divided, threadlike. Flowers 8–10mm across. Fruits beaded, pointing upwards. A small, delicate and very attractive species.

Schizopetalon walkeri Sims (*Cruciferae*) A winter annual with narrow, pinnate, greyish leaves and white flowers with deeply pinnately lobed petals, native of Chile, in the S Atacama desert, growing in dry, sandy and rocky places on foggy hills near the coast, flowering in September. Stems to 45cm. Flowers about 2.5cm across, scented of almonds. An easily grown and unusual plant, which will flower for several months into autumn if kept moist; best planted in late spring in frosty areas. The flowers open in evening or dull weather, as do many *Silene* and *Zalusianskya*.

Heliophila coronopifolia 'Mediterranean Blue'

Heliophila africana

Moricandia moricandioides near Ronda

Moricandia moricandioides

Lunaria annua subsp. *annua*

Lunaria annua L. (*Cruciferae*) **Honesty**
A biennial with stalked and toothed lower leaves, purple or white flowers and large, round, papery fruits, native of SE Europe and Italy, growing in woods and shady, rocky places, flowering in April–May. Stems to 1m. Petals 1.5–2.5cm long. Fruits around 5cm across, with 3–4 flattened seeds on either side of a silvery persistent septum. The commonly cultivated variety is subsp. ***annua***, which generally has a slender tap root and reddish-purple or white flowers, and is usually found as an escape from cultivation. Both the white-flowered and variegated forms are available in strains that come true from seed. 'Atrococcinea' is intensely red, 'Munstead Purple' less so.

Subspecies ***pachyrhiza*** (Borbás) Hayek from the Balkans, Romania and S Italy has tuberous roots and bluish-purple flowers. This needs a warm, sunny position; plants collectted by W. M. M. Baron flowered well in Devon, but set little good seed, and even that tended to rot before ripening. The other two *Lunaria* species are perennial; the familiar *L. rediviva* L. is large with pale lilac flowers, sweetly scented in the evening, and elliptical fruits; *L. telekiana* Jav. from NE Albania has the base of the sepals distinctly saccate for 2.5mm, and the fruit ciliate on the margin.

Moricandia arvensis (L.) DC. (*Cruciferae*)
An annual or short-lived perennial with grey, fleshy, amplexicaul leaves and lilac flowers veined with dark purple, native of the Mediterranean region in SW Europe, Greece and NW Africa, growing in waste places and cornfields on limestone, flowering in March–November. Stems to 65cm. Basal leaves obovate, not in a rosette. Flowers delicately scented with petals 2.1–2.9cm. Fruits linear straight, 3–6cm long. An easily grown plant with a long flowering season, lasting 2–3 years in mild areas.

Moricandia arvensis

Lunaria annua wild in the Ardèche, France

Orychophragmus violaceus at Hanshow Botanical Garden

Lunaria annua

Lunaria annua with leaves of daylilies in Eccleston Square

Moricandia moricandioides (Boiss.) Heywood   A winter annual with a rosette of almost round basal leaves and bright purple flowers, native of S, C and E Spain, growing on rocky slopes, screes and roadside banks at 300–700m, flowering in February–June. Stems to 80cm. Petals 1.8–2.9cm long. Fruits slightly curved, 7–11cm long. A striking plant, common in rocky places in SE Spain.

Orychophragmus violaceus (L.) Schultz (*Cruciferae*)   A winter annual or biennial with pinnatifid lower leaves, large lavender-blue flowers, native of NE China, growing in woods flowering in April–June. Stems to 1m. Upper leaves simple, amplexicaul. Petals to 3cm long. Fruit linear, 7–12cm. An honesty-like plant with rather fleshy leaves, which are eaten in China as a spring vegetable. As this species grows in woods north of Beijing, it should be very hardy. It grows well in full sun in cool climates.

Lunaria annua subsp. *pachyrhiza*

Isatis platyloba on rocky hills north of Salamanca

Isatis tinctoria seeds

Woad The genus *Isatis* contains around 30 species of annuals, biennials and perennials in Europe and W Asia, of which 26 are found in Turkey. *Isatis tinctoria* is the famous woad with which the Ancient Britons are said to have painted themselves. It was the usual source of navy-blue dye until the introduction of indigo from the East in 1631. The largest fruits, obovate and 2–3cm long, are found in the Turkish perennial species *I. cappadocica* Desv.

Isatis tinctoria L. (*Cruciferae*) **Woad**
A biennial or winter annual with tall stems forming a flat-topped, branching plant with small, yellow flowers followed by elongated, black, hanging fruits, native of the Mediterranean area, growing in waste places and open ground, flowering in May–July. Stems to 1.2m; stem leaves oblanceolate to linear-lanceolate. Flowers 3–4mm long; fruits 1.5–2cm long, 2–4mm wide, tapering from near the rounded or emarginate apex. Easily grown in well-drained, preferably chalky soil.

Isatis platyloba Link ex Steud. A winter annual or rarely biennial with tall stems forming a flat-topped, branching plant with small, yellow flowers followed by rounded, black, hanging fruits, native of the C Spain and NE Portugal, growing on bare rocky granite hills and roadsides, flowering in March–July. Stems to 1m; stem leaves ovate to almost linear, with acute auricles. Flowers 3.5–5.5mm long; fruits 8–14mm long, 6–10mm wide, suborbicular or ovate, rounded at base and apex. A striking species, found mainly around Salamanca and Zaragosa, and in the Miranda do Douro. *I. lusitanica* L., an annual with even narrower fruits than *I. tinctoria*, comes from Greece, North Africa and SW Asia.

Mignonette The genus *Reseda* contains about 55 species of annuals, perennials and subshrubs, found mainly around the Mediterranean region. All have small, palmately lobed, generally greenish-yellow

Woad, *Isatis tinctoria* in Eccleston Square

Reseda odorata at Quince House, with catmint and *Nemesia*

petals, and strange, open-ended capsules containing few large seeds. Several contain a yellow dye, particularly the biennial *R. luteola* L., the dyer's weed or weld used by the Romans. It is now found wild on chalky soils in Britain and in North America, and is easily recognised by its rosettes of linear, dark green leaves and very narrow, upright spikes of pale green flowers to 1.5m tall.

Reseda odorata L. (*Resedaceae*) **Mignonette**
A leafy winter annual or perennial with spikes of dull whitish flowers with a heavy, sweet scent, and red or brownish-orange anthers, native of Egypt, but naturalised elsewhere in the Mediterranean and in California, growing in open ground, flowering in May–September or until the first frost. Stems to 50cm. Leaves thin, soft, and fleshy. Petals 4–4.5mm long; Stamens 20–25. Fruit nodding. Mignonette is an old favourite, grown in gardens for its scent, and still used by the perfume industry. 'Red Monarch' has deep red anthers; 'Grandiflora' is more yellow.

Reseda phyteuma L.   A branching winter annual to perennial with glandular spikes of whitish flowers, native of C and S Europe, N Africa and SW Asia, growing in stony places, dry scrub and waste ground, flowering in March–August. Stems to 40cm, prostrate, then ascending. Leaves often fleshy, bluish-green with wavy margins. Sepals 6, enlarging in fruit. Petals 3–7mm long, with around 12 long, linear lobes. Stamens 17–20. Fruit with 3 obtuse teeth. A very variable species, common around the Mediterranean coasts.

Reseda odorata

Reseda phyteuma near Granada

Cleome hassleriana 'Violet Queen'

Cleome (*Capparidaceae*) A genus of around 150 species of annuals, perennials and shrubs, mainly from tropical America and Africa. A few are cultivated as summer annuals. Fruits are carried on a long gynophore, the stalk of the ovary, which elongates as the fruits develop.

Cleome aculeata L. A stiff tropical annual with spidery pinkish flowers, native of Mexico and the West Indies to South America, flowering much of the year. Stems to 90cm. Leaves with 3 leaflets, short stalked. Petals around 6mm long. Fruits to 6.5cm.

Cleome gynandra L. A widely branching annual with white or pink flowers and long, red filaments, native of Central America, but now found throughout the tropics, growing in rocky places, flowering much of the year. Stems to 1.3m. Leaves with 3–7 leaflets, long-stalked. Petals around 2cm long. Fruits to 10cm.

Cleome hassleriana Chodat, syn. *C. spinosa* auct., *C. sesquiorygalis* Naudin ex C. Huber A tall, sticky and aromatic summer annual with palmate, hemp-like leaves and spikes of spidery, pink, mauve or white flowers with long stamens, native of SE Brazil to Argentina, but widely naturalised elsewhere in the warmer parts of America, growing in fields and waste places, flowering in summer and autumn. Stems to 2m. Leaves with 5–7 leaflets. Leaf stalks often with a spine at the base. Petals 2.5–4cm; stamens 6, to 6cm. Fruits 5–15cm long. This is now available in the following colours: **'Helen Campbell'** syn. 'White Queen'; 'Cherry Queen'; 'Mauve Queen'; 'Pink Queen'; 'Rose Queen'; **'Violet Queen'**; and 'Colour Fountain' mix. Sow at 15–20°C, and plant out after the last frost.

Cleome serrulata Pursh **Rocky Mountain Beeplant** A summer annual with 3 leaflets and dense spikes of small, pink flowers, native of E Washington and N California and on the Great Plains to New Mexico and N Texas, growing on plains and in sagebush scrub in the foothills, flowering in May–September. Stems branched to 1.5m. Leaflets 2–7.5cm long. Petals 4, 1–1.2cm long. Stamens 6, much longer than the petals. Fruits 2.5–6.5cm long. An attractive species, not common in cultivation. *Cleome lutea* Hook., also from western North America, has smaller, yellow flowers and 5–7 leaflets. Both have abundant nectar and are beloved by bees.

Cleome serrulata, wild in Arizona

Cleome hassleriana 'Helen Campbell' at Cothay

Cleome aculeata in Mexico

A mixed planting of *Cleome hassleriana*

Cleome gynandra on the ruins of Monte Albán in Oaxaca in April

Tropaeolum majus naturalised on the west coast of Madeira

Tropaeolum peregrinum at Kew

Nasturtium The genus *Tropaeolum* in the family *Tropaeolaceae* has around 87 species native from Mexico to South America, most of which are perennial climbers with tuberous roots. The leaves are peltate, and round, lobed or deeply divided, and the flowers have the lowest sepal modified into a long spur. The hardiest species include the scarlet *T. speciosum* and the yellow *T. ciliatum*, both fleshy-rooted perennials from S Chile. The English name Nasturtium is confusing, as it is also the Latin name for watercress, a member of the family *Cruciferae*. *T. majus* was formerly called Indian Cress, and does contain the hot mustard oil found in the *Cruciferae*; like cabbage, it is also eaten by the Large White and Small White butterflies.

Tropaeolum majus L. A robust summer annual climber or creeper with round leaves and cream, yellow, orange, red or brown flowers. Not known in the wild, but perhaps a hybrid between *T. minus* and *T. ferreyrae* Sparre formed long ago in the Lima area and introduced to Europe from Peru before 1656. It is now naturalised elsewhere in cool, frost-free climates, especially along coasts. Stems to 3m or more. Leaves 5–15cm wide. Flowers 3–6cm across, originally red. Spur 2–3.5cm. Fruits to 1cm across. Both leaves and flowers are edible. Numerous new hybrids have since been raised in Europe, aiming to produce more floriferous varieties with flowers held well above the leaves. Some single varieties are shown here; many of the double ones are on the following pages.

'Moonlight' An old variety, grown since 1899. Flowers single, pale creamy-yellow; leaves light green. Stems trailing to 180cm.

'Strawberry Ice' Flowers single, deep yellow with a red spot on each petal. Leaves bluish-green. Height around 20cm, not trailing.

Tropaeolum peregrinum

Tropaeolum majus 'Moonlight'

Tropaeolum at Monet's garden, Giverney, photographed by Jonathan Lloyd

'Tip Top Apricot'   Flowers single, pale apricot with red feathering on the upper petals, held well above the leaves to around 30cm, not trailing. 'Tip Top' is also available as a mixture or in gold, mahogany or scarlet. 'Tip Top Alaska' has variegated leaves.

Tropaeolum minus L.   A trailing or scrambling summer annual with round leaves and yellow flowers with red spots, native of Peru and Ecuador, flowering in summer. Stems to 2m. Leaves downy beneath and indented with a minute point at the end of each vein. Flowers to 3.5cm across, with a spur 2.5–3cm long. Petals yellow or pale orange, the upper larger, with a red spot on each. Fruit 5–6mm.
    Tropaeolum peltophorum Benth., from Colombia, Ecuador and Peru, has leaves with veins ending in a point, with wavy edges, and orange or red flowers 2.5cm across, the lower petals with fringed edges. The cultivar 'Spitfire', which is rare but in cultivation, has reddish stems and orange flowers with red markings in the throat.

Tropaeolum peregrinum L. **Canary Creeper**   A climbing summer annual with deeply 5-lobed leaves and small, yellow flowers with fringed and feathery petals, native of Peru, where it is common around Tarma, Cuzco and Chinceros, at around 3000m, flowering in summer in cultivation. Stems to 2.5m. Leaves 3.5–8cm across. Flowers to 2.5cm across, the upper 2 petals deeply fringed, finely spotted with red, the lower 3 narrow and feathery. Fruit 1–1.4cm. A common and easily grown climber, best started indoors at 15–20°C.

Tropaeolum majus 'Tip Top Apricot'

Tropaeolum majus 'Strawberry Ice'

Tropaeolum minus in the order beds at Kew

Tropaeolum 'Strawberries & Cream'

Tropaeolum 'Jewel Primrose'

Tropaeolum 'Jewel of Africa'

Tropaeolum 'Whirlybird Cherry'

Nasturtiums in the trial grounds of Kees Sahin in Holland

Tropaeolum 'Gleam Apricot'

Tropaeolum 'Alaska'

Nasturtium (*Tropaeolaceae*) Shown on these pages are a selection of *Tropaeolum* cultivars of mixed parentage, most of which are readily available. Do not sow until after the last frosts. 'Tom Thumb' (not shown) is an old dwarf strain, grown since 1859, with single flowers and stems to 25cm, not trailing. It was formerly available in separate colours and with variegated leaves.

'Alaska' A semi-trailing strain, with pale green leaves marbled with white. Flowers single, in mixed colours.
'Empress of India', syn. 'Pride of India' An old variety, but still one of the best, grown since 1882. Flowers single, dark crimson scarlet; leaves dark bluish-green with a red edge. Height around 20cm, not trailing.
'Gleam Apricot' Flowers semi-double. This series also available in gold, scarlet, orange and mixed. Plant semi-trailing, to 40cm.
'Jewel of Africa' perhaps the same as 'Out of Africa' Stems trailing to 2m. Leaves with

white spots and streaks. Flowers single, in mixed colours including peach and cream.
'Jewel Dwarf Double' mixed Flowers semi-double; height to 25cm.
'Jewel' mixed, **'Jewel Primrose'** Flowers double, in a mixture of colours; height to 25cm. Also available in 'Cherry Rose' an unusual red, gold, mahogany and scarlet.
'Red Tiger' Flowers semi-double, orange, with darker stripes.
'Salmon Baby' A dwarf with salmon-pink double flowers.
'Strawberries & Cream' Flowers double, creamy-yellow with red blotches on all the petals. Height to 30cm, not trailing.
'Tall Single-flowered' mixed Flowers single, of various colours. A trailing strain with stems to 2m.
'Whirlybird Cherry' The Whirlybird series has single, actinomorphic flowers, i.e. with all the petals the same shape, and without spurs. Stems to 20cm, not trailing. Available also in gold, orange, tangerine, scarlet, red, or as a mixture, **'Whirlybird' mixed**.

'Jewel' mixed

'Gleam' mixed

'Tall Single-flowered' mixed

'Jewel' mixed

'Red Tiger'

'Empress of India'

'Salmon Baby'

'Alaska'

'Jewel Dwarf Double' mixed

'Whirlybird' mixed

Specimens from Eccleston Square, July 8th, ½ life-size

Limnanthes douglasii var. *sulphurea*

Limnanthes douglasii

Meadow Foam The genus *Limnanthes* in the small family *Limnanthaceae* is a genus of around 8 species of annuals from western North America. Most are found in wet ground, and have white, pink or yellow flowers, much visited by bees. The family *Limnanthaceae* is sometimes placed close to *Linaceae*, sometimes to *Tropaeolaceae*.

Limnanthes douglasii R. Br. var. ***douglasii*** **Poached Egg Plant** A branched, spreading winter annual with bright green leaves and sweetly scented white flowers with yellow centres, native of the Coast Ranges from S Oregon and N California southwards to San Benito Co., growing in moist places, springs and vernal pools, at below 1000m, flowering in March–May. Stems to 40cm. Leaves pinnate, with 5–11 lobes. Flowers around 3cm across. Seeds drupe-like, 3–5 per flower. Var. *sulphurea* C.T. Mason has all-yellow flowers, and is confined to the Point Reyes area in Marin Co.; var. *nivea* C.T. Mason has white flowers, often with dark purple veins, and is found from San Luis Opispo Co. northwards; var. *rosea* (Hartw. in Benth.) C.T. Mason has pink-veined flowers, becoming pink all over as they fade and is found in the Sierra Nevada foothills south to Madera Co.

All are easily grown as spring annuals, sown in moist ground after the worst frosts have passed, or in autumn in mild areas.

Limnanthes vinculans Ornd. A low, branching annual with undivided leaves and white flowers with green veins, native of California, in Sonoma Co., growing in marshy meadows, flowering in March–May. Stems to 20cm. Leaves oblanceolate. Flowers around 2cm across, with emarginate petals.

Flax Well-known as the source of linen and linseed oil, *Linum* has been cultivated since 8000 BC. About 180 species of *Linum*, either annuals (mostly small-flowered), perennials or low shrubs, are found all around the northern hemisphere. In many species the flowers are heteromorphic: the style and stamens are of different lengths, to ensure cross-pollination.

Limnanthes vinculans in Berkley Botanical Garden

Linum grandiflorum

Linum grandiflorum 'Bright Eyes'

A field of *Linum usitatissimum* on Salisbury Plain

Linum grandiflorum Desf. (*Linaceae*)
A winter annual with spectacular large, usually red flowers, native of North Africa, (and occasionally naturalised in California), growing in fields and waste places, flowering in March–May. Stems upright, little-branched, to 60cm. Leaves lanceolate, greyish-green. Petals 1.5–2.5cm long. The commonest variety, var. *rubrum*, has bright crimson-red flowers; in the past, there were varieties with more crimson and more scarlet flowers, and one with purple flowers. Var. *album* is pure white. **'Bright Eyes'** has pure white, shining flowers set off by a chocolate-brown centre. All are easy to grow and fast to flower from seed sown outdoors in spring. *Linum pubescens* Banks & Sol., an attractive annual with pink petals with bluish veins and base, 1.8–2.7cm long, does not seem to be in cultivation. Subsp. *pubescens* grows on dry limestone hills and fields from S Turkey and W Syria to N Israel and Cyprus, flowering in April–May. Subsp. *sibthorpianum* (Margot & Reut.) Davis, is found in Albania, Greece and W Crete.

Linum usitatissimum L. **Common Flax**
A slender annual with narrow leaves and pale blue flowers, not known as a wild plant, but long cultivated for linen and linseed. Stems 40–90cm or more depending on the variety. Flowers blue, to about 3cm across. 'Skyscraper' is a tall variety. 'Sutton's Blue' a shorter one, grown for its flowers. European Common Agricultural Policy subsidies encouraged the planting of flax fields such as the one shown here. The small, yellow-flowered *Linum sulcatum* Riddell, from dry fields in eastern North America is sometimes cultivated.

Tuberaria guttata (L.) Fourr., syn. *Xolantha guttata* (L.) Raf. (*Cistaceae*) A winter annual with stiffly hairy leaves and bright yellow, usually red-spotted flowers, native of Europe from W Ireland to the Mediterranean region, growing in dry, rocky and sandy places, flowering in April–July. Stems to 30cm. Leaves obovate to broadly linear. Petals 3–9mm long, or even absent. An attractive annual rock rose, found wild in NW Europe only on rocky exposed headlands and offshore islands. The dwarf, branching form with wide leaves, found in Ireland and NW Wales, is sometimes distinguished as subsp. *breweri* (Planch.) E.F. Warb. The generic name *Xolantha* Raf. is used in the recent *Flora Iberica* (1993).

Tuberaria guttata in Spain in May

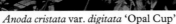
Anoda cristata var. *digitata* 'Opal Cup'

Lavatera trimestris in S Spain near Cadiz

Anoda cristata 'Snow Cup'

Malva hispanica

Anoda cristata (L.) Schlecht. (*Malvaceae*) An upright summer annual with triangular, lobed to narrowly hastate leaves and purplish flowers, native of Arizona, W Texas and Mexico, growing in moist meadows and along streams at 1100–1900m, flowering in August–October. Stems to 1m, long-haired. Leaves 2–6cm long, very variable in shape, the lowest digitately lobed in var. **digitata** (Gray) Hochr. Petals 2–2.5cm long. Epicalyx lacking. Calyx with 5 long, acuminate lobes, accrescent. Carpels 9–20, bristly hairy. **'Opal Cup'**, with pinkish-purple flowers, appears to belong to var. *digitata*. **'Snow Cup'**, with white flowers, has broader leaves. They should be sown at 15–20°C, and planted out in mid-summer in cool areas. They do best in moist, rich soil. Most of the around 23 *Anoda* species are found in Mexico and S America.

Lavatera arborea L. (*Malvaceae*) An upright, shrubby biennial with velvety-hairy leaves and purplish flowers, native of the W coasts of Europe, from Ailsa Craig southwards to the Mediterranean region, growing in shrubby and rocky places and waste ground near the sea, flowering in March–June. Stems to 3m. Leaves to 20cm across, shallowly lobed. Petals 1.5–2cm. Epicalyx of 3 large, broad, accrescent segments, 8–10mm long. Sepals about 4mm, oblong-lanceolate, acute. Carpels 6–8, smooth or downy. A striking plant, usually found near the sea, and sometimes grown in gardens there.

Lavatera trimestris L. An upright, branching winter annual with vine-like, large, pink or white flowers, native of Portugal and the Mediterranean region, growing in open fields, waste ground and sandy places, at up to 900m, flowering in March–June. Stems to 120cm. Leaves 3–7cm across, the lower less lobed. Petals 2–4.5cm. Epicalyx of 3 segments, forming a cup, accrescent. Sepals 9–14mm, oblong-lanceolate, acute. Carpels 9–20, glabrous. A showy and easily-grown annual, now available in dwarf (60–70cm), and normal sizes and ranging in colour from deep pink to white.

Lavatera trimestris mixed colours

Lavatera arborea on the coast of Cornwall

Lavatera trimestris 'Silver Cup'

Lavatera trimestris 'Silver Cup' This beautiful variety has pale silvery pink petals with darker veins, and stems to 70cm. In 'Pink Beauty' the flowers are a little darker, while 'Ruby Regis' has deep pink flowers with crimson veins, about 10cm across, and stems to 70cm. 'Mont Blanc' is pure white, with stems to 70cm. All do well, sown where they are to flower, in spring, in not too heavily manured soil. In mild areas they may be sown in autumn.

Malope trifida Cav. (*Malvaceae*) An upright and almost glabrous annual with deep purplish-red flowers, native of NW Africa, and possibly native though probably naturalised in SW Spain and S Portugal, growing in stony places and waste ground, flowering in April–June. Stems single, to 1.5m. Upper leaves with 3–5 broad lobes. Petals 3.5–6cm long, narrowed towards the base. Epicalyx segments 3, cordate, wider than the sepals. Easily grown as a summer annual, planted in light soil in early spring.

Available in mixed colours from purplish-red to pink and white, and as 'Pink Queen', 'Red Queen' and 'White Queen'; 'Tetra Vulcan', said to be a tetraploid, has branching stems and large deep purplish-red flowers. *Malope malacoides* L. from S Europe, SW Asia and NW Africa has ovate, crenate leaves and trumpet-shaped, bright pink or purplish flowers with petals 2–6cm long.

Malva hispanica L. (*Malvaceae*) A winter annual with semicircular leaves and pale pink flowers, native of Spain, Portugal and western North Africa, growing in meadows and sandy open places, flowering in April–September. Stems to 90cm, with long, soft hairs. Leaves 2–3cm across. Petals 1.5–2.5cm long. Epicalyx segments 2, linear, pubescent. Sepals 8–15mm, ovate or triangular-ovate. This is one of the larger-flowered of the annual species of *Malva*; *M. trifida* Cav., syn. *M. stipulacea* auct., from C and S Spain, has petals 1.5–3cm long, and leaves deeply dissected into 3-fid lobes.

Malope trifida in the Chelsea Physic Garden

A field of cotton, *Gossypium hirsutum*

Flowers of cotton, *Gossypium hirsutum*

Hibiscus trionum at Suttons

Alcea pallida near Antalya in May

Alcea pallida (Willd.) Walsdt. & Kit. (*Malvaceae*)   A tall and very variable perennial with shallowly lobed leaves and white, lilac or pink flowers, yellow at the base, native of E Europe from Hungary southwards to Turkey, growing on open fallow fields and rocky places at up to 1500m, flowering in May–October. Stems to 2m, hispid-setose. Petals 3.5–5cm. Epicalyx segments around half as long as the sepals. Requires a hot, dry position.

Alcea setosa (Boiss.) Alef.   A tall and very variable perennial with often deeply divided leaves and white or pink flowers, native of Cyprus, Crete, W. Syria and Turkey, growing on rocky places at up to 700m, flowering in May–July. Stems to 2m, hispid-setose. Petals 3.5–5cm. Epicalyx segments around half as long as the sepals. Requires a hot, dry position.

Gossypium hirsutum L. (*Malvaceae*) A woody annual with lobed leaves and yellow flowers followed by a capsule with cotton among the seeds, native perhaps of Peru, but now widely cultivated for its cotton. Stems to 1.5m. Leaves 3–7-lobed. Flowers yellow. Epicalyx segments 3, deeply toothed. Capsule 4–6cm. Thrives best in great heat, with irrigation at the root. Sow seed in spring.

Hibiscus trionum L. (*Malvaceae*) A shrubby summer annual with deeply divided, lobed leaves and pale yellow flowers with a dark purple centre, native of SW Asia and Africa, but now widely naturalised throughout the drier parts of the tropics. Stems to 1.2m. Leaves 3–5-lobed, the lobes narrow, sometimes further lobed and toothed. Flowers about 5cm across. Epicalyx segments linear, numerous, deeply toothed. Calyx inflated, papery, strongly veined. 'Lyonia', in creamy-yellow, 'Simply Love', in silvery-yellow, and 'Sunnyday', in lemon-yellow are three selections of the species. Very easily grown; sow seed indoors at 15–20°C in early spring.

Alcea setosa on the coast of Turkey, south of Antalya

Hollyhocks in a village garden in Dorset

A single cultivated hollyhock

Alcea rosea L. syn. *Althaea rosea* (L.) Cav.
(*Malvaceae*) **Hollyhock**   A biennial or
perennial with hairy, lobed leaves and tall
spikes of flowers of various colours, of
uncertain origin and long cultivated both in
SW Asia and China, but probably a hybrid
between two species from Turkey, *A. setosa*
and *A. pallida* (see below). Stem to 7.39m,
(which Mabberly mentions as the UK
record), but usually around 3m, glabrous
when mature. Leaves finely crenate, with
shallow, rounded lobes. Flowers to 12cm
across. Epicalyx with 6–8 broadly triangular
segments. Angles of the seeds almost winged.

The hollyhock is an old garden flower,
grown in England since the 16th century and
now widely naturalised around the world. The
black-flowered single 'Nigra' was illustrated in
1585 (Istanbul), and by 1613 Besler's *Hortus
Eystettensis* showed double and single
hollyhocks in shades of red, white, and purple.
In this period, many new plants were being
introduced to W Europe from Istanbul.

Most species and cultivars are affected by
rust in moist climates, which disfigures, though
rarely kills plants. Spray at the first sign of the
disease, and as the new leaves emerge in
spring. Hollyhocks do best in well-drained,
limy soil in a sunny, sheltered position.

'Peaches 'n' Dreams' is a recent double
with stems to 2m, and pale peach-pink
flowers; 'Double Apricot' is similar, if not the
same. 'Nigra' is still available, as is 'Nigra
Plena' and one called 'Black Beauty'. Doubles
and singles are also sold as seed in single or
mixed colours.

Hollyhocks at Leiden Botanical Garden

Hollyhock 'Peaches 'n' Dreams' at
Thompson and Morgan's trial grounds

Alcea rosea

Alcea rosea

Viola altaica, yellow and purple forms near Medeo

Viola altaica in alpine meadows near Medeo, above Alma Ata, in May

Viola lutea wild in Aberdeenshire in May

Pansies and Violas (*Violaceae*) Both pansies and violas have long been grown in cottage gardens, loved and admired for their ability to flower in winter and spring. In *A Midsummer Night's Dream* (1595) Shakespeare refers to them as "love-in-idleness", while in *Hamlet*, Ophelia raves of "pansies, that's for thoughts", punning the French for thoughts, *pensées*, the origin of the common name of pansy for *Viola tricolor,* also called heartsease.

However, the development of garden pansies as we know them dates only from the early 19th century. During the 1820s, two keen English amateur gardeners, Lord Gambier, of Iver, Buckinghamshire and Lady Tennet (later Lady Monke), of Walton-upon-Thames began to grow the common heartsease, *V. tricolor*, as a garden plant, and made attempts to "improve" it.

Lady Tennet's gardener, William Richardson, raised several new cultivars, while Gambier's gardener, Mr T. Thompson, collected as many varieties as he could of the variable British natives *V. tricolor* and *V. lutea* (see below), and selected out the finest and largest forms. Encouraged by their employers, both men also used a "darker sort, said to be imported from Russia" (probably a form of *V. altaica*) and started to breed larger-flowered varieties.

At first, the only colours available were blue, white, and yellow. Eventually, Thompson was lucky enough to find a self-sown seedling which had the dark blotch and characteristic "face" markings of the most desirable pansies, and he used this and another chance seedling of bronze to extend the colours and range of markings available for breeding. An idea of these early varieties can be seen in the "Bouquet de Pensées", in Redouté's *Choix de plus Belles Fleurs,* published from 1827–33.

By the mid-19th century around 400 named varieties of pansies were available, and they were classified in Britain as Show or Florists' flowers. For exhibition purposes the flowers were divided into two categories: the Selfs, with petals all of the same colour and an inconspicuous eye, and the White or Yellow Ground category. Rules for admittance to these categories were so strict that further development of the pansy was almost stifled.

Luckily, the French and Belgians, who had also started to grow pansies seriously, were not so constrained, and produced flowers in a wide array of colours; these were known as Fancy Pansies, and were imported to England by an enterprising Englishman named John Salter, who had, until the Revolution, run a nursery in Versailles specialising in florists' flowers. In 1848 he left France and came to London, where he founded the Versailles Nursery in Hammersmith, growing and distributing pansies and other flowers. The Fancy pansies eventually eclipsed the Show pansies in popularity, leading to the numerous varieties available today, most of which are treated as annuals or biennials and used as bedding plants or in containers.

Viola altaica Ker-Gawl.   A creeping perennial, with pale to deep yellow or violet flowers, native of the Altai and Tien-Shan mountains, with subsp. *oreades* in Turkey, the Caucasus and the Crimea; it grows in grassy, open places at 2000–2600m, flowering in May–July. Plant spreads underground to form clumps of elliptic to ovate leaves with crenate margins. Flowers to 2.5cm across, with broad, overlapping petals. This species is probably Thompson's "darker sort, said to be imported from Russia".

Viola lutea Huds. **Mountain Pansy**
A creeping perennial, with small flowers,
1.5–2.5cm across, the lower petal to 1.5cm
wide, usually yellow, occasionally violet or
bicoloured. Native of W Europe, from
Scotland and Ireland to Spain, eastwards to
Switzerland, growing in grassy meadows,
usually in the hills, forming loose patches and
spreading by means of underground stolons,
flowering in May–June. Subspecies *sudetica*
(Willd.) W.Becher, with thicker stems and
larger flowers, to around 2.3cm across, is
found from the Alps eastwards to the former
Czechoslovakia, and it was this subspecies
that was crossed with *V. tricolor* to produce the
cultivated pansy.

Viola tricolor L. **Heartsease, Johnny-
Jump-up** An annual, or sometimes
short-lived perennial, with flowers variously
coloured, often bicoloured blue and yellow,
native of most of Europe and Asia, southwards
to C Turkey and eastwards to Siberia and the
Himalayas, growing in grassy places and
arable fields, flowering from April–September.
Stipules conspicuous, with the terminal
segment lanceolate, leaf-like and larger than
the others. The wild type shown here from NE
Scotland, is often perennial, common in the
north of England and Scotland, rare in the
south; it grows in pastures and disturbed
grassland, where it forms mats of creeping
stems. Subspecies *curtisii* (E.Forster) Syme is
similar, but often has yellow flowers, and is
usually found on sand dunes near the sea in
W Europe and the Baltic. Other subspecies
are found in the mountains of the Balkan
peninsula and S and C Europe.

'Blackjack' A small, black-flowered
V. tricolor, similar to 'Bowles' Black' or
'Sawyer's Black'. There are also black pansies
with larger, rounder flowers, such as 'Black
Devil' raised in Japan.

'Blue Moon' A dwarf with blue and yellow
flowers, very like the wild Scottish heartsease.

'Yesterday, Today and Tomorrow' A new
variety, in which the small flowers change
colour from white through pale blue to deep
blue. A seed-raised F$_1$ strain.

Pansy 'Yesterday, Today and Tomorrow' with flowers that fade after opening

Pansy 'Blue Moon'

Pansy 'Blackjack'

Viola tricolor, wild form

Old-fashioned pansies in the trial fields of Kees Sahin in Holland

Pansies, hyacinths and tulips in Monet's garden at Giverny in April

Garden Pansies (*Violaceae*) The collective name for garden pansies is *V.×wittrockiana*, after the Swedish botanist V. B. Wittrock (1839–1914) who studied them in detail. There is much similarity and confusion between pansies and violas, but the main difference can be seen in the root system: pansies are single-rooted, while violas are either multi-rooted or have underground stolons.

Pansies are easily raised from seed, which can be sown in pots in the summer and kept outside in a cool, moist spot, before pricking out and planting in the autumn. In good conditions, and with mild winter weather, hardy strains such as 'Universal' will start to flower during the autumn and continue throughout the winter into the spring and early summer.

Alternatively, seed of later-flowering groups can be sown in the autumn, and kept at a temperature of about 20°C to ensure good germination; seedlings should then be grown on at about 10°C, before being overwintered in a cold frame and planted out in spring. A third option is to sow seed of summer-flowering strains such as 'Imperial' or 'Majestic Giants' in early spring for hardening off and planting out in early May.

To flourish, pansies need a good, moist soil. If you have time, snip off dead heads and any seed pods as they appear, as this will prolong the flowering season. Try to avoid areas where

Pansy 'Universal Light Blue' with *Narcissus* 'Hawera' at Kew

Pansy 'Rose Bedder' at Giverny

Pansy 'Ultima Lavender Shades' at Kew

Pansy 'Universal Mixture' in Spain

they have been previously grown, as the plants can be susceptible to certain soil-borne fungi.

Some of the photographs of pansy cultivars here were taken in France, during April, when we visited Monet's garden at Giverny; the planting and colour combinations were so attractive that we decided to include many of them as a model of good planting and a source of inspiration. Note the way in which pansies and violas have been mixed together, providing a contrast in flower size, with tulips and other bulbs providing extra height.

More pleasing results are achieved through obtaining single colour forms and then mixing them with similar or complementary colours, rather than buying one of the ready-mixed selections from seed suppliers. Some, such as 'Antique Shades' (see page 80–81), are now sold as mixtures in a single colour range. We have given the cultivar names where known, although many very similar-looking pansies are offered for sale under different names, depending on which catalogue you consult, and the selection is always changing. Single colours of strains such as 'Aalsmeer Giant' (early flowering), 'Clear Crystal', 'Imperial', 'Swiss Giant', 'Tempo' and 'Universal' are available from some seed suppliers, and some very distinctive named varieties, such as the Joker types, are available separately.

'Rose Bedder'   This is notable for its unusual rose colour, and received a Highly Commended award from the RHS in 1985.

'Ultima Lavender Shades'   A new F_1 hybrid, with flowers ranging from pale lavender to light blue. Does well in containers.

'Universal'   A well known strain of winter-flowering pansies, available from seedsmen either in mixed colours, as **'Universal Mixture'** shown here or in single colours, e.g. 'Blue Blotch', deep blue, tinged with purple, and a dark blue blotch, or **'Light Blue'**, pale blue with a darker blue blotch.

Mixed blue and mauve pansies, with tulips and *Fritillaria persica* in Monet's garden

Pansies and tulips with a border of lilac forget-me-nots in Monet's garden at Giverny

'Imperial Antique Shades' A recent F_1 hybrid introduction, using 5 pastel shades, attractive, subtle colours that change as they mature. Not available as separate colours at the moment.

'Imperial Gold Princess' Plant to about 20cm high, large-flowered, with golden petals and a deep raspberry-red blotch. Introduced in 1991.

'Joker Poker Face' Plant to about 15cm high, with a very distinctive flower, consisting of orange and violet petals and a dark eye.

'Jolly Joker' An F_2 hybrid to about 15cm high, with bright orange petals and contrasting purple wings. Spring flowering.

'Prince John' A compact, tufted viola-type, with pure yellow flowers over a long season. Best sown in the autumn.

'Universal' The following colours are shown: **'Orange'**, apricot orange, with slightly paler upper petals and no blotch; **'Red Wing'**, deep rusty-red upper petals, and gold lower petals with a dark blotch.

Pansies at Versailles in May

Pansy 'Prince John' with *Muscari*

Pansy 'Imperial Gold Princess'

Pansy 'Joker Poker Face' at Giverny

Pansy 'Universal Red Wing'

Pansy 'Universal Orange'

Pansies with wallflowers and tulips in Monet's garden

Pansy 'Jolly Joker' at Giverny

Pansy 'Imperial Antique Shades'

Agrostemma gracilis 'Milas'

Gypsophila elegans 'Covent Garden'

Agrostemma gracilis

Agrostemma gracilis 'Ocean Pearl'

Agrostemma githago L. (*Caryophyllaceae*)
Corn Cockle An upright winter or spring
annual with narrow leaves and reddish-
purple, sometimes whitish, flowers, native of
the Mediterranean region, but naturalised
through much of the world, growing in
cornfields and waste places, flowering in
April–August. Stems to 1m. Leaves lanceolate
to linear, opposite. Calyx tube with spreading
hairs, the teeth 2–3.5cm long, 2–3mm wide,
extending beyond the petals. Petals 3–3.5cm,
usually unspotted. Seeds large, 3mm or more.
This was once often seen in cornfields, even in
England, but is now increasingly rare in areas
where the corn is sprayed. The large seeds
survived primitive cleaning, and it was formerly
a common and poisonous adulterant of wheat.

Agrostemma gracilis Boiss. A branching
winter annual with narrow leaves and purplish
or reddish flowers with lines of spots, native of
C Greece, near Farsala, and W and S Turkey
east to Hatay, growing in fields and dry hills,
flowering in May–June.
   This differs from *A. githago* in having stems
to 60cm, narrower leaves, and petals longer
than the calyx teeth, which are 1.1–1.6cm
long, 1–1.5mm wide. Seeds 1.5–2mm across.
   'Milas', syn. 'Rose Queen' pinkish, with
stems to 1m, **Milas Cerise**, syn. 'Purple
Queen' purplish-pink, 'Rose Queen' and
'Ocean Pearl' a beautiful white, are cultivars
of this species, rather than of *A. githago*, under
which they are sometimes listed. 'Milas' is said
to be named after the village of Milas near
Mugla in SW Turkey, from where it was
brought into cultivation. These cultivated corn
cockles are among the loveliest and easiest of
annuals to grow. They are best sown in spring,
and in succession, where they are to flower.

Gypsophila elegans 'Giant White'

Gypsophila elegans var. rosea

Gypsophila elegans Bieb. (*Caryophyllaceae*)
A much-branched spring annual with masses
of white, pink or crimson flowers, native of
S Russia, the Caucasus, E Turkey and Iran,
growing on stony steppes and banks at
650–2600m, flowering in June–July. Plants to
60cm across, glabrous. Leaves opposite, linear
or linear-lanceolate, 1–6cm long, more than
3mm wide. Petals 5–10mm, long, usually
white with purple veins, emarginate.
Numerous varieties of this quick-growing
annual are cultivated. **'Covent Garden'** has
stems to 70cm with large, pure white flowers,
and was grown for cutting in spring and early
summer; **'Giant White'** is as tall, with masses

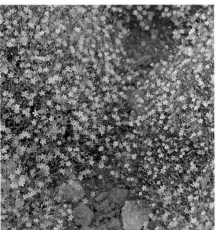

Gypsophila muralis 'Gypsy'

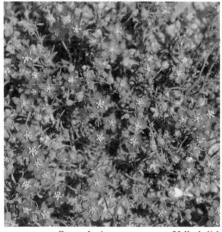

Spergularia purpurea near Valladolid

Agrostemma gracilis 'Milas Cerise'

of smaller flowers; 'White Elephant' is said to have the largest flowers of all. Var. **rosea** has small, pale pink flowers, and 'Carminea', 'Crimson' and 'Kermesina' have deeper reddish flowers. All germinate very easily and grow fast, but are particularly attractive to slugs and snails. The plants are hardy, but are best planted in spring except in mild areas.

Gypsophila muralis L.   A cushion-forming dwarf annual with masses of very small, pink or white flowers on hair-like stalks, native of much of C Europe, (not the Mediterranean), the Caucasus and Siberia, and naturalised in eastern North America, growing in dry, sandy places, flowering in July–September. Stems finely hairy at the base, 5–25cm. Leaves linear, 5–25mm long, less than 3mm wide. Petals 4–7mm, usually pink with darker veins. 'Garden Bride' has pink flowers with white centres; **'Gypsy'** has deeper pink flowers, both single and double. Both are easily grown provided they can be kept away from slugs and snails.

Spergularia purpurea (Pers.) G. Don fil. (*Caryophyllaceae*)   A mat-forming winter annual or biennial with masses of small purple flowers which open in the sun, native of Spain, Portugal, and North Africa, growing in sandy but not salty places, flowering in May–July. Stems 2–25cm. Leaves linear. Petals 2.5–4mm long. Stamens 10. This is one of the more striking annual species of this usually salt-loving genus. Similar perennials are found on coastal cliffs and dunes and in salt marshes.

Wild corn cockle, *Agrostemma githago*, with poppies

Silene coeli-rosa and *Silene armeria* mixed with white *Iberis* at Quince House

Silene coeli-rosa and *Silene armeria* mixed

Silene armeria

Silene compacta at Kew

Silene alba (Mill.) Krause (*Caryophyllaceae*)
White Campion   An annual, biennial or
short-lived perennial with softly hairy leaves
and pure white flowers, native of most of
Europe, North Africa and W Asia, and widely
naturalised in North America, growing in
cornfields, roadsides and waste places,
flowering in April-September. Stems to 1m.
Lower leaves oblanceolate. Flowers 2.5–3cm
across, male and female on separate plants.
On field edges by woods, this often hybridises
with the deep pink-flowered **Silene dioica**
(L.) Clairv. The hybrids are conspicuous
plants with flowers in shades of pale pink.

Silene armeria L.   A biennial or spring
annual, with stems sticky below the leaves and
loose heads of bright magenta-pink flowers,

Silene coeli-rosa 'Royal Celebration' at Wisley

native of Europe from Portugal and Spain eastwards to the Ukraine and Turkey, and naturalised in eastern North America, growing in open woods and rocky places, flowering in June–August. Stems to 40cm. Stem leaves ovate-cordate to lanceolate, the uppermost leaves not surrounding the base of the inflorescence. Calyx 1.2–1.5cm. Flowers 1.2–1.6cm across, the petals usually slightly emarginate. Easily grown from seed sown in spring or early summer. 'Electra' has more purple flowers.

Silene compacta Fischer   A biennial or short-lived perennial with stems sticky below the leaves and compact heads of bright pink flowers, native of SE Europe, and S Russia to the Caucasus, Iran, NW Iraq and Turkey, growing on rocky slopes and open forests at up to 2100m, flowering in May–August. Stems to 1.2m. Stem leaves ovate, amplexicaul, the uppermost surrounding the flowerheads. Calyx 1.6–2cm. Flowers around 1.5cm across, the petals rarely slightly emarginate. Easily grown from seed sown in spring, in a warm, sunny position.

Silene coeli-rosa (L.) Godron, syn. *Lychnis coeli-rosa* (L.) Descr., *Viscaria oculata* Lindl. A winter or spring annual with smooth, upright stems and large, pink flowers, native of SW Europe, eastwards to Sicily and North Africa, growing in damp, grassy places, flowering in April–May. Stems 20–50cm. Leaves linear-lanceolate. Calyx 1.5–2.8cm. Flowers 2–4cm across, in wild plants usually notched. Commonly cultivated, at least since the 18th century, and now grown in several colours. **'Cherry Blossom'** has deeply emarginate petals, pink with a white centre, and stems to 60cm. 'Blue Pearl' is also tall, with flowers of sky-blue. **'Angel' series**, including 'Blue Angel' and 'Rose Angel' has stems to 25cm, flowers with a dark eye, and is often sold in mixed colours, including some white. 'Cardinalis', an old variety with flowers to 6cm across and stems to 50cm, is available again; it is a particularly rich, deep red, as shown here included in the mixture **'Royal Celebration'**.

Silene coeli-rosa 'Angel' series at Suttons Seeds trial grounds

Silene coeli-rosa 'Cherry Blossom'

Silene alba with *Silene dioica* behind

Silene conica, wild near Dungeness, Kent

Saponaria calabrica

Silene pendula 'Peach Blossom'

Silene pendula 'Snowball'

Saponaria calabrica Guss. (*Caryophyllaceae*)
A winter annual with small, pink flowers with
spoon-shaped petals, native of SE Europe,
from S Italy eastwards to European Turkey,
growing on rocky hillsides and waste ground,
flowering in April–June. Stems branched;
upper leaves oblong-ovate, glandular. Petals to
2cm long. Fruiting pedicels often deflexed. A
modest plant with unusually shaped petals,
easily grown from a late spring sowing.

Silene colorata Poir. (*Caryophyllaceae*)
A winter annual with hairy leaves and bright
pink to white flowers with lobed petals, native
of Portugal and the Mediterranean area,
southwards to Sinai and Arabia, growing in
sandy and rocky places often in great quantity,
flowering in March–June. Stems 10–50cm.
Stem leaves obovate to linear. Flowers
1–1.8cm across. A *Silene* with magenta-pink
flowers with emarginate petals, now in
cultivation and sold under the name
S. caroliniana 'Hot Pink', may in fact belong
to this species.

Silene conica L.   A winter annual with
upright stems, small pink flowers and large
green capsules, native of Europe from England
to the Ukraine, and from North Africa
eastwards to Turkestan and Arabia, growing in
sandy places, flowering in April–June. Stems
to 50cm. Leaves linear-lanceolate. Flowers
6–10mm across, the petals usually curled in
daytime. Capsules 7–12mm long, with
conspicuous parallel veins. The cultivar
'Balletje Balletje' with stems to 60cm, is grown
as a cut flower for its slightly larger capsules.

Silene gallica L. var. ***quinquevulnera*** (L.)
Mert. & Koch **Small-flowered Catchfly**
A winter or spring annual with stickily hairy
stems and small flowers, each petal with a
crimson spot, in a long, one-sided
inflorescence, native of S Europe, but now
found throughout the world, growing in waste

Vaccaria hispanica   Vaccaria hispanica var. grandiflora

ground and weedy fields, flowering in
April–June in Europe. Stems to 45cm. Leaves
spathulate to oblanceolate. Flowers about 1cm
across, the petals rounded or emarginate.
A rare weed in mainland Britain, but more
common in the Scilly Isles, the warmer parts
of Europe and California.

Silene pendula L.   A winter annual with
softly hairy, spreading stems and pale pink or
white flowers, native of S Italy, Sicily, and
North Africa, growing in open, rocky places,
flowering in May–July. Stems much branched
to 40cm. Leaves opposite, ovate to ovate-
lanceolate, acute. Flowers 1.5–2cm across.
Seed pods hanging. Long-cultivated and
variable; the varieties cultivated at present
include 'Alba', 'Rosea' and 'Ruberrima', a
single carmine-rose with stems to 30cm, and
the double-flowered **'Peach Blossom'**, pale
pink, and **'Snowball'**, white, both dwarf,
growing to 15cm.

Vaccaria hispanica (Mill.) Rauschert, syn.
V. pyramidata Medic., *Saponaria vaccaria* L.
(*Caryophyllaceae*) **Cow Cockle**   A winter or
spring annual with glaucous, glabrous stems
and pale pink flowers on stiff, slender stalks,
native of Europe and Asia eastwards to
Afghanistan and Sinjiang, growing in
cornfields and steppe, flowering in April–July.
Stems 30–60cm. Leaves opposite, ovate to
lanceolate. Inflorescence repeatedly
branching. Calyx winged. Petals 1.4–2.3cm.
Seeds subglobose, 2–2.5mm.

In var. ***hispanica*** the claw extends only
slightly beyond the calyx; the more showy
cultivated plants, such as 'Pink Beauty' seem
to belong here. In var. ***grandiflora***, syn.
V. grandiflora (Fisch. ex DC) Jaub. & Spach,
the claw clearly extends beyond the calyx. This
variety is found throughout Turkey. Both are
attractive and easily grown from a spring
sowing in the open garden.

Silene pendula, with *Vinca* in the Ventnor Botanic Garden, Isle of Wight

Silene colorata in C Spain in May

Silene gallica var. *quinquevulnera*

Dianthus superbus 'Crimsonia' at Thompson and Morgan's trial grounds

Dianthus armeria L. **Deptford Pink** (*Caryophyllaceae*) An annual or biennial with a flat rosette of narrow green leaves in the first year, followed by tall, upright stems with heads of a few small reddish flowers, native of Europe from S England eastwards to the Caucasus, N Turkey and N Iran, growing in open, grassy places and on the edges of woods, flowering in June–August. Stems 25–85cm, usually about 40cm. Basal leaves green, 4–8cm long, 4–6mm wide. Flowers 6–8cm across; calyx teeth 5–8mm, bristle-like; petals narrowly ovate, toothed. Easily grown and self-seeding in a sunny place. Called in England the Deptford pink because it was found by Gerard around 1590 "in the great field next to Detford by the path side as you go from Redriffe [Rotherhithe] to Greenwich".

Dianthus chinensis 'Heddewigii', large-flowered double at Suttons

Dianthus armeria

Dianthus chinensis 'Heddewigii' mixed

Dianthus superbus 'Rainbow Loveliness'

Dianthus barbatus L. **Sweet William**
A biennial or short-lived perennial with
rosettes of wide, green, lanceolate leaves and
flat heads of many scented flowers. Native of
Europe from the Pyrenees to Poland and
European Turkey, naturalised elsewhere and
also reported wild across N Asia to China,
growing in clearings in mountain meadows
and woods, flowering in June–July. Stems
40–60cm. Flowers in the wild about 2cm
across, pinkish-purple or red, finely spotted
with white.

Sweet Williams have been grown in gardens
since at least the 16th century, and numerous
colour variations are established in cultivation.
The annual strains 'Wee Willie', 'Rondo' and
'Roundabout' have stems 15–20cm, and
another annual, 'Summertime' has stems to
70cm, which are suitable for cutting. Double-
flowered varieties are also available.
'Oeschberg' and 'Nigricans' have very dark
purple leaves, stems and flowers. Seed is
usually sown in June or July in a seed bed, and
the young plants planted out where they are to
flower in September.

Dianthus chinensis L. **Chinese**, **Japanese**
or **Indian Pink** A summer annual or
short-lived perennial with narrow green leaves
and heads of a few purplish-pink flowers, with
a purple ring near the base, native of NE
China and common in the hills near Beijing,
growing in rough grassy places, flowering in
May–October. Stems to 30cm, thin and
straggling. Flowers about 2.5cm across, the
petals with toothed edges. This wild form is
illustrated and described in Roy Lancaster's
'Travels in China', and was introduced to the
Jardin des Plantes in Paris in 1705. It is close
to *D. amurensis* Jacq., which is said to be longer
lived, with 1–3 flowered heads.

Numerous cultivars of *D. chinensis* were
grown in both China and Japan from the 18th
century, and in England by the late 19th. In
Japan in 1838 there were around 300 of these
old varieties, collectively called Nadeshiko,
named, and some of them are still grown in
Japan today. Many have beautifully fringed
petals, derived from hybridisation with
D. superbus. Rather similar are some of the
surviving old Heddewigii varieties, such as
'Rag Doll', with stems 30–45cm. Modern
varieties of this species are shown on the
following pages.

'Heddewigii' mixed Stems upright, to
35cm. Flowers mainly solitary, about 5cm
across, in many colours, and variably marked
and picoteed.

'Heddewigii' large-flowered double
Stems to 35cm. Flowers double or
semi-double, variable in colour.

Dianthus superbus L. A perennial often
better grown as a biennial, with beautifully
fringed petals, native of N Europe from
France and Holland eastwards to Siberia and
Japan, growing in damp grassy places, on
dunes, in open woods and mountain
meadows, flowering in June–October. Stems
30–80cm; flowers scented, pink or lilac in the
wild, with the petals deeply laciniate.
'Crimsonia' has rich, crimson flowers with a
pale centre. **'Rainbow Loveliness'**, an old
hybrid strain between *D. superbus* and
D. × allwoodii, has flowers in many shades of
pink and purple to white, often beautifully
marked as well as fringed. It can be grown as
an annual but is very good treated as a
biennial, sown in late summer and planted out
in spring to flower through the summer.

Dianthus barbatus at Littlewood Park, Aberdeenshire

Dianthus barbatus

Dianthus 'Parfait Strawberry'

Dianthus 'Pink Charm'

Dianthus 'Crimson Charm'

Dianthus 'Baby Doll' mixed

Dianthus 'White Charm'

Chinese, Japanese or **Indian Pink cultivars** (*Caryophyllaceae*) The modern European and Californian varieties of *Dianthus chinensis* L. shown here have sadly aimed mostly for compactness, freedom of flowering and bright colours, and lost the interesting shapes and markings that were the hallmark of old cultivars. Some groups such as the 'Telstar' varieties are intermediate between *D. chinensis* and the Sweet William, *D. barbatus*, under which they are sometimes listed. In the south of England these annual *Dianthus* are best sown in heat indoors in late February, and grown on before planting out in late April or early May in rich, well-drained sandy soil. In Mediterranean climates they can be sown outdoors in autumn.

'Charm' series A group of F$_I$ hybrids raised by Goldsmith Seeds Inc., California. Plants to 15–20cm tall, about 25cm across. Flowers 4–5cm across, without scent: **'Crimson Charm'** flowers bright crimson with faint black lines; **'Pink Charm'** flowers rose pink with a darker eye; 'Scarlet Charm' flowers deep scarlet with a pale eye; **'White Charm'** flowers pure white.

'Baby Doll' mixed Raised by L. Clause S. A. France. Plants to 20cm tall, 25cm across. Flowers large, 4–7cm across. Ground colour varying from white to purple, magenta or rose red, variously zoned and speckled with maroon and scarlet.

'Colour Magician' One of the 'Telstar' strain of hybrid origin, probably between *D. barbatus* and *D. chinensis*. Flowers in small heads in white to many shades of pink. Other 'Telstar' varieties are described below.

'Ideal' series A group of F$_I$ hybrids, derived from crosses between *D. chinensis* and *D. barbatus*. Plants to 25cm tall, about 25cm across. Flowers about 3cm across, deep purplish-red in **'Ideal Deep Violet'**.

'Princess' series Stems upright, to 30cm. Flowers about 4cm across, in various colours from white to pink and red; a rich plum-purple in **'Princess Purple'**.

'Parfait Raspberry' and **'Parfait Strawberry'** A pair of F$_I$ hybrids, with stems 15–20cm. Flowers about 5cm across; pink with a dark eye, becoming reddish in 'Parfait Raspberry' and remaining bicoloured in 'Parfait Strawberry'.

'Snow Fire' One of the 'Carpet' series, with stems 15–20cm. Flowers about 5cm across, white with a red eye.

'Telstar' series A group of F$_I$ hybrids, derived from crosses between *D. chinensis* and *D. barbatus*. Plants to 20cm tall, about 25cm across. Flowers about 3cm across, in flattish heads, continuing well into autumn. Colour strains include **'Crimson'**, **'White'** and **'Picotee'**, often sold together.

'Snow Fire'

'Parfait Raspberry'

'Parfait Strawberry'

'Colour Magician'

'Telstar' mixed

'Telstar' mixed

'Princess Purple'

'Telstar Purple Picotee'

'Telstar' mixed

'Ideal Deep Violet'

'Telstar Picotee'

'Telstar Crimson'

'Telstar White'

Specimens from Unwins, June 15th, ½ life-size

DIANTHUS

Dianthus 'Enfant de Nice' from Thompson and Morgan's trial grounds

Dianthus 'Chabaud Giant Superb' (yellow)

Dianthus 'Chabaud Giant Superb' (scarlet)

Dianthus 'Chabaud Giant Superb' (crimson)

Dianthus caryophyllus L. (*Caryophyllaceae*)
Carnation   A perennial with bluish-grey, narrow leaves and sweetly scented purple, pink or white flowers on tall stems, native probably of islands in the C Mediterranean area, but long cultivated, perhaps since Roman times, and now not known for certain in the wild. Stems to 80cm. Leaves 2–4mm wide. Epicalyx scales 4, broadly obovate, cuspidate. Calyx 2.5–3cm. Flowers 2–3cm across. Most cultivated carnations are perennial, and propagated regularly by cuttings, but strains have been developed which do well as biennials or annuals.

'Chabaud Giant Superb'   A strain of mixed colours ranging from white to yellow, pink and red. Flowers double, well scented. stems to 60cm. Best grown as a biennial, sown without heat in autumn, and planted out in spring. 'Lillipot' has a similar range of colours, but is bred especially for growing in small pots. It has stems 20–25cm tall.

'Enfant de Nice'   An old strain of annual carnations with a large range of colours.

Single Crimson   This fine single-flowered carnation appears to be rare in cultivation.

Stems 45–60cm. Flowers 4–5cm across. 'Fenbow's Nutmeg Clove', which can be raised from seed, is similar, but is illustrated as semi-double, and the young plants I have grown have not yet flowered. Both should have excellent clove-like scent.

***Dianthus* Allwoodii Alpinus**   A strain of seed-raised dwarf pinks, with flowers in various shades of pink and red with darker markings, raised from crossing *D. caryophyllus*, *D. plumarius* and *D. alpinus* in various combinations. The plants may be treated as biennials or perennials.

Dianthus caryophyllus single crimson at Ventnor Botanic Garden, Isle of Wight

Dianthus Allwoodii Alpinus group

Conicosia pugioniformis wild in sandy fields near Clanwilliam, Western Cape

Dorotheanthus gramineus, near Ceres

Dorotheanthus bellidiformis (yellow)

Dorotheanthus bellidiformis

Dorotheanthus bellidiformis
on the Cape Peninsula

Dorotheanthus bellidiformis (red), with
Senecio cakilefolius

Conicosia pugioniformis (L.) N.E. Br.
(*Mesembryanthemaceae*) A biennial or
perennial with fleshy, grey-green leaves, and
large, pale yellow flowers, native of South
Africa in the Western Cape from
S Namaqualand southwards to Bellville, (and
naturalised in North America on the coast
near San Francisco), growing in deep sandy
soils, flowering in September–October. Plants
to 60cm across, 20cm tall. Leaves 15–20cm
long, triangular in section. Flowers 7cm
across, with threadlike petals and staminodes.
   Carpanthea pomeridiana (L.) N.E. Br., a
sprawling annual, which has similar flowers
but flat leaves with hairy margins and coarsely
woolly stems, grows in the same areas as
Conicosia. Apatesia helianthoides (Ait.) N.E. Br.
looks almost identical, but has stems without
hairs; it is found from Saldanha Bay to the
Peninsula. All are easy in a warm, frost-free
climate, quick to grow from seed, but liable to
be attacked by snails in wet seasons.

Dorotheanthus bellidiformis (Burm. fil.)
N.E. Br., syn. *D. oculatus* N.E.Br.,
Mesembryanthemum criniflorum hort.

Dorotheanthus bellidiformis at Rinsey Cross in Cornwall

(*Mesembryanthemaceae*) **Livingstone Daisy**
A winter or, in cultivation, a summer annual
with flattish, fleshy leaves covered in frost-like
cells, and shining, daisy-like flowers varying
from purple and pink to white, yellow and
orange, sometimes with a dark red centre
(*D. oculatus*). Native of South Africa from the
Cape Peninsula and Bredasdorp northwards
to the Bokkeveld near Nieuwoudtville,
growing in open sandy and rocky places,
flowering in July–September. Stems to 10cm.
Leaves spathulate. Flowers 3–4cm across.

Different colour forms may be found
growing separately in the wild; cultivated
strains are mostly sold in mixed colours, but
'Lunette' (see below), 'Gelato White', with a
red centre, and 'Gelato Deep Pink' are also
available. Easily grown in sandy or very
shallow soil. In frosty climates sow in gentle
heat in early spring, keeping the plants on the
dry side. Always plant out into a position in
full sunlight.

'Lunette' syn. 'Yellow Ice' is a selection of the
yellow form, with lovely, pale yellow,
red-centred flowers, easy to grow and very
quick to flower from seed.

Dorotheanthus gramineus (Haw.)
Schwantes   A winter or, in cultivation, a
summer annual with short, thin, fleshy leaves
and shining, daisy-like flowers varying from
purple and pink to white, native of South
Africa, in the Western Cape from Clanwilliam
to Malmesbury, growing in open sandy and
grassy places, flowering in August–September.
Stems to 6cm. Leaves terete or linear, to 5mm
wide. Flowers 3.5cm across. Judging by its
habitat, this species should tolerate more damp
than *D. bellidiformis*; it is equally easy to grow.

Dorotheanthus bellidiformis

Dorotheanthus bellidiformis 'Lunette'

95

Claytonia perfoliata

Portulaca grandiflora 'Sun State White'

Portulaca oleracea cultivar in Tanzania

Portulaca oleracea 'Wildfire' in Tanzania

Calyptridium umbellatum L.
(*Portulacaceae*) **Pussy Paws**   A dwarf annual
or short-lived perennial with fluffy pink flower
heads, native of western North America from
British Columbia to Baja California and
eastwards to the Rockies, growing in open,
sandy and loose gravelly places, mainly in the
mountains at 800–3000m, flowering in
May–August. Rosette leaves spathulate,
2–7cm long. Flowering stems to 25cm long.
Flowers crowded into coiled spikes, with
2 pink or white, scarious sepals 5–8mm long
and 4 minute white petals. An attractive plant,
which may soon appear in cultivation.

Claytonia perfoliata Willd., syn. *Montia
perfoliata* (Willd.) Howell (*Portulacaceae*)
Miner's Lettuce   A quick-growing winter
annual with fleshy, spathulate basal leaves and
clusters of small white flowers surrounded by
cup-like, fused stem leaves, native of western
North America from British Columbia to Baja
California, growing in moist, shady places,
below 1500m, flowering in February–May.
Stems to 30cm, usually around 10cm. Petals
4–6mm long. Seeds black and shining. Easily
grown in sandy soil, and can become a weed.
It is said to have been eaten as salad by the
forty-niners in the Californian gold rush, and
I have found that the chickens love it when
there is a shortage of greenery in the winter.

Portulaca grandiflora L. (*Portulacaceae*)
A mat-forming summer annual with terete
leaves and usually reddish or orange flowers
with thin petals that open in the sun, native of
Brazil and Uruguay, and reported naturalised

Portulaca grandiflora 'Sundial Mango'

Portulaca grandiflora 'Sundial Peppermint'

Portulaca oleracea 'Silver Pink'

in S Europe, growing in dry, sandy places, flowering in summer. Plant to 15cm across, with scattered hairs. Leaves to 2.5cm long. Flowers around 2.5cm across, often semi-double in cultivated varieties. Sow in spring in heat in sandy soil, and be very careful not to over water when young. 'Cloudbeater' has semi-double flowers which stay open in cloudy weather, as does the 'Sundial' series. **'Sundial Mango'** is bright orange; **'Sundial Peppermint'** has striped flowers; **'Sun State White'** is large, semi-double and pure white. Single-flowered strains are also still available.

Portulaca oleracea L. **Purslane** A trailing winter or summer annual with flat, spathulate leaves and small, yellow flowers; possibly originally from India, but long cultivated as a vegetable, and a common weed, so its native range is uncertain. Plants to 30cm across. Flowers 1.2–1.6cm, but around 2.5cm across in cultivated ornamental strains such as **'Wildfire'**, which is sometimes found under the name *P. umbraticola*. **'Silver Pink'** seems to be a selection of 'Wildfire'. Subsp. *sativa* (Haw.) Celakovsky is generally grown as a salad and pot herb. It has more upright stems.

Calyptridium umbellatum in the trials field of Kees Sahin in Holland

Allionia incarnata in the Joshua Tree National Monument Reserve, Mohave Desert, California

Mirabilis multiflora at Harry Hay's

Abronia villosa Wats. (*Nyctaginaceae*) **Sand Verbena**   A creeping annual with glandular-hairy stems and leaves and dense heads of scented, pinkish-purple flowers with a white centre, native of California in the Mojave and Colorado deserts, and of Arizona in the Sonoran desert southwards into Mexico, growing on open, sandy places below 1000m, flowering in February–July. Stems to 50cm. Leaves opposite, 1–3cm long, the blades almost round. Flowers 1.2–1.6cm long. Fruits with 3–4 wings. Sow seed in warmth in deep pots of sand in early spring, keeping rather dry. The closely related *A. umbellata* Lam. and its subspecies are perennial, found on sandy strands all along the California coast.

Allionia incarnata L. (*Nyctaginaceae*) **Windmills, Trailing Four O'Clock** A trailing winter annual or perennial with opposite leaves and magenta flowers, in tight groups, so apparently with many petals, native of S California to Colorado, Mexico, and South America, growing on dry, stony and sandy slopes and washes below 1500m, flowering in April–September. Stems to 1m long, glandular-pubescent. Leaves ovate, 2–3cm long, in unequal pairs. Flowers occasionally white, in tight clusters of 3, each corolla 1.5–2cm across, 4–5-lobed, opening in the morning, with 4–7 stamens.

Calandrinia umbellata L. (*Portulacaceae*) A perennial often grown as a summer annual, with heads of red-purple flowers, native of Chile and Peru, growing in sandy deserts, flowering in late summer. Leaves mostly basal, fleshy, grey-green, hairy and linear, 1.5–2cm long. Stems to 15cm. Flowers to 2cm across, crowded in a flat head. This requires very sandy soil and careful cultivation if it is not to get too wet. Sow in spring and plant out in as dry and sunny a place as possible.

Calandrinia umbellata at Chelsea Physic Garden

Calandrinia ciliata, in the hills above Malibu Beach, California

Sand verbena, *Abronia villosa*, carpeting the desert outside Palm Springs after heavy spring rains

Calandrinia ciliata (Ruiz & Pavon) DC.
var. ***menziesii*** (Hook.) Macbr. **Red Maids**
A winter annual with fleshy leaves and bright,
shining, purplish-red or rarely white flowers,
native of western North America from British
Columbia southwards to Baja California and
eastwards to Arizona, (with var. *ciliata* in Peru
and Ecuador), growing on grassy hills below
1800m, and as a weed on cultivated land,
flowering in February–May in California.
Stems to 40cm, leafy, the lower leaves
oblanceolate, the upper linear. Flowers
1–1.8cm across; pedicels suberect. Capsule
scarcely longer than the calyx. A common
early spring annual from coastal California to
Arizona. *C. grandiflora* Lindl. from Chile, a
perennial often grown as an annual, has
flowers 2.5–5cm across.

Mirabilis multiflora (Torr.) Gray
(*Nyctaginaceae*) A perennial usually grown
as an annual, with grey-green, heart-shaped
leaves and several purple flowers from calyx-
like, fused bracts, native of Colorado, Utah,
Arizona and N Mexico, growing on hillsides
and plateaux among rocks and scrub at
1000–2000m, flowering in April–September.
Stems to 1m. Leaves about 8cm. Flowers
4–6cm. Sow seed in heat in spring. Shown
here is Archibald 10753 from Washington Co.,
Utah. *M. longiflora* L., also from Arizona and
Mexico, has solitary white or pinkish flowers
with a long slender tube 6–15cm long.

Abronia villosa near Palm Springs

Amaranthus caudatus var. albiflorus

Amaranthus var. viridis 'Green Tails'

Amaranthus hypochondriacus 'Green Thumb'

Amaranthus cruentus 'Hot Biscuits' at Thompson and Morgan's trial grounds

Amaranthus caudatus

There are around 50 species of *Amaranthus*, found throughout the tropics, but the ones shown here are mostly from South America, where they have been grown since ancient times as grain crops; the young leaves are also edible. There is still some confusion in the naming of the species, and anyone who wants to follow up the subject in more detail can consult J.D. Sauer, "The Grain Amaranths and Their Relatives: A Revised Taxonomic and Geographic Survey" in *Annuals of the Missouri Botanic Garden* 54:103–137 (1967).

Amaranthus caudatus L. (*Amaranthaceae*)
Love-lies-bleeding A summer annual with green leaves and long, drooping, dense, usually red spikes, native of the Andes of South America, flowering in late summer to autumn. Stems 1–2m, red or purple. Leaves green, stalked. Terminal spike of the compound inflorescence more than 30cm, drooping from the base. Best sown in heat in early spring, and grown on before planting out

in early summer. The seeds of this species were used as a grain by the Incas.
Var. ***albiflorus*** A variety with greenish-white flowers.
'Green Tails' A form of the green-flowered var. ***viridis***.

Amaranthus hypochondriacus L.
An erect summer annual with green or purple leaves and erect, dense spikes of often reddish flowers, native of the southern USA and Mexico, flowering in late summer. Stems 1–1.5m. Leaves stalked, green to purple. Terminal spike of the compound inflorescence to 20cm, upright.
'Green Thumb' A variety with green leaves and flowers. Stems around 60cm.
'Pigmy Torch' A variety with deep purple leaves and flowers. Stems around 1m.

Amaranthus cruentus L., syn.
A. paniculatus L. A summer annual with upright stems and numerous, rather loose

Amaranthus tricolor 'Aurora Yellow'

Amaranthus tricolor, seedlings grown as a vegetable in Sichuan

Amaranthus hypochondriacus 'Pigmy Torch' at Levens Hall

Amaranthus caudatus

spikes of flowers of various colours, but usually reddish or yellowish, native of S Mexico and Guatemala, flowering in summer–autumn. Stems 1–2m. Leaves stalked, pubescent beneath. Terminal spike of inflorescence much-branched, upright.
'Hot Biscuits' has stems to 1m, and orange-brown flowers in a much branched inflorescence. 'Red Cathedral' has dense, scarlet foliage.

Amaranthus tricolor L., syn. *A. gangeticus* L. **Tampala** A tropical summer annual with narrow leaves, often red-veined or in a range of colours from yellow to orange and red, native of tropical Asia, and widely grown in China and India as a substitute for spinach. Stems to 1.5m. Flower spikes mostly in the leaf axils. Leaves in var. *salicifolius* (Veitch) Aellen are narrowly lanceolate, drooping towards the tips.
'Aurora Yellow' has bright creamy-yellow leaves in the rosette at the top of the stem. 'Joseph's Coat' has bright red, yellow, brownish and green leaves. 'Splendens' has bright red leaves, paler at the top. These tropical amaranths do best in tropical areas; they should be started in heat and be put outdoors only when the weather has become really warm.

Celosia cristata 'Golden Triumph' at Longwood gardens, Pennsylvania

Celosia cristata 'Apricot Brandy'

Fagopyrum esculentum in Sichuan

Gomphrena globosa L. (*Amaranthaceae*)
A tropical summer annual with tight heads of usually red-purple flowers, native of India, but now widely cultivated throughout the tropics, flowering in summer. Stems to 1m, with swollen nodes. Leaves hairy, oblong or elliptic. Flower heads 2–3cm across, lavender, red, pink or white in cultivars, and orange in hybrids with *G. haageana* Klotsch. Easily grown in warm climates when sown directly into the ground, or started in heat and planted out in early summer.

Celosia cristata L., syn. *C. argentea* L. var. *cristata* Kuntze (*Amaranthaceae*) **Cockscomb**
A tropical summer annual with plumes or cockscombs of very small flowers in various colours, native of the tropics, flowering in summer. Stems to 1.5m. Leaves 4–15cm long, linear to ovate-lanceolate. Flowers 6–10mm long, with papery bracts; sepals 5, petals absent. Two main groups are cultivated, often sold as *C. cristata*, with combs, and *C. plumosa*, with plumes; semi-dwarf or dwarf varieties with stems to 15cm are found in both groups. *C. argentea* has silvery-white plumes and stems to 2m tall. Its variety, var. *spicata*, has tall bushy tail-like spikes to 1m in soft pink, as in 'Flamingo Pink Feather', or purple. All celosias are best in the tropics, or in temperate areas started in warmth and planted out only when summer's heat has arrived.
'Apricot Brandy' (Plumosa group)
Stems to 40cm. Flowers orange-yellow.
'Golden Triumph' (Plumosa group)
Flowers bright yellow.
'Fairy Fountains' mixed (Plumosa group)
Stems to 30cm. 'Kimono' mixed forms very compact plants on stems to 10cm. The 'Century' strain have stems to 60cm.
'Floradale Rose Pink' (Cristata group)
Stems to 85cm.

Fagopyrum esculentum Moench, syn. *Polygonum fagopyrum* L. (*Polygonaceae*)
Buckwheat A spring annual with triangular leaves and white or pink flowers, native of Asia, and cultivated for grain since ancient

Celosia cristata 'Fairy Fountains' mixed in Regent's Park, London

Gomphrena globosa

times, flowering in summer. Stems to 1m. Leaves to 12cm long, with a stalk shorter than the blade. Flowers 3–5mm long. Nut 5–8mm long, dark brown, triangular in cross section. Hardy and easily grown if sown in early spring. The grain can be either cooked whole or made into flour. *Polygonum orientale* L. is an attractive annual from China, now naturalised in C and S Europe, with spikes of red or purple flowers on stems 1–3m tall. It was popular in gardens in the 18th and 19th centuries, being first cultivated in England in 1707. Now, however it is hardly ever seen, though available from Chiltern Seeds.

Celosia cristata 'Floradale Rose Pink'

Salicornia europaea in autumn colour in Hokkaido on the north coast of Japan

Salicornia europaea

Atriplex hortensis

Chenopodium giganteum

Atriplex hortensis 'Rubra'

Bassia scoparia, a centrepiece in the summer bedding at Southsea

Atriplex hortensis L. (*Chenopodiaceae*)
An upright spring annual with purple stems and leaves, native of Asia and Siberia but naturalised elsewhere, flowering in May–August. Stems to 2.5m. Leaves to 20cm, ovate-triangular to broadly lanceolate, mealy when young. Flowers in tall spikes, the fruiting bracteoles 5–15mm, heart-shaped to circular, not toothed. The green form is used as a substitute for spinach. It is the coloured varieties that are usually grown as ornamentals and called red orache: **'Rubra'**, syn. var. *atrosanguinea* or var. *rubra*, is entirely blood-red. 'Cupreatorosa' has coppery-red leaves.

Bassia scoparia (L.) A. J. Scott f. ***trichophylla*** (Schmeiss) Schinz & Thell., syn. *Kochia scoparia* (L.) Schred. (*Chenopodiaceae*) **Summer Cypress**, **Burning Bush**   An upright, shrubby spring annual with narrow, bright green leaves, turning red and orange in autumn, native of Central Asia, and naturalised in a few places in S California, growing in dry, sandy places. Plant to 1.5m. Leaves to 5cm, narrowly lanceolate, glabrous. Flowers inconspicuous; fruit 3–4mm across. This old favourite can be sown indoors in early spring, or sown directly outside where it is to grow in late spring.

Beta vulgaris L. (*Chenopodiaceae*) **Beet**
The wild sea beet, subsp. ***maritima*** (L.) Archangeli, is an annual, biennial or perennial with fleshy, triangular leaves and small green flowers, native of the coasts of Europe and the Mediterranean, and in saline areas inland, growing on dunes and shingle beaches, flowering most of the year. It has dark green, fleshy leaves and usually sprawling stems, often marked with red. The cultivated subsp. *vulgaris* includes the vegetables spinach beet, grown for its leaves, Swiss chard, grown for its fleshy, flattened leaf stalks, and beetroot, grown for its swollen stem base. Some varieties are now grown as ornamentals. **'Rhubarb Chard'** has striking red leaf stalks, and in 'Rainbow Chard' or 'Bright Lights' they are yellow, orange, purple and white as well. In ornamental beetroot **'MacGregor's Favourite'** the leaves are narrow and recurved, of a deep blackish-purple colour.

Beta vulgaris 'MacGregor's Favourite' at Levens Hall

Chenopodium foliosum L.

(*Chenopodiaceae*) A spring annual with creeping stems and round, red, fleshy seed clusters in the axils of the leaves, native of S Europe from Portugal eastwards to Turkey and across Asia to NW China, growing in steppes and rough places in the mountains, fruiting in June–August. Stems to 70cm. Lower leaves triangular, becoming linear towards the top of the stem. Sepals 3–5, green, becoming red and fleshy in fruit. A frequent plant in the dry mountains of Turkey and Iran, but the fruits are disappointing, even when you are hungry and thirsty, as they are neither very juicy nor have any flavour. Sometimes sold with the name 'Strawberry Sticks'.

Chenopodium giganteum D. Don, syn.

C. amaranticolor Coste & Reynier A tall summer annual with leaves suffused reddish-purple when young, native of N India, and naturalised near Marseilles, flowering in late summer. Stems 2–3m, but usually much less in the cool summers of N Europe. Leaves to 14cm long and wide, triangular to rhomboid with rounded teeth. Inflorescence farinose when young. An attractive plant for its handsome foliage, needing a hot and humid summer to reach its full size. Sow indoors in heat and plant out in early summer.

Salicornia europaea L. (*Chenopodiaceae*)
Glasswort, **Samphire** or **Sea Asparagus**
A spring annual with fleshy stems, leaves reduced to scales, and hidden flowers, native of most of the N hemisphere, growing in salt marshes, flowering in late summer. The remarkable view opposite, in which a whole shallow estuary near Shari in Hokkaido is red with *Salicornia*, is a famous phenomenon in Japan in October. Though similar masses of *Salicornia* may be seen in Europe, it does not usually turn such a striking colour.

Beta vulgaris 'Rhubarb Chard' in the vegetable garden at Hope End House

Chenopodium foliosum, with strawberry-like fruit

Euphorbia marginata 'Kilimanjaro'

Euphorbia lathyris

Ricinus communis 'Carmencita Pink'

Cannabis sativa L. (*Cannabaceae*) A tall, upright or branching annual with 5–7 jaggedly toothed, greyish leaflets and small green flowers, native of C Asia, but cultivated at least since 4000BC in China and often found apparently naturalised in warm areas. Stems to 8m or more. Leaflets around 10cm long. Male and female flowers are found on separate plants. Seeds shiny, whitish and almost spherical. Two main types are grown; subsp. *sativa* is the taller, hardier, almost unbranched hemp type, used for fibre, and subsp. *indica* is the shorter, more branching hashish or marijuana type, used as a drug. The cultivation of either subspecies has been illegal since 1951 in Britain, but some farms grow the hemp type under licence. It makes a very handsome, aromatic plant for a tall border.

Euphorbia lathyris L. (*Euphorbiaceae*) **Caper Spurge** A tall biennial, forming, in the first year, an unbranched stem thickly covered with opposite pairs of stiff leaves, and in the second, a widely branching bright green inflorescence, flowering in May–August; it is found wild as a weed in much of the warmer parts of Europe, North America and China, but is native probably only in the E and C Mediterranean, where it grows in damp places. Stems to 1.5m. Stem leaves linear, 3–15cm long, 5–25mm across. Bract leaves broadly ovate. Glands with 2 curved horns. Capsule spongy, about 1.3–1.7cm across; seeds 5mm across.

This spurge has a way of appearing unexpectedly in borders and abandoned parts of the garden. It is also called mole plant, and said to keep moles (the burrowing kind) away, but I have found it useless; perhaps the very poisonous juice was used to burn away moles on the skin.

Euphorbia marginata Pursh An upright summer annual with soft leaves and bracts with white edges, native of North America from Montana to S Mexico, (and naturalised E of the Mississippi and in SE Europe), growing in moist, open places, flowering in May–August. Stems 40–80cm. Stem leaves ovate. Bract leaves oblong, the upper almost all white. Glands peltate, with petal-like appendages. An easily grown annual, needing ample water and warmth while it is growing. Three cultivars are available: 'Icicle' to 45–60cm; **'Kilimanjaro'** to 90cm and 'Snow Top' to 1.2m.

Ricinus communis L. (*Euphorbiaceae*) **Castor Oil Plant** A shrub often grown as an annual, with deeply lobed leaves and often bright red, spiny capsules, native of the SE Mediterranean and E Africa but now naturalised throughout the tropics, flowering in summer. Stems to 12m, but usually only to 2m in the first year. Leaves to 60cm across, often reddish. **'Carmencita Pink'** has red stems to 1.5m, dark green leaves and spiny, deep pink seed pods. **'Carmencita Bright Red'** has red stems to 1.5m, dark purplish-brown leaves and spiny, bright red seed pods. **'Gibsonii'** has stems to 1.5m, leaves dark with reddish veins, and greenish-pink seed pods.

The whole plant, and especially the seed coat, is very poisonous. The seeds contain valuable oils. Plant the seeds in heat of over 20°C, and grow the seedlings on at this temperature until outside temperatures have reached it as well.

Ricinus communis 'Carmencita Bright Red' on the front at Southsea

Euphorbia marginata, wild form

Cannabis sativa subsp. *indica*

Ricinus communis 'Gibsonii' in the greenhouse at Wisley

Geranium biuncinatum in the greenhouse at Quince House

Geranium lucidum, leaves in winter

Erodium gruinum in Turkey near Antalya in April

Geranium bohemicum

Erodium gruinum (L.) L'Hérit.
(*Geraniaceae*) A winter annual with 3-lobed
lower leaves and lavender-blue, unmarked
flowers, native from Sicily and North Africa
eastwards to Iran, growing in open, grassy,
sandy and rocky places, mostly near the coast,
flowering in February–May. Stems to 15cm.
Leaves with the terminal lobe much the
largest. Petals 2–2.5cm. Beak of the fruit
6–11cm. A modest, early-flowering annual for
a warm position.

Geranium biuncinatum Kokwaro
(*Geraniaceae*) An upright winter annual with
small, bright magenta flowers with a black
centre, native of the Yemen in the Jebel Bura
and of adjacent E. Africa, growing in the
mountains, flowering in early spring. Stems to
20cm. Leaves about 6cm across, deeply
divided, soft, with blunt lobes. Flowers about
2cm across, (but often on feeble plants only
cleistogamous flowers are formed.) Fruits
with a short beak, the edges modified into
2 sharp hooks, to catch in the fur of passing
animals. An easily grown, tender annual for a
frost-free climate, but not free with its
remarkable flowers.
  G. ocellatum Camb. has smaller flowers
about 1.8cm across, with the petals not
overlapping. It is found from W Africa across
to Arabia, the Himalayas and SW China,
growing in shady rocks, forest edges and as a
weed of cultivated areas.

Geranium bohemicum L. A biennial with
much-branched, sprawling stems and small,
blue flowers, the petals veined and notched,
native of E and C Europe, from S Norway and
E France to Albania, N Turkey and the
Caucasus, growing in clearings in forest,
flowering in June–July. Stems to 60cm. Leaves
3–6cm across. Petals 8–11mm long. An
attractive plant for a wild garden, germinating
most freely after a fire.

Geranium lucidum L. A winter or spring
annual or biennial with small, shining, fleshy,
often reddish leaves and small, bright pink
flowers, native of Europe from Ireland
southwards to North Africa and Central Asia,

Grielum humifusum in the Western Cape near Nieuwoudtville in early September

growing on limestone rocks and old walls, flowering in March–June. Stems to 30cm, spreading from a central rosette. Leaves 1–4cm across. Petals 8–9mm long. Attractive for its leaves, which are fresh green through the winter. A white-flowered form was collected by P. H. Davis on Rhodes.

Grielum humifusum Thunb. (*Neuradaceae*) A prostrate winter annual with deeply divided leaves and pale yellow flowers with a white centre, native of South Africa in the Western Cape from Namaqualand to Malmesbury, growing in dry, sandy places, flowering in August–September. Stems to 30cm long. Leaves with blunt lobes. Flowers 3–4cm across. Fruit a dry, papery disk. A beautiful plant, but rarely cultivated; it requires a hot, sunny, Mediterranean climate. *G. grandiflorum* (L.) Druce, with larger, deeper yellow flowers with a greenish centre and silvery leaves with pointed divisions, is also available. It is found mainly near the coast from Clanwilliam southwards to the Cape Peninsula.

Tribulus terrestris L. (*Zygophyllaceae*) **Caltrops** A creeping annual with pinnate leaves and yellow flowers, native of S Europe and SW Asia, and now found as a weed almost throughout the world, growing in dry, sandy places, flowering in May–October. Stems to 80cm. Leaves with 10–16 leaflets. Petals 4–5mm long. Fruits with stiff horns. An attractive annual, but now a serious pest in many areas, as it is poisonous to cattle. Most of the other 24 species of *Tribulus* are found in the drier parts of Africa.

Grielum humifusum, with *Osteospermum pinnatum*, *Felicia* and *Zaluzianskya*

Tribulus terrestris in Oaxaca, Mexico

LUPINUS

Lupinus sparsiflorus subsp. *inopinatus*

Lupinus densiflorus in Marin Co.

Lupins Of the 200 or so species of the genus *Lupinus* in the world, 6 are native of Europe, 82 of California. Of the latter, 31 are annuals, 11 are shrubby and the rest are herbaceous perennials, including *L. polyphyllus* Lindl., the main ancestor of the garden lupin. Lupins have spike-like racemes of flowers, usually in whorls, but often scattered. The leaves consist of a whorl of narrow and often silky-hairy leaflets. The plants are poisonous, and the seeds even more so, as they often contain high concentrations of toxic alkaloids.

Annual lupins are best planted where they are to flower. Most prefer very well-drained, sandy, acidic soil and full sun. In mild areas the seed may be sown in autumn, but where winters are cold or very wet, seed is best sown in spring, when the weather has begun to warm up. Soaking the seed in hot water overnight may hasten germination. Plant a good distance apart to give the plants room to develop. Most species grow and flower very quickly from seed.

Lupinus bicolor Lindl. subsp. ***microphyllus*** (Wats.) D. Dunn (*Leguminosae*) A hairy winter annual with oblanceolate leaflets and short spikes of bright blue and white flowers in whorls, native of Oregon and most of California west of the Sierras, growing on grassy slopes on sand and gravel below 1500m, flowering in March–June. Stems 10–40cm. Leaflets 5–7, oblanceolate to cuneate. Spikes 1–5cm long, with 1–9 whorls of flowers, the pedicels 1.5–3mm. Flowers 4–7mm long, the upright petal with a pale centre; keel ciliate on upper edge towards the tip. Seeds 2–3mm long, pale pinkish, scarcely mottled.

Lupinus densiflorus Benth. A low-growing, hairy winter annual with oblanceolate leaflets and spikes of white, pinkish or yellowish flowers in whorls, native of the Coast Ranges from Santa Clara to Butte Co. and Humboldt Co. southwards, growing on grassy slopes and dry banks below 1800m, flowering in April–June. Stems 20–40cm, often hollow. Leaflets 7–9, oblanceolate. Spikes around 20cm long, the pedicels 2–3mm. Flowers around 1.4cm long, the upright petal often veined with red or violet; keel ciliate on the upper edges near the claws. Seeds 4–5mm long, dark to pale. Variable in hairiness and flower colour. Var. *aureus* (Kell.) Munz, with pale yellow flowers, is found from Mendocino Co. to Santa Barbara Co.

Lupinus sparsiflorus Benth. subsp. ***inopinatus*** (C.P.Smith) Dziekanowski & D. Dunn A silky-hairy winter annual with linear to oblanceolate leaflets and spikes of bright blue and white flowers, not in whorls, native of California in the foothills of the Sierras from San Deigo Co. to Baja California, growing in open fields below 1200m, flowering in March–May. Stems 15–40cm. Leaflets 5–9, 2–3mm wide, linear. Spikes 3–10cm long, the pedicels 3–5mm. Flowers 7–11mm long, the upright petal with a pale centre; keel ciliate on lower edge, near claws. Seeds 2–3mm long, marbled or mottled. An attractive species with neat leaves and loose spikes of flowers, often found in recently burnt areas. Subspecies *sparsiflorus* is found from Ventura to Riverside Co.

Lupinus vallicola Heller, syn. *L. nanus* Dougl. in Benth. subsp. *vallicola* C.P. Sm. A small, hairy winter annual with linear leaflets and spikes of bright blue and white flowers in whorls, native of California in the foothills of the Sierra Nevada from Kern Co., northwards to Shasta, growing on grassy slopes below 1200m, flowering in March–June. Stems 15–35cm. Leaflets 6–8, around 2–3mm wide, linear. Spikes 3–10cm long, the pedicels 3–5mm. Flowers 6–10mm long, the upright petal with a pale centre; keel ciliate towards apex. Seeds 2.5mm long, pale pinkish, scarcely mottled.

A very beautiful dwarf lupin, close to *L. nanus* Dougl., which is found in the Coast Ranges. *L. subcarnosus* Hook., the Texas bluebonnet, is similar, with oblanceolate, rounded leaflets, silky-hairy beneath, and dense spikes of flowers.

Lupinus bicolor subsp. *microphyllus*, growing on dry hills in Marin Co., California

Lupinus sparsiflorus subsp. *inopinatus,* with *Eschscholzia*, wild oats and other annuals near Aguanga, San Diego Co.

Lupinus vallicola in a graveyard in the California goldrush country

Lupinus arizonicus San Andeas Canyon, above Palm Springs, California

Lupinus succulentus in the hills above Malibu beach

Lupinus arizonicus (Wats.) Wats. (*Leguminosae*)   A stout, fleshy winter annual with oblanceolate leaflets and loose spikes of purplish-pink flowers, native of W Arizona, SE California and Baja California, growing on rocky slopes and in sandy washes in the desert below 1000m, flowering in January–May. Stems 30–60cm, hollow, with sparse, spreading hairs. Leaflets 5–10, 4–12mm wide, oblanceolate. Spikes 5–30cm long, the pedicels 2–3mm. Flowers 8–10mm long, the upright petal with a pale centre; keel ciliate near the base. Seeds 2–3mm long, marbled or mottled. Close to *L. sparsiflorus*.

Lupinus hirsutissimus Benth.   A stout winter annual with nettle-like, stinging hairs, broad leaflets and long spikes of reddish-purple or magenta flowers, not in whorls, native of California in the Coast Ranges, from San Mateo Co., to Baja California, growing in grassy places and scrub, below 1300m, flowering in March–May. Stems 20–80cm. Leaflets 5–8, broadly cuneate-obovate. Spikes 10–25cm long, the pedicels 3–4mm. Flowers 1.3–1.5cm long, the upright petal with a yellowish blotch; keel ciliate on the lower edges towards the base. Seeds 3–4mm long, pale, marbled with brown.

Lupinus mutabilis Sweet var. ***cruckshanksii*** (Hook.) L.H.Bailey syn. *L. hartwegii* Lindl. subsp. *cruckshanksii* Hook. A tall, almost hairless, bluish-green summer annual with spikes of blue and yellow, or sometimes white flowers, native of the

Lupinus texensis

Lupinus mutabilis var. *cruckshanksii*, cultivated in Devon

mountains of Colombia and Peru, flowering in summer. Stems 75–150cm. Leaflets 6–8, around 1.2cm wide, oblanceolate or spathulate, sometimes with short hairs beneath. Flowers not in whorls, around 2cm across, with a yellow blotch, turning crimson and purple. Seeds 6–8mm long, greyish-white, smooth and shiny. Easily grown and fast to flower; best planted where it is to flower, or kept in a large pot.

Lupinus succulentus Dougl. ex Koch.
A fleshy winter annual with hollow stems, broad leaflets and spikes of deep purple-blue flowers in whorls or groups, native of Arizona and California in the foothills of the Sierra Nevada from Butte Co. to Shasta Co. and southwards in the Coast Ranges to Baja California, growing on grassy slopes in heavy soil below 1500m, flowering in February–May. Stems 20–60cm. Leaflets 7–9, cuneate to cuneate-obovate. Spikes 6–30cm long, the pedicels 4–6mm. Flowers 1.2–1.4cm long, the upright petal with a yellowish centre; keel ciliate near base. Seeds 4–5mm long, marbled with dark brown.

Lupinus texensis Hook. **Texas Bluebonnet**
A spring annual with 5 leaflets and deep blue flowers with a white, yellow, or reddish blotch, native of Texas, growing in dry meadows and on roadsides, flowering in early summer. Stems to 25cm, branching at ground level. Leaflets lanceolate, silky beneath, glabrous above. Flower spike to 8cm, the flowers scattered, around 1cm across. *L. subcarnosus* Hook., also called Texas Bluebonnet, has obovate-lanceolate, fleshy leaflets, and longer spikes of flowers, around 15cm long; it is also found in Texas.

Lupinus truncatus Nutt. ex Hook. & Arn.
An almost hairless winter annual with linear, blunt leaflets and loose spikes of flowers, not in whorls, opening purple and becoming red after pollination, native of California from Monterey Co. to N Baja California, growing on grassy slopes and in open woods below 1000m, and often common after a fire, flowering in March–May. Stems 30–70cm. Leaflets 5–7, around 4mm wide. Spikes 5–15cm long, the pedicels 2–3mm. Flowers 1–1.2cm long. Keel ciliate on both edges. Seeds 3mm long, pale pinkish mottled with brown.

Lupinus hirsutissimus above Malibu Beach, California

Lupinus truncatus in hills near Los Angeles

Lupinus hispanicus

Lupinus hispanicus in the northern foothills of the Sierra de Gredos in May

Lupinus albus subsp. *albus*

Lupinus angustifolius

Lupinus luteus in northeast Portugal near Braganca

Lupinus albus L. subsp. *albus*
(*Leguminosae*)   An upright annual with white
flowers and large seeds, native of S Europe,
but known mainly or perhaps only as a
cultivated plant, flowering in April–June.
Stems to 120cm. Leaflets obovate, 1.4–1.8cm
wide, hairy on both sides. Upper lip of calyx
with 2 shallow teeth. Flowers pure white, the
keel sometimes tipped with pale blue. Seeds
10–14mm across, evenly coloured. The wild
subsp. *graecus* (Boiss. & Sprun.) Franco &
Silva, from open ground in the south Balkan
peninsula and NW Turkey, has bright blue
flowers and smaller, variegated seeds, 8–9mm
across. The seeds of the cultivated variety are
eaten roasted, and were used for flour in
ancient Egypt, Greece and Rome. Most other
lupin seeds are very poisonous.

Lupinus angustifolius L.   An upright
annual with narrow leaflets and blue flowers,
native of S Europe, North Africa, and Turkey
to Syria, growing in open places on light soil,
flowering in March–May. Stems to 80cm.
Leaflets flat, linear, 4–5mm wide, hairy only
beneath. Upper lip of calyx deeply 2 lobed.
Flowers blue, 1.1–1.3cm long. Seeds 6–8mm
long. An alkaloid-free form is planted for
fodder in both Europe and South Africa.
Subspecies *reticulatus* (Desv.) Coutinho, from
coastal sands in SW Europe, Morocco and the
W Mediterranean, is a smaller plant to 40cm,
with channelled leaflets 2mm across and seeds
4.5–5mm long.

Lupinus hispanicus Boiss. & Reut.
An upright annual with obovate-oblong
leaflets and flowers that open cream, then
become pink, native of N and C Portugal and
W Spain, growing on roadsides and in open
fields, flowering in May–June. Stems to 80cm.
Leaflets 9–12mm wide, hairy only on the
edges above. Upper lip of calyx deeply
2-lobed. Flowers 1.3–1.6cm long. Seeds
4.5–6mm long, pale reddish-brown with
darker spots. A conspicuous roadside weed in
the northern Sierra de Gredos, variable in

Lupinus varius

Lupinus varius on the beach at Phaselis, near Antalya, Turkey

flower colour, perhaps through hybridisation with *L. luteus*.

Lupinus luteus L. An upright annual with bright yellow, scented flowers, native of Portugal, Spain, Corsica, Sardinia, Italy, Sicily and North Africa to Israel, growing in open ground and abandoned fields, flowering in May–June. Stems to 80cm. Leaflets 8–12mm wide, mucronate, sparsely hairy above. Upper lip of calyx deeply 2-lobed. Flowers 1.3–1.6cm long. Seeds 6–8mm long, black, marbled with white. Often grown for fodder or green manure in other parts of Europe where it is not native.

Lupinus micranthus Guss., syn. *L. hirsutus* L. p.p. An upright annual with brownish hairs and long, dense spikes of bright blue flowers, native of Portugal and the Mediterranean region, growing in open ground and abandoned fields on acidic soil, flowering in March–June. Stems to 40cm. Leaflets 5–15mm wide, obovate-cuneate to obovate-oblong, mucronate, sparsely hairy. Upper lip of calyx deeply 2-lobed. Flowers 1–1.4cm long, the keel blackish-violet at the apex. Seeds 5–8mm long, pinkish-grey to brown, with dark veins and dots.

Lupinus varius L., syn. *L. pilosus* L. An upright annual with brownish or white hairs and deep blue flowers, native of Portugal and the Mediterranean region, growing in open ground and abandoned fields, flowering in March–May. Stems to 50cm. Leaflets 6–9mm wide, oblong-obovate, mucronate, hairy. Upper lip of calyx deeply 2-lobed. Flowers 1.5–1.7cm long, with a white and yellow or pale purple blotch. Seeds 7–12mm long, papillose, cream or purple, marbled cream or black. Some authorities distinguish the western subsp. *varius*, with rusty hairs and seeds 7–9mm long, and subsp. *orientalis* Franco & P. Silva, syn. *L. pilosus* L., with white hairs and seeds 1–1.2cm. A striking plant easily grown in dry climates, but apt to rot in damp areas.

Lupinus micranthus in south-west Spain, near Cadiz

Lablab purpureus in the kitchen garden at Longwood, Pennsylvania

Lablab purpureus in Tresco Abbey gardens

Lablab purpureus 'Ruby Moon'

Arachis hypogea

Phaseolus coccineus 'Sunset'

Arachis hypogea L. (*Leguminosae*) **Peanut, Ground Nut**   A tropical annual with rounded leaflets and yellow flowers followed by underground seed pods, originating in S Bolivia and N Argentina, but now also widely cultivated in Africa and Asia. Stems to 50cm, upright or trailing. Leaves with 2 pairs of leaflets 2.5–6cm long. Flowers 1.5–2cm long. After fertilisation, the stem at the base of the ovary grows downwards, pushing the young pod into the ground. Peanuts require high temperatures to grow well and a long season to produce a good crop; they thrive in the same areas as cotton, but elsewhere are interesting in a warm garden, or planted in sandy soil in a large pot in the greenhouse, with a night minimum of 10°C.

Lablab purpureus (L.) Sweet, syn. *Dolichos lablab* L., *Lablab niger* Medik. (*Leguminosae*) **Hyacinth Bean, Lablab Bean**   A strongly climbing tropical annual, biennial or short-lived perennial, with 3 leaflets and spikes of loose groups of pinkish-purple or white flowers, widely cultivated as a vegetable in the tropics and possibly native of tropical Africa, where subsp. *uncinatus* Verdc. is found. The plants flower in late summer in temperate areas, and in the cooler seasons, mainly spring and autumn, in the tropics. Stems twining to 6m. Leaflets to 15cm long, broadly ovate, cuneate at the base, with a long point. Flowers around 15mm long, the very broad upper petal reflexing when the flower is ready for pollination. Seed pods curved and flattened, to 20cm long.

Some varieties have deep purple leaves and pods, and others are short-day, long-day or day-neutral plants. In temperate areas, long-day or day-neutral varieties are more likely to flower well; start the plants in heat, and put out after all chance of frost is past. **'Ruby Moon'** is an attractive cultivar with purplish flowers and leaves and dark purple pods, and succeeds outdoors as far north as S England.

Phaseolus coccineus L. (*Leguminosae*) **Runner Bean**   A tropical climber, in the wild a perennial with annual stems, but usually grown as an annual, with scarlet flowers, native of W and S Mexico and Guatemala, growing in deep valleys in oak and pine forest with dahlias, shrubby senecios and salvias, at 1800–2500m, flowering in September–November. Climber to 3m or more. Leaflets 3, to 10cm long. Flowers 3cm long. Pods in the wild around 8cm long, to 35cm or more in cultivated varieties. Runner beans were first cultivated by the Mexicans around 2200 years ago, and first grown in England in around 1630, when they were valued as ornamentals. Attractive varieties include **'Desirée'** with white flowers; **'Sunset'** with pink flowers; **'Painted Lady'** with white lower petals and a red upper petal. Most of the other commercial varieties have the usual scarlet flowers. Sow the beans in late spring or early summer when the soil is warm. Runner beans tolerate cooler temperatures than French beans (*Phaseolus vulgaris* L.), and prefer a moist, sheltered and partially shaded site. More details of these edible beans and peas can be found in our book 'Vegetables' (Pan 1993).

Pisum sativum L. subsp. **elatius** (Bieb.) Aschers. & Graebn. (*Leguminosae*) A scrambling or climbing winter annual with purplish-red flowers, and pods of finely papillose seeds, native of S Europe and Turkey eastwards to Turkmenia, growing in rough grassy places and scrub at up to 1700m, flowering in March–May. Stems to 1.5m. Leaves with 2–4 pairs of leaflets, and branched tendrils. Flowers 2–3cm across, solitary or paired on stalks 2–4 times as long as the leafy stipules. Seed pods 7–12mm thick, exploding when ripe. The cultivated pea differs in its larger, smooth or wrinkled seeds; the wild variety of this, var. *arvense* (L.) Poiret, has bicoloured flowers and small, black-blotched seeds. There is also a decorative cultivated pea, 'Purple Podded' with pink and red flowers and dark purple pods.

Psophocarpus tetragonolobus (L.) DC. (*Leguminosae*) **Four-angled Bean**

A climbing tropical perennial, often grown as a summer annual, with 3 leaflets and blue flowers followed by edible, 4-winged pods, widely cultivated in the Old World tropics and not known wild, though possibly derived from *P. grandiflorus* Wilczek, from Zaire. Stems to 2m or more, flowering in the first year, and then forming a tuberous, edible root. Leaflets rounded at the base, around 8cm long. Flowers 5cm across; pods 15–20cm long when mature, with 4 wide, wavy wings, but best eaten young, at 10–15cm. Flowers and young shoots may be added to salads. An attractive bean, which will flower in 3–4 months from seed in hot, humid weather.

Psophocarpus tetragonolobus

Pisum sativum subsp. *elatius* in the ancient Greek theatre in Side

Phaseolus coccineus 'Desirée'

Phaseolus coccineus 'Painted Lady'

Lathyrus tingitanus in southern Spain, near Gibraltar

Lathyrus chloranthus

Lathyrus tingitanus

Lathyrus (*Leguminosae*) A genus of 160 species, including *L. odoratus*, the sweet pea. Most species are found in Europe (54) and Turkey (59). *Lathyrus* is not easy to distinguish from *Vicia*. In *Vicia*, the style is pubescent all round, or bearded on the lower side, and the stem is not winged. In *Lathyrus*, the style is pubescent only on the upper side, and may be straight or twisted; the stem is often winged.

Lathyrus chloranthus Boiss.   A climbing
winter or spring annual with leaves with
2 leaflets and greenish-yellow flowers, 1–2 on
the stem, native of Turkey from Konya
eastwards to N Iraq, Iran and Armenia,
growing in wheatfields and on the banks of
streams in scrub, at 600–1800m, flowering in
June–July. Stems to 2m, winged, roughly
hairy. Leaflets elliptic, 2–6cm long. Flowers
1.5–2.5cm long. Pods 4–5cm, with 5–9
papillose seeds. Easily grown in well-drained
soil and a warm, airy position.
   Lathyrus chrysanthus Boiss. has narrower
leaflets and 2–4 golden-yellow flowers,
2–2.2cm long. It is rarer, confined to SE
Turkey, Lebanon and the Syrian desert,
growing mainly in abandoned fields. A new
species, *L. belinensis,* which has 2–4 flowers
with red-veined upper petals and yellow wings
and keel, was described from SW Turkey as
recently as 1987. It is described as strong-
growing, and as annual or perennial. *L. gorgoni*
Parl., from Sardinia and Sicily to North
Africa, Turkey and N Iraq, has solitary,
orange-brown, veined flowers 1.5–1.8cm long,
and speckled pods.

Lathyrus clymenum L., syn. *L. articulatus* L.
A scrambling winter or spring annual with
2–4 pairs of narrow leaflets on a winged stalk
and 1–4 flowers varying from lilac to pink and
white, native of the Mediterranean region and
Portugal, growing in scrub and rough ground,
usually damp in winter, below 100m,
flowering in April–May. Stems to 80cm.
Leaflets 2–6cm long, 1–11mm wide, linear to
lanceolate. Flowers 15–20mm long, either with
crimson upper petal and purplish wings
(*L. clymenum*), or, as shown here, crimson
with white or pink wings (*L. articulatus*). Pods
3–7cm long, with 5–7 seeds. Some authorities
recognise *L. articulatus* as a separate species or
as a variety. Apart from the colour of the
flowers, it tends to have narrower leaflets and
pods, but these three characters are not always
well correlated. *L. ochrus* (L.) DC has white or
yellowish flowers and 1–2 pairs of ovate
leaflets on a very flat, wide stalk.

Lathyrus sativus L.   A slender climbing
or sprawling annual with 1 pair of linear-
lanceolate to linear leaflets and solitary,
usually sky-blue flowers, of uncertain origin
but cultivated since early Neolithic times for
fodder, and the seeds as food, flowering in
April–July. Stems to 1.2m, subglabrous.
Leaflets 2–10cm long, 1.5–11mm wide.
Flowers 1.4–2cm long, the upper petal blue
with a white and pink spot, rarely purplish or
white. Pods 2.5–3cm with 3–4 seeds. A
delicate plant, lovely if planted in a large
terracotta pot.

Lathyrus tingitanus L.   A robust, climbing
or sprawling annual with 1 pair of linear-
lanceolate to ovate leaflets and 1–3 usually
purplish-crimson flowers, native of the Azores,
Portugal, S Spain Sardinia and North Africa,
growing in rough ground and hedges,
flowering in March–June. Stems to 1.2m,
glabrous. Leaflets 2–8cm long, 4–18mm wide.
Flowers 2–3cm long. Pods 6–10cm with 6–8
seeds. An attractive and robust species,
frequently and easily grown in a sunny
position. 'Roseus' has pink and white flowers.
L. tremolsianus Pau, from SE Spain, has
narrower leaflets, 1–4cm wide, and large
flowers, 2–3cm long, with a pink upper petal
and blue wings.

Lathyrus sativus

Lathyrus clymenum

Lathyrus sativus

Lathyrus lycicus

Lathyrus lycicus among the ruins of Phaselis, near Antalya

Lathyrus lycicus Boiss. (*Leguminosae*)
A slender, scrambling annual with 1 pair of
elliptic leaflets and 2–6 pink and white
flowers, native of the south coast of Turkey,
growing in rough places beneath pine trees
and in scrub, from sea level to 420m,
flowering in May–June. Stems to 1m, with
sparse, short hairs. Leaflets 2.5–5cm long,
7–15mm wide. Flowers 1.4–1.8cm long, the
upper petal pink, veined with crimson,
pubescent on the back. Pods with 4–6 seeds.
An attractive species for a warm, sunny place.
A closely related species, *L. phaselitanus*
Hub.-Mor. & Davis, is known only from
Phaselis. It differs in having no hairs, linear-
elliptic leaflets 4–8mm wide, and 1–2 violet
flowers 2cm long.

Vicia hybrida L. (*Leguminosae*)   A climbing
or sprawling annual with 4–8 pairs of
oblanceolate to obovate leaflets and solitary,
pale yellow or purplish flowers, native of the
Mediterranean area, eastwards to Transcaspia
and Iran, growing in grassy places and scrub,
and among limestone rocks, often by the sea,
flowering in March–June. Stems to 80cm,
hairy. Leaflets 5–20mm long, 3–8mm wide.
Flowers 2–3cm long, usually sessile, the upper
petal hairy on the back. Pods 2–4cm with 2–5
seeds. This is one of the largest flowered of the
vetches, needing a warm, sunny position.

Vicia villosa Roth. subsp. **varia** (Host)
Corb.   A climbing or sprawling annual with
4–12 pairs of linear to elliptic leaflets and
racemes of 10–30 purplish flowers, native of
the Mediterranean area, eastwards to
Transcaspia and Iran, planted for fodder and
now naturalised over much of Europe,
growing in grassy places and scrub, flowering
in May–August. Stems to 2m, sometimes with
flatteded hairs. Leaflets 1–3cm long, 2–8mm
wide. Flowers 1–1.6cm long, with purple, blue
or white wings. Pods 2–4cm with 2–8 seeds.
Subspecies *villosa* has hairy stems, long lower
calyx teeth and flowers 1–2cm long.
Subspecies **eriocarpa** (Hausskn,) P.W.Ball,
which is common in the Aegean and
W Turkey, has 5–15 purple flowers in the
raceme and pubescent pods. *Vicia tenuifolia*
(Roth.) subsp. *dalmatica* (A. Kern.) Greuter is
similar to *V. villosa*, but is perennial and has
narrowly linear leaflets 0.5–2mm wide.

Vicia villosa subsp. *varia* near Valladolid, Spain

Vicia hybrida near Marmaris in Turkey

Vicia villosa subsp. *varia*

Vicia villosa subsp. *eriocarpa* on Kos

Antique Fantasy Mixed

pea from Sicily, and it was from Sicily that a monk named Franciscus Cupani is reported to have sent seeds to Dr Uvedale in England in 1699. The flowers of the original plants were apparently dull purple or maroon and purple, and possibly also red and white, and it is thought that during the 16th century the Spanish were responsible for taking the maroon and purple form of the plant (called at various times 'Cupani' and 'Lord Nelson') to South America, where it became naturalised.

Stems to 2m tall, winged, with small, green leaflets arranged in pairs, each leaf stalk ending in a tendril. Flowers to about 3cm across, in racemes of 2–4, highly scented, standard purplish-red, keel and wings purple.

'Painted Lady' A popular old red and white variety, probably a bicolour sport of *L. odoratus*, the exact origins of which are unknown, although it was growing in the Chelsea Physic Garden in London by 1737. It has fairly small flowers and a strong, slightly spicy, scent.

'America' syn. 'Toreador' An old Grandiflora variety introduced into cultivation in Britain in 1896 by Morse. Flowers white, striped and stippled with red, well-scented.

Antique Fantasy Mixed This commercial selection of older-style varieties comes in a range of colours. The flowers are smaller than those of most modern varieties, plain (i.e. not frilled) and well scented.

'Chatsworth' Flowers large, slightly ruffled, light blue, sometimes with 5–6 flowers on a stem. (See also individual photograph and full entry on p.124.)

'Cupani' Close to the wild type, this is the original *L. odoratus*, named after Franciscus Cupani, the Sicilian monk credited with sending the first sweet pea seeds to England in 1699. Possibly the same as 'Matucana', which was illustrated in Curtis' *Botanical Magazine* in 1788.

'Edward Unwin' Flowers very large and ruffled, light lavender-blue from green-tinted buds. Plant very strong and free-flowering. New from Unwins in 1998.

'Janet Scott' Flowers small, plain pink, with an excellent scent, and produced in great numbers.

'Her Majesty' Flowers of formal shape, a rich pinkish-red, becoming paler. New from Unwins in 1998.

'Mars' Flowers very large and ruffled, white with red shading, stippling and stripes. New from Unwins in 1998.

'Miss Willmott' An old Grandiflora variety, first introduced into cultivation in 1901, and relaunched commercially in 1910 after being improved. Flowers scented, orange-pink shaded with rose veins. Named after the great and eccentric English amateur gardener.

'Mrs Collier' syn. 'Ceres', 'Dora Cowper' An old Grandiflora variety, raised by Dobbie in 1905. Flowers small, creamy-white, with an erect standard and pale yellow buds. Strong vanilla-like scent, particularly noticeable in the evening.

Lathyrus odoratus 'Painted Lady'

Sweet Peas The genus *Lathyrus* contains about 100 annual, shrubby and perennial species of the pea family (*Leguminosae*), most of which climb by tendrils. The name sweet pea is generally used to refer to the large-flowered cultivars that are derived from *L. odoratus* (see below), an attractive, scented, small-flowered annual species which is itself well worth growing.

In Victorian times, sweet peas became popular as cut flowers and were bred and grown in huge quantities in Britain; one group, known generally as Grandifloras, was raised chiefly by Henry Eckford (1823–1905), a nurseryman at Wem in Shropshire. In the early 20th century, the popularity of the flower was further boosted by the arrival of the larger, wavy-edged 'Spencer' types. These originally occurred as mutants from Eckford's 'Primadonna' in 1900, were raised by Silas Cole, and named after his employer's wife, Countess Spencer of Althrop. It is these 'Spencer' types that have been developed throughout recent years, giving rise to the sweet peas now offered by commercial suppliers, and frequently named after celebrities, or the raisers and their families.

Sweet peas are easy to grow from seed, sown indoors in autumn or spring, or directly outdoors once the soil has begun to warm up; spring sowing in pots is easiest, as it removes the need to look after the young plants throughout the winter, while still giving the young plants a head start over those grown directly outside. Young, pot-grown plants should be put out into good, rich soil in a sunny, sheltered place once the weather warms up, kept moist, and given some kind of support up which to climb. The flowers are normally produced from about the beginning of June through until early autumn but it is very important to pick them regularly, for once they have run to seed, flower production will stop.

Lathyrus odoratus L. A climbing annual the exact origins of which are uncertain, though it is probably native of Italy and Sicily. The plant was recorded by John Ray in his *Historia Plantarum* (1686) as a sweet-scented

Lathyrus odoratus 'Cupani' at Tapeley Park, Devon

'Janet Scott'

'America'

'Her Majesty'

'Mrs Collier'

'Miss Willmott'

'Mars'

'Chatsworth'

'Edward Unwin'

Specimens from Quince House greenhouse, May 17th, ½ life-size

Lathyrus odoratus 'Comet'

Lathyrus odoratus 'Snoopea'

Lathyrus odoratus 'North Shore'

Lathyrus odoratus 'Chatsworth'

Sweet peas with *Onopordum acanthium* and *Agapanthus* at Sellindge, Kent

'Alan Titchmarsh'   A modern variety with light red flowers, named after the British gardening television presenter and writer.

'Anniversary'   A variety with wavy, delicate, rose-pink flowers, edged with darker shade of pink. Slight scent.

'Blue Danube'   A vigorous variety, with long, stout stems and well-scented, large, ruffled flowers. The mid-blue colour is fairly weather resistant.

'Chatsworth'   A beautiful variety with waved, well-scented, pale lavender-blue flowers. Stems to 2m, with 5–6 blooms per stalk. Raised by Harvey Albutt, and first offered commercially in 1998. (For flower detail see photograph on p.123.)

'Colin Unwin'   Plant to 1.8m high, with about 4 lightly scented flowers per stem. Flowers to about 6cm in diameter, wavy, with red standards and paler red wings. Unlike many other reds, the colour does not fade in the sun. Raised by the Rev. T.K. Colledge of Christchurch, Dorset in 1984.

'Comet'   A new variety, bred by Unwins of Cambridge, this has white petals streaked and edged with cerise.

'Esther Rantzen'   A modern variety with pale lilac flowers, named after the British television presenter.

'Felicity Kendal'   A modern variety with pale red flowers, named after the actress.

'Mrs Bernard Jones'   A vigorous plant, to about 2.3m high, with long, stout flower stems, each bearing about 4 heavily scented

flowers. Flowers waved, pale pink flushed with purplish-pink, to about 6cm in diameter. Raised by Bernard Jones, a keen amateur breeder, in the 1980s.

'Noel Sutton'   A vigorous plant, to about 2.1m high, with long, stout flower stems, each bearing 3–4 strongly scented blooms. Flowers waved, to about 6.5cm in diameter, with deep violet standards and purplish-blue wings.

'North Shore'   This sweet pea, which was raised by Dr K.R.W. Hammett of New Zealand in the early 1980s, is one of the best varieties for growing in the garden, and has the distinction of having been given two awards after trial at Wisley. It grows to about 1.6m tall, with long, stiff, flower stems, each bearing an average of 4 well-scented, violet-purple flowers.

'Red Arrow'   A modern variety with deep scarlet, weather-resistant flowers on stiff stems. Raised by Bernard Jones.

'Sally Unwin'   Large, scented, salmon-pink flowers, fading to white at the base. Long stems. Raised by Unwins in 1977.

'Sarah'   A variety with purplish-magenta flowers.

'Snoopea'   This name refers to a strain of dwarf plants, distinguished by their lack of tendrils. These are available in 4 different colours, and are good for growing in containers. Raised by E.W. King, of Colchester, Essex.

'Sutton's Beaujolais'   Rich burgundy-maroon. Highly Commended in 1967 at the R.H.S. trials.

'Sutton's Beaujolais'

'Red Arrow'

'Sarah'

'Felicity Kendal'

'Alan Titchmarsh'

'Blue Danube'

'Mrs Bernard Jones'

'Esther Rantzen'

'Anniversary'

'Sally Unwin'

'Noel Sutton'

'Colin Unwin'

Specimens from Eccleston Square, June 28th, ½ life-size

Hare's-foot clover, *Trifolium arvense*, at Braunton Burrows, Devon

Trifolium stellatum

Trifolium stellatum near Cadiz in Spain

Melilotus cretica

Trifolium incarnatum

Melilotus cretica L., syn. *Trigonella cretica* (L.) Boiss. (*Leguminosae*)   An upright, often branched winter annual with broad, toothed leaflets and loose racemes of small, yellow flowers, native of the E Aegean islands and W Turkey – but, in spite of its name, not found in Crete – growing in bare ground, flowering in April–June. Stems to 25cm. Leaflets 3, 1–2cm long. Flowers 6–7mm long. Pods like parchment, broadly elliptic, flattened, 1–2 seeded. Most melilotus have upright spikes of many small, yellow flowers, white in *M. alba*. Sow seed in winter or early spring; I have found that in some species late-sown seed will not flower until the following year.

Tetragonolobus purpureus Moench., syn. *T. palaestinus* Boiss., *Lotus tetragonolobus* L. (*Leguminosae*)   A creeping, hairy winter annual with crimson flowers and winged seed pods, native of S Europe from Spain eastwards to S Russia, W Turkey and North Africa, growing in dry, grassy places, flowering in March–June. Stems to 40cm. Leaflets 3, to 4cm long. Flowers solitary or in pairs, 1.2–2.2cm long. Pods 3–9cm, with 4 wings 2–4mm wide. An attractive plant, sometimes grown for its edible pods, which are called asparagus pea, and best eaten when around 2.5cm long. Easily grown from a spring sowing, and more ornamental if grown in not-too-rich soil, to discourage them from producing masses of leaves at the expense of the flowers. *T. palaestinus* was described as having smaller flowers 1.2–1.5cm long, and more narrowly winged fruit, but the two merge in parts of Turkey.

Trifolium arvense (*Leguminosae*)
Hare's-foot clover   A small, upright winter annual or biennial with soft, woolly, often pinkish flowerheads, native of Europe from Ireland eastwards to the Caucasus, N Iran and Syria, growing in sandy places, usually on acidic soils, flowering in March–July. Stems to 30cm. Leaflets 1–2cm long, narrowly elliptic, finely toothed. Calyx and corolla both pinkish, purplish or silvery, in oval heads to 2.5cm long. A charming annual, common in sandy soils and on dunes. Widely naturalised in eastern North America, and associated with poor soil.

Trifolium incarnatum L.   A robust, upright winter annual with broad leaflets and large, oval heads of crimson flowers, native of S and W Europe, and widely naturalised elsewhere, growing in grassy places, flowering in May–August. Stems to 50cm. Leaflets 8–25mm long, obcordate. Flowers 1–1.2cm long, in heads 1–4cm long. A striking and easily grown plant, good for meadow gardens, and widely naturalised in eastern North America, where it is planted as a green manure. *T. purpureum* Loisel. is similar, but has narrow leaflets and purplish-red flowers in heads 2–11cm long.

Trifolium stellatum L.   A low, branching annual with small, round flowerheads and conspicuous, starry fruiting calyces, native of S Europe and the Mediterranean to W Iran, growing in open ground and in scrub, flowering in April–June. Stems to 20cm. Leaflets 8–12mm, obcordate. Flowers 8–12mm long, in heads 1.5–2.5cm across. Attractive for its starry and woolly fruiting heads, which often become reddish. It is common around the Mediterranean, and needs to be planted in a sunny, dry place.

Trifolium incarnatum

Tetragonolobus purpureus near Ronda, Spain

Crassula dichotoma, on the Cape Peninsula, South Africa

Saxifraga cymbalaria subsp. *huetiana*

Saxifraga tridactylites on a ruined wall in Bideford, Devon

Crassula dichotoma L. (*Crassulaceae*)
A winter annual with opposite, fleshy leaves and bright yellow flowers with red spots in the centre, native of South Africa in the Western cape from the Peninsula and Caledon, northwards to Namaqualand, growing in sandy and rocky places, flowering in September–October. Stems 5–20cm. Flowers around 1cm across. Of around 300 species of *Crassula*, most are succulent perennials, but some are annuals and some, such as the weedy *C. helmsii* and *C. natans* Thunb. from southern Africa, are aquatics.

Saxifraga cymbalaria L. subsp. **cymbalaria** (*Saxifragaceae*)   A brittle, fleshy winter annual or biennial with 7–9-lobed lower leaves and small, shining, bright yellow flowers, native of Romania and the Caucasus, N Iran, Turkey, W Syria and Lebanon, growing on rocks by mountain streams and on damp cliffs, flowering in March–September. Stems to 25cm. Leaves with pointed lobes. Petals 4.5–5mm. An attractive, sprawling annual for a damp, shady position, sowing itself around in a quiet way.

Subspecies **huetiana** (Boiss.) Engl. & Irm. is a shorter, denser plant with shallower, rounded leaf lobes. It is found scattered in Turkey and NW Syria. This is the plant commonly cultivated. Subspecies *atlantica* Batt., with narrow petals 5–6mm long, is found in the Djebel Babor in E Algeria.

Other annual saxifrages have very small, white flowers. *S. hederacea* L., from the E Mediterranean, has leaves with 3–7 short lobes. *S. adscendens* L. is a biennial with stems to 25cm, a rosette of usually 3-lobed leaves and petals 3–5mm long.

Saxifraga tridactylites L.   A small annual, often with red stems and leaves, and with white flowers, native of most of Europe and North Africa eastwards to the Caucasus, Iran and Iraq, growing in dry places, on old walls and rocks, flowering in March–July. Stems 2.5–10cm. Basal leaves spathulate, lower stem

Saxifraga cymbalaria subsp. *cymbalaria* from Boludag, Turkey

Sedum sempervivoides, near Malatya, Turkey in July

leaves divided into 3 narrow lobes. Petals 1.5–2.5mm, obovate. An attractive dwarf, flowering very early in the spring.

Sedum caeruleum Vahl (*Crassulaceae*)
A small, fleshy winter annual with pale blue, starry flowers, native of Corsica, Sardinia, Sicily, Tunisia and Algeria, growing on mossy rocks, flowering in April–June. Stems much branched, 5–20cm, often tinged bright red. Leaves around 1cm, terete, succulent. Flowers with 7 petals and 14 stamens. Attractive and easily grown, and will sow itself, the seedlings appearing in autumn, and in danger from slugs, or from frost in the winter in cold and wet areas.

Sedum oreades (Decne.) Raym.-Hamet
A dwarf annual with bright yellow, starry flowers, native from Kashmir to SW China (W Sichuan), growing on rocky slopes and thin pastures at 3200–5500m, flowering in July–September. Leaves fleshy, narrowly lanceolate, 3–6mm long. Flowers around 1cm across. A common plant at high altitudes in the Himalayas, flowering with the autumn gentians.

Sedum sempervivoides Fisch. ex M. Bieb. syn. *Sedum sempervivum* Ledeb. A biennial forming a houseleek-like rosette of leaves in the first year, and in the second sending up a red stem topped by a flat inflorescence of scarlet flowers. Native of Georgia, Armenia, the Caucasus, NW Iran and N, E and S Anatolia in Turkey, growing on dry, rocky, usually limestone slopes, at 1200–2900m, flowering in June–August. Plant pubescent; stems 7–20cm. Inflorescence 5–12cm wide, with 30–150 flowers each 1.2–1.5cm across. Petals 5, stamens 10. A striking plant, bright red among the dead summer grasses. It rots in winter or summer wet, though it tolerates frost, and needs a dry climate to thrive outdoors. Under cover, water mainly in spring and early summer, sparingly in autumn.
S. pilosum M. Bieb., from NE Turkey, the Caucasus and the Talysh, is also a biennial, but has smaller rosettes of narrow leaves 8mm long, 3mm wide, densely leafy stems and a smaller head of pink flowers.

Sedum oreades, above Kanding, Sichuan at 3500m in October

Sedum caeruleum

Cuphea silenoides

Cuphea hyssopifolia

Cuphea (*Lythraceae*) A genus containing around 260 species of shrubs, perennials and annuals, mostly native of South America and Mexico, but with 2 or 3 species extending northwards into eastern North America and Arizona. The few, large seeds are ejected from the split calyx before they are completely ripe. *Cuphea cyanea* and *C. ignea* are the so-called cigar flowers, tender perennials with a tubular orange calyx tipped with yellow. *Cuphea* is related to the familiar purple loosetrife, *Lythrum salicaria* L., native in Europe, but a serious pest in parts of Canada.

Cuphea calcarata Benth. A summer annual with opposite, narrow leaves and bright purple flowers, native of C Mexico, in Zacatecas, Jalisco, Guanajuato, and Michoacan, growing by streams in rocky places, flowering in September–October. Stems 30–60cm. Leaves opposite, linear, 3.2–7cm long, 3–13mm wide. Inflorescence leafy only at the base. Calyx 1.1–2.1cm long, with an ascending or straight spur. Upper petals obovate or round; the lower ⅓ shorter, cuneate, oblong to obovate. We photographed this graceful and attractive species growing with *Eryngium*, *Lobelia*, *Milla* and *Tagetes*, near Zacatecas in N Mexico in 1991, but it did not live long in cultivation.

Cuphea hyssopifolia H. B. & K. A dwarf subshrub, often grown as a summer annual, native of S Mexico and Guatemala, flowering most of the year. Stems spreading to 60cm. Calyx 6–8mm long. Petals more or less equal,

Cuphea calcarata, with *Tagetes* near Zacatecas, Mexico in October

Cuphea lanceolata 'Firefly'

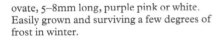

Trapa natans on the lower Shire river in Malawi

ovate, 5–8mm long, purple pink or white. Easily grown and surviving a few degrees of frost in winter.

Cuphea lanceolata Ait.   A softly sticky summer annual with opposite, ovate-lanceolate leaves and bright pinkish-red or purplish-red flowers, native of Mexico in San Luis Potosi, Guanajuato, Zimapan, Mexico and Michoacan, growing in damp places, flowering in August–October. Stems to 1m. Leaves 2–4.5cm long, 6–20mm wide. Inflorescence leafy to near the top. Calyx around 1.6–2.4cm long, with purple hairs, with an unequal base. Upper petals heart-shaped or round; the lower ⅓ shorter, broadly obovate. Easily grown in good, rich, moist soil, and very striking, with a long flowering season, into autumn until the frost. The variety shown here is sold under the name **'Firefly'**.

Cuphea llavea La Llave & Lexarza
A summer annual with opposite leaves and purple and red flowers, native of Mexico, growing in wet places in Chihuahua, Zacatecas, Jalisco, Michoacan, and Oaxaca, flowering in August–October. Stems 30–60cm, with stiff, white hairs. Leaves 2–8cm long, 5–25mm wide, ovate to lanceolate, often bristly-hairy. Inflorescence very leafy to the top. Calyx with white hairs, not sticky, with a rounded base, 2–4cm long. Upper petals obovate or round, around 1cm long; lower petals absent. Easily grown in good, rich soil.

Cuphea procumbens Cav.   A softly sticky summer annual with opposite, lanceolate leaves and pinkish flowers, native of S Mexico, growing in wet places in Morelia, Patzcuaro, Angangeo, Mexico and Jalapa, flowering in

August–October. Stems 20–50cm, with purple hairs. Leaves 3–7cm long, 5–20mm wide, often bristly-hairy. Inflorescence leafy to near the top. Calyx up to 2cm long with purple hairs, with a swollen base. Upper petals obovate or round; the lower ¼–⅓ shorter, oblong to obovate. Easily grown in good, rich soil.

Cuphea silenoides Nees   A softly sticky summer annual with opposite, ovate leaves and deep purple flowers, native of Mexico, (but described from cultivated plants), flowering in August–October. Stems to 80cm. Leaves 2–4cm long, 6–20mm wide. Inflorescence leafy to near the top. Calyx with purple hairs, up to 2cm long, with a swollen base. Upper petals heart-shaped or round, with a pale edge; the lower ⅔ shorter, almost round. Easily grown in good, rich, moist soil.

Trapa natans L. (*Trapaceae*) **Water Chestnut**   An aquatic summer annual or short-lived perennial with feathery, submerged roots and a rosette of rhombic, dark green, floating leaves, native of C and S Europe, Africa, N and SE Asia, and naturalised and sometimes a pest in North America, growing in ponds and the margins of lakes, flowering in summer. Stems to 2m. Leaves with swollen stalks to 17cm, the toothed blade 1.5–6cm across. Flowers around 1.5cm across, with 4 white or lilac petals. Fruits angular, with 2, 3 or 5 horns or spines, to 7.5cm across. Sow the seeds in spring in shallow water, and put the plants in deeper water as the stems elongate. *Trapa* is an interesting curiosity which formerly grew in England in warmer periods before and during the Ice Ages. The seeds are edible when well cooked, and are a regular constituent of Chinese cooking.

Cuphea llavea

Cuphea procumbens

Clarkia tenella

Clarkia bottae with *Gilia* at Quince House, Devon

Clarkia deflexa

Clarkia speciosa subsp. *polyantha*

Clarkia (Onagraceae) A genus named after Captain William Clark who, with Merriweather Lewis, led the first expedition across the rockies to northwestern North America in 1806. Around 30 species of *Clarkia* are native in California, with some extending northwards to Oregon and Washington, and one species, *C. tenella,* in Argentina. In the past, the species with cup-shaped flowers were called *Godetia,* while *Clarkia* was reserved for the species with lobed and long-clawed petals, and *Eucharidium* for the species with narrow, 3-fid petals.

Clarkia bottae (Spach) Lewis & Lewis, syn. *Godetia bottae* Spach A slender winter or spring annual with delicate, purplish-pink, cup-shaped flowers with 4 petals, native of California, in Monterey Co., growing in dry, grassy places in sage scrub and pine forest near the coast, flowering in May–July. Stems 20–50cm. Leaves lanceolate to linear-lanceolate, 2–5cm long. Top of stem and buds nodding. Sepals on one side of flower. Petals fan-shaped, sometimes shallowly toothed, 1–3cm long, white at the base, sometimes with darker flecks. Stigmas white. Capsule 4-grooved when young. A very attractive and easily grown plant, quick from seed. Sold under various names such as 'Amethyst Glow', 'Lilac Blossom' and 'Lilac Pixie'.

Clarkia cylindrica (Jeps.) Lewis & Lewis, syn. *Godetia bottae* var. *cylindrica* Jeps. A slender winter or spring annual with delicate, reddish-purple to pinkish, cup-shaped flowers with 4 petals, native of California from Los Angeles Co. northwards to Monterey and Mariposa Cos, growing in dry, grassy places below 1200m, in chaparral, valley grassland and open woodland, flowering in April–July. Stems 20–50cm. Leaves lanceolate to linear-lanceolate, 2–5cm long. Top of stem and buds nodding. Sepals on one side of flower. Petals fan-shaped, 1–3.5cm long, white in the middle

and bright red-purple at the base, sometimes with darker flecks. Capsule 4-grooved when young, very slender. Similar to *C. bottae,* but less restricted in distribution.

Clarkia deflexa (Jeps.) Lewis & Lewis, syn. *Godetia deflexa* Jeps. A tall, upright winter or spring annual with delicate, pale pink or lavender, cup-shaped flowers with 4 petals, native of California, from S Monterey to Orange and W Riverside Cos, growing in dry, grassy open places in sage scrub, chaparral and open woodland in the Coast Ranges, flowering in April–June. Stems 30–90cm. Leaves lanceolate, 3–8cm long. Top of stem erect, buds nodding. Sepals on one side of flower. Petals fan-shaped, sometimes shallowly toothed, 1–3cm long, white at the base, sometimes with darker flecks. Capsule 4-grooved when young.

Clarkia rubicunda (Lindl.) Lewis & Lewis, syn. *Godetia rubicunda* Lindl. An upright or sprawling winter or spring annual with lavender to bright red, cup-shaped flowers with 4 shining petals, native of California, from S Marin and Alameda to Santa Clara and Santa Cruz Cos, growing in dry, grassy and stony open places in sage scrub and open woodland, flowering in May–July. Stems 30–100cm. Leaves lanceolate, 1–6cm long. Top of stem and buds erect. Sepals on one side of flower. Petals fan-shaped, sometimes shallowly toothed, 1–3cm long, red or red-purple at the base. Capsule with 4 shallow grooves when young, 2–4cm long, blunt. Similar to *C. amoena,* but rather more delicate, with fewer markings on the petals, and with a red base.

Shown here are two colour forms: a lavender one, in cultivation in England, and a bright red form, in the wild south of San Francisco. Both are sometimes found in seed catalogues in Europe, and a cultivated mixture is also available.

Clarkia bottae and other Californian annuals in a mixed planting

Clarkia speciosa Lewis & Lewis subsp.
polyantha Lewis & Lewis An upright,
many-branched winter or spring annual with
purple, lavender or yellowish, cup-shaped
flowers with a red spot on each petal, native of
California in the foothills of the Sierra
Nevada, Fresno, Tulare and Kern Cos,
growing in dry, grassy and stony open places
below 1500m, flowering in May–July. Stems
10–60cm. Leaves linear to linear-lanceolate,
1–6cm long. Top of stem and buds erect.
Sepals on one side of flower or splitting into
groups. Petals fan-shaped, 1–2.7cm long, pale
at the base, with a purple-red spot near the
middle. Capsule 4-sided, 1–2.5cm long, blunt.
Subspecies *speciosa*, found in the Coast
Ranges from Monterey to Santa Barbara Cos,
is very similar, but usually has fewer branches,
and sometimes unspotted flowers.

Clarkia tenella (Cav.) Lewis & Lewis,
A slender winter or spring annual with
delicate, lavender-blue, cup-shaped flowers
with 4 petals, native of Argentina and Chile.
Stems 20–50cm. Leaves greyish, linear-
oblanceolate, 2–8cm long. Top of stem and
buds upright. Sepals on one side of flower or
splitting into groups. Petals fan-shaped,
1–3cm long, paler below, dark at the very base.
Capsule curved. A very attractive and
easily grown plant, quick from seed. Sold
under various names; 'Blue Pigmy' is an old
variety from Messrs Benary in Germany;
'Blue Magic' and 'Lady in Blue' are modern
varieties. Sometimes apparently sold under
the name *Godetia bottae*.

Clarkia rubicunda, cultivated form

Clarkia cylindrica in the Sierra Madre

Clarkia rubicunda, wild form, south of San Francisco

Clarkia unguiculata, wild near San Antonio

Clarkia concinna 'Pink Ribbons' at Quince House

Clarkia unguiculata at Kew

Clarkia pulchella 'Passion for Purple' at Suttons Seeds

Clarkia biloba (Durand) Nelson & Macbride, syn. *Godetia biloba* Wats. (*Onagraceae*) A tall, slender winter or spring annual with delicate, pale-pink to purplish-pink, cup-shaped flowers with 2-lobed petals, native of California, from Contra Costa Co. and Eldorado to Mariposa Cos, growing in dry, stony and grassy places in open forest below 1200m, flowering in May–July. Stems 30–100cm. Leaves lanceolate to linear, 2–6cm long. Top of stem and buds nodding. Sepals on one side of flower. Petals cuneate, bilobed for up to half their length, 1–2.5cm long. Pollen white or blue. Capsule 4-sided, straight.

Clarkia concinna (F. & M.) Greene, syn. *Eucharidium concinnum* F. & M. A branching winter or spring annual with spidery, magenta to purplish-pink flowers with 3-lobed petals, native of California in the coast ranges from Santa Clara Co. northwards to Humboldt Co., and in Butte and Yuba Cos, growing on dry, loose, stony slopes below 1200m, flowering in May–July. Stems 10–40cm. Leaves ovate-lanceolate to narrowly elliptical, 6–20mm wide. Top of stem and buds more or

less erect. Sepals on one side of flower. Petals streaked with white, clawed and 3-lobed for up to half their length, 1.5–2.6cm long, the middle lobe equal to or slightly longer than the laterals. Stamens 4; anthers red to lavender. Capsule 1.5–2cm long. Sold under the name **'Pink Ribbons'**.

C. breweri (A. Gray) Greene, from the inner coast ranges from Alameda to Fresno Cos, differs in having narrower leaves 1–7mm wide, the petals 1.5–2.6cm long, with the outer two lobes broad, the inner much longer, and linear to spathulate.

Clarkia pulchella Pursh An upright and branching winter or spring annual with purplish-pink or white flowers with shallowly 3-lobed, long-clawed petals, native of S British Columbia to SE Oregon and eastwards to W Montana, growing on dry, loose, stony slopes below 1200m, flowering in May–July. Stems 10–50cm, the top erect or nodding in bud. Leaves 2–10cm, linear to lanceolate or oblanceolate. Sepals on one side of flower. Petals with a winged claw, and with 3 wide, equal lobes, 1–3cm long, sometimes veined

with white or purple. Inner stamens sterile. Capsule 1–3cm long. An attractive and much-cultivated species, available in mixed colours and in white, semi-double **'Snowflake'**, and purple **'Passion for Purple'**. There is also a double form.

Clarkia unguiculata Lindl., syn. *Clarkia elegans* Dougl. An upright and branching winter or spring annual with lavender to purplish-red, salmon or white flowers with unlobed, long-clawed petals, native of California, in the Coast Ranges from Mendocino and Lake Cos to N San Diego Co., and in the Sierra foothills in Butte and Kern Cos, growing on dry, often shaded slopes below 1500m, flowering in May–June. Stems 30–100cm, the top of the stem erect, the buds nodding. Leaves 1–6cm, lanceolate to ovate. Petals 1–2cm long, with a narrow, unwinged claw which equals the deltoid to rhombic blade. All 8 stamens fertile, the outer stamens reddish. Capsule 1–3cm long. This has the typical starry flowers of the traditional *Clarkia*, and is especially common in its double form, shown over the page.

Clarkia concinna, wild form in California

Clarkia biloba

Clarkia pulchella 'Snowflake'

Clarkia pulchella mixed at Suttons Seeds

Clarkia biloba on a rocky roadside bank in goldrush country, California

Clarkia amoena 'Sybil Sherwood'

Clarkia amoena 'Memoria'

Clarkia amoena 'Satin Pink'

Clarkia 'Tall Double' mixed

Clarkia amoena (Lehmann) Nelson & Macbride, syn. *Godetia amoena* G. Don (*Onagraceae*) Godetia   An upright or sprawling winter or spring annual with white to lavender cup-shaped flowers with 4 shining petals, usually marked with bright red, native of NW California, from Humboldt to Marin Co., growing on dry, grassy cliffs and coastal bluffs, flowering in June–August. Stems 30–100cm. Leaves lanceolate, 1–6cm long. Top of stem and buds erect, in a congested inflorescence. Sepals on one side of flower. Petals obovate to fan-shaped, 1–3cm long, pink or lavender at the base. Capsule with 4 grooves when young, 2–5cm long, blunt.

Three subspecies are recognised in California, and were formerly cultivated in Europe, as separare species: subsp. *amoena*, as described above; subsp. *whitneyi* (Gray) Lewis & Lewis, syn. *Godetia grandiflora* hort., with coarse, erect or sprawling stems to 50cm, broad leaves, a congested inflorescence and large petals 4–6cm long, lavender with a large, central, red blotch, is found on coastal bluffs in a few places in Humboldt and Mendocino Cos; and subsp. *huntiana* (Jeps.) Lewis & Lewis with slender, much-branched stems to 1m tall, narrower leaves, a lax inflorescence, and smaller petals 1.5–3cm long with a red blotch. It grows inland in forest clearings from SW Oregon to Marin and Napa Cos.

There are numerous cultivars of *C. amoena*, which was first brought to Europe in 1818, and they are among the flashiest of all annuals. 'Shaminii' (not shown) is an old, semi-double variety with tall stems and lavender flowers with a red base.

Clarkia unguiculata 'Double Salmon'

Clarkia amoena on a Cornish hedge at Rinsey

The F$_I$ 'Grace' series are available in single colours. Sow seeds outdoors where they are to flower in late spring, or indoors in gentle heat in late winter or early spring, putting out the young plants in late spring. In Mediterranean areas, with a winter minimum of −5°C, the plants can be sown outdoors in autumn, and kept well watered in early spring.

'Furora' Flowers bright, shining crimson; stems around 75cm.

'Memoria' Flowers pure white; stems to 75cm. Pure white is also available in the 'Grace' series of F$_I$ hybrids. The first pure whites were named *Godetia venosa* Lindl.

'Satin Pink' Flowers palest pink, single; stems around 20cm. This group, which are F$_I$ hybrids, are also available as a mixture, including reds, lavenders, and pink with a red blotch.

'Sybil Sherwood' Flowers pale salmon-pink, semi-double; stems around 30cm; a novelty in 1932.

'Tall Double' mixed Flowers double, in shades of pink and red. Stems around 65cm.

Clarkia unguiculata Lindl., syn. *Clarkia elegans* Dougl. Wild *C. unguiculata* is shown on the previous page. Two double varieties are shown here, which have been grown at least since 1861. **'Double Salmon'** and **'Double Purple'** both have stems around 45cm, and make long-lasting cut flowers.

Clarkia unguiculata 'Double Purple'

Clarkia amoena 'Furora'

Oenothera brevipes in the Mojave desert

Oenothera versicolor 'Sunset Boulevard'

Oenothera bistorta Nutt. ex Torrey & Gray, syn. *Camissonia bistorta* Raven (*Onagraceae*) A small, sprawling winter or spring annual or biennial with yellow, cup-shaped flowers opening in the morning, native of S California, from Los Angeles Co. to N Baja California, growing on beaches and rocky clifftops, in sage scrub and open ground, flowering in March–June. Stems 5–80cm. Leaves linear-lanceolate, 3–7cm long. Buds erect. Petals 8–14mm long, often with a dark spot at the base. Capsule 1.2–1.5cm long, curved, quadrangular, sessile. A modest but attractive plant for dry, sandy soil.

Var. *veitchiana* Hook. is a stemless, inland form with longer, beaked capsules, growing in open places in chaparral and oak woodland from Ventura and Kern Cos southwards to N Baja California.

Oenothera brevipes Gray, syn. *Camissonia brevipes* Raven **Desert Primrose** A winter or spring annual, often rather coarse, with leaves mostly at the base and crowded, small, yellow, cup-shaped flowers, native of SW California, Nevada and W Arizona, growing in deserts in dry, sandy places and washes, flowering in February–May. Stems often reddish, 10–40cm. Leaves stalked, ovate to oblong-cordate, entire or pinnate, reddish beneath. Buds nodding. Petals 7–15mm long, often with a dark spot at the base. Capsule linear, spreading, 5–9cm long, curved. Quick-growing in dry, sandy soil.

Oenothera glaziouana Mart., syn. *O. erythrosepala* Borb., *O. lamarckiana* de Vries A tall and often branched biennial with leafy stems and yellow flowers opening in the evening, of uncertain origin but probably a garden hybrid, now naturalised throughout the world in suitable climates, growing in waste places and on dunes, flowering in July–September. Stems to 1.8m. Leaves lanceolate, entire, sometimes wavy, stalked, 8–20cm long. Buds upright, the sepals often reddish. Petals 3.5–6cm long, sometimes turning reddish as they fade. Capsules 2–3cm long, sessile, thickest near the base, some of the hairs with swollen red bases. Because of the unusual behaviour of their chromosomes at meiosis, forming an irregular ring of 14 rather than the usual 7 pairs, the taxonomy of these weedy, hybrid evening primroses is very complex; many small variants come true from seed, and the one shown here is paler than many forms of *O. glaziouana*.

Oenothera kernensis Munz subsp. **mojavensis** Munz, syn. *Camissonia kernensis*

Oenothera bistorta var. *veitchiana* in San Diego Co., S California

Oenothera kernensis subsp. *mojavensis*, growing wild in the Joshua Tree National Monument, California

Oenothera bistorta in cultivation

Oenothera stricta

Raven   A slender, much-branched winter or spring annual with linear leaves and few, yellow, cup-shaped flowers, native of SW California, in the Mojave desert, growing in deserts, dry, sandy places and washes, flowering in March–May. Stems 5–20cm. Leaves 3–4mm wide, with wavy margins. Buds erect. Petals 1–1.5cm long, rounded. Capsule 2–2.5cm long, curved. A particularly delicate and attractive species.

Oenothera stricta Ledeb. ex Link   A little-branched biennial with narrow leaves and yellow flowers opening in the evening, native of Chile, but now naturalised in Europe and, rarely, in North America, growing in waste places, flowering in June–September. Stems to 80cm. Leaves linear-oblanceolate, ciliate, finely toothed, sometimes wavy, only the lower leaves stalked, 3–10cm long. Buds upright, the sepals often reddish. Petals 1.5–4cm long, turning reddish as they fade. Capsules 2–3cm long, sessile, thickest near the tip, without hairs, with swollen red bases. A more slender plant than *O. glaziouana,* with flowers distinctly orange as they fade.

***Oenothera versicolor* 'Sunset Boulevard'** syn. *O. campylocalyx*   A little-branched, hairy annual or biennial with narrow leaves and orange flowers, opening at night, reddening as they fade, native of South America, flowering in June–September. Stems 30–80cm. Leaves linear-lanceolate, finely toothed, only the lower stalked, 10–15cm long. Buds upright. Petals 1.5–2.5cm long. Capsules 1–2cm long, sessile, thickest near the middle. Distinct in its orange but rather small flowers.

Oenothera glaziouana

Lopezia racemosa in Mexico

Oenothera deltoides in the Anza-Borrego Desert

Oenothera claviformis in the Anza-Borrego Desert

Oenothera pallida 'Innocence'

Oenothera boothii

Oenothera claviformis subsp. *claviformis*

Oenothera kunthiana in Mexico

Oenothera deltoides with *Abronia* outside Palm Springs after heavy spring rains

Lopezia racemosa Cav. **Mosquito Flower**
(*Onagraceae*)   An annual or short-lived
perennial with masses of small, pink, white or
purple flowers on thread-like stems, like
hovering mosquitos, native of C Mexico south
to El Salvador, growing in damp places by
waterfalls and springs, and along ditches,
flowering in October–December, but from
June in cultivation. Stems to 1.5m, usually
around 50cm or sprawling. Leaves ovate to
lanceolate. Petals 4–10mm long, the lower
wing-like with a long claw. Anthers blue or
greenish; staminode white. Capsules globose.
The variety 'Pink Brush' is available. For
good, rich, moist soil. Raise the plants in
warmth and keep cooler at flowering time.

Oenothera boothii Munz, syn. *Camissonia
boothii* (Munz) Raven (*Onagraceae*)   An erect,
rather slender spring annual with small, white
flowers and sessile, downward-pointing fruit,
native of California, from Inyo Co. and the
Mojave desert to N Arizona, Utah, Idaho and
E Washington, growing on open, sandy slopes
at 1000–2500m, flowering in June–August.
Stems reddish, 10–40cm. Leaves short-
stalked, ovate to oblong-ovate, entire, often
reddish. Buds erect. Petals to around 9mm
long. Stigma capitate. Capsule linear, to
2.5cm long, with a long beak. A very confusing
group of 8 subspecies, some with exfoliating
epidermis on the stems, some with almost
coiled fruit.

Oenothera claviformis Torr. & Frém., syn.
Camissonia claviformis Raven   An erect winter
annual with heads of small, white, pinkish,
creamy or yellow flowers and stalked,
spreading fruit, native of California, Baja
California, S Oregon and Nevada, growing on
open, sandy slopes in deserts below 1500m,
flowering in March–May. Stems 10–40cm.
Leaves short-stalked, ovate, dentate or
pinnatifid. Buds and top of inflorescence
nodding. Petals 4–6mm long. Stigma capitate.
Capsule clavate to 1.2–2cm long. A group of
7 subspecies in California and adjacent states,
some with yellow flowers, some with pinnate
leaves, with varying pubescence. The one here
seems closest to subsp. *claviformis*, with
white flowers, a glabrous inflorescence and
pinnate leaves, found in the W Mojave desert.

Oenothera deltoides Torr. & Frém.   A large
winter or spring annual with large, white
flowers that open in the evening, native of
Californiain the Mojave and Colorado deserts
to Arizona and Baja California, growing in
sandy desert below 1200m, flowering in
February–May. Stems to 30cm, with spreading
branches from the base. Leaves rhombic-ovate
to lanceolate or oblanceolate. Buds nodding,
obtuse. Petals 2–4cm long, fading to pink.
Stigma with 4 linear lobes. Capsule woody,
2.5–7cm long. The whole plant breaks off from
the root when dead, and acts as a tumbleweed,
with the hard capsules protecting the seeds.

Oenothera kunthiana (Spach) Munz
A winter or spring annual or short-lived
perennial with large, pink flowers that open in
the evening, native of W Texas to SE Arizona
and C Mexico, growing in open ground and
on roadsides, flowering in April–October.
Stems to 30cm, with branches spreading from
the base. Leaves lanceolate or oblanceolate.
Buds upright. Petals 1–1.5cm long, white to
pink. Stigma with 4 linear lobes. Capsule
4-angled, tapering at the base.
 O. rosea Ait. is a similar but more upright,
weedy plant with small flowers with petals
5–10mm long, now found naturalised in many
warm countries.

Oenothera pallida Lindl.   A spring annual
or biennial with large, white flowers that open
in the evening, fading to pink, native of
E Washington State to New Mexico and
Arizona, growing in dry, open ground and
sandy fields at 200–2000m, flowering in
May–September. Stems to 50cm, often with
branches spreading from the base, more or
less glabrous, sometimes with scattered hairs.
Leaves lanceolate, toothed. Buds and top of
inflorescence upright. Petals 2.5–4cm long.
Stigma with 4 linear lobes. Capsule
cylindrical, contorted, not woody. Easily
grown and fast (2 months) to flower from
seed, but not good in cold, wet summers.
'Innocence' is a white variety, available as
seed.

Caiophora lateritia at Harry Hay's

Blumenbachia insignis

Loasa triphylla var. *vulcanica*

Mentzelia involucrata, in the Anza-Borrego desert, California

The family *Loasaceae*, mainly from South America and the southern States of North America, but with odd species in Africa and Arabia, often have stinging hairs and unusual flowers with bag-like petals and curved staminodes and nectaries. The most familiar is *Mentzelia*, or *Bartonia*, a mainly Californian genus with large, yellow flowers and numerous stamens.

Blumenbachia insignis Schräd. (*Loasaceae*) A climbing or scrambling annual or biennial with opposite, stinging leaves and white flowers with unusual bag-like petals, native of Brazil and Argentina, flowering in summer. Stems to 70cm; leaves lobed or pinnatifid to 7.5cm long. Flowers 2.5cm across. Nectary scales with wings on the back. Capsules short and strongly twisted. Winter-growing in frost-free climates, or can be started under glass and planted out in early summer.

Caiophora lateritia Benth. (*Loasaceae*) A summer annual, biennial or perennial climber with greyish leaves with stinging hairs, and nodding, orange-yellow to reddish flowers, native of Argentina, flowering in summer. Stems twining to 3m; leaves opposite, 8–18cm long, cordate, lobed or deeply toothed. Flowers to 6cm across, with bag-like petals with a crested keel along the back. Nectary scales without wings. Capsules curiously twisted in fruit. Usually grown as a tender annual, though the rootstock may survive the winter if kept dry and protected from frost.

Loasa triphylla Juss. var. **vulcanica** (André) Urban & Gilg (*Loasaceae*) A climbing or scrambling summer annual with alternate, divided leaves with stinging hairs, and white flowers with bag-like petals and yellow and red nectaries, native of Ecuador, flowering in summer. Stems to 70cm; leaves mainly 3-lobed; the upper leaves may be simple. Flowers 5cm across. Nectary scales with wings on the back. Capsules long, not twisted. Can be started under glass and planted out in early summer. Other cultivated *Loasa* species have yellow, orange or red flowers.

Mentzelia involucrata Wats. (*Loasaceae*) A winter annual with upright stems, white, scarious, deeply lobed, green-tipped bracts and pale yellow flowers, native of California from Inyo Co. southwards to Baja California, growing on dry, rocky hills and sandy places in desert areas, flowering in January–May. Stems to 40cm. Bracts 1.5–3cm long. Petals obovate, acuminate, reddish-veined at the base, 1.5–3cm long, or to 6.5cm on var. *megalantha* Jtn. from Coachella Valley. For hot, dry conditions.

Mentzelia lindleyi Torr. & Gray, syn. *Bartonia aurea* Lindl. A winter or spring annual with deeply cut leaves and intensely yellow flowers with numerous thread-like stamens, native of S California, in the Coast Ranges from Alameda and Santa Clara Cos to W Fresno Co., growing on sunny rocky slopes below 1000m, flowering in April–June. Stems much branched, to 60cm. Leaves alternate, amplexicaul. Petals 2–4cm long, obovate, acutely mucronate, with an orange-red base. Capsule papillose. Subspecies *crocea* (Kell.) C.B. Wolf has petals 2–3cm long, with a less pronounced spine; it is found in the Sierra foothills from Tuolumne Co. to Tulare Co. Commonly cultivated, and lovely for its silky, shining petals. Sow in late spring where it is to flower, in full sun and well-drained soil. There is also a double-flowered variety listed.

Lagenaria siceraria (Molina) Standl. (*Cucurbitaceae*) **Bottle Gourd** A tropical, annual climber with white flowers and large variably shaped fruit, native probably of Africa, but now found throughout the tropics, flowering in summer. Stems to 3m or more. Flowers to 12cm across, the male with a very long stalk. Much used for containers, but needing hot, humid conditions to flower and fruit satisfactorily. The small, yellow, orange or green, hard-shelled ornamental gourds are the fruits of *Cucurbita pepo* L. subsp. *ovifera* (L.) Alefeld, a subspecies of the marrow or summer squash; it has yellow, cup-shaped flowers with pointed lobes.

Mentzelia lindleyi, often called *Bartonia aurea* Lindley

Lagenaria siceraria

Semperflorens begonias at Herrenhausen

'Olympia Light Pink'

'Olympia Rose' at Colegrave Seeds

'Olympia Starlet'

'Devil Light Pink'

Semperflorens Begonias *Begonia ×
carrieri* hort., syn. *Begonia semperflorens* hort.
(*Begoniaceae*) is a complex hybrid group,
originally derived from *B. cucullata* Willd.
var. *hookeri* (Steud.) from Paraguay and
N Argentina, crossed with *B. schmidtiana*
Regel from Brazil. Later *B. fuchsioides* Hook.
fil., *B. gracilis* H. B. & K. and *B. minor* Jacq.
were added to some strains. Most of these can
be found in our *Conservatory and Indoor
Plants*, vol. 2, pp. 74–75.

The older varieties were fibrous-rooted
perennials with stems to around 30cm,
flowering almost continuously, given sufficient
light and warmth. Modern varieties are
designed as bedding annuals: compact, free-
flowering, and quick to develop from seed.
Some have bronze leaves, some are variegated,
and some have double flowers.

The very fine seed needs planting thinly on
the surface of peaty compost at 21°C in early
spring, and growing on in moderate warmth
until planting out after all danger of frost is
past. In bedding schemes, these begonias
would follow the wallflowers, pansies or
forget-me-nots, and flower through the
summer until the frost. Like *Impatiens,* they
do best in partial shade in hot areas. Shown
here are:

'Devil Light Pink' Leaves bronze. Stems
15–20cm.

'Excel' mixed An F_1 hybrid strain with
clear colours and leaves either bronze or
green. Stems 15–20cm.

'Olympia Light Pink' An F_1 hybrid with
green leaves. Stems 15–20cm.

'Olympia Rose' An F_I hybrid with green leaves. Stems 15–20cm.

'Olympia Starlet' An F_I hybrid with green leaves. Stems 15–20cm. The flowers are particularly attractive pale pink with darker edges.

'Victory White' An F_I hybrid with green leaves. Stems 15–20cm. 'Whisky', not shown, is a white-flowered variety with bronze leaves.

Tuberous Begonias *Begonia × tuberhybrida* Voss. are complex hybrids of tuberous species from the Andes. The first hybrids were produced in 1868, and aimed for larger flowers of perfect shape, and both upright and pendulous habit. These are plants for greenhouses or sheltered cool places outside, and are generally grown from tubers, kept dry in winter and started in spring. More recently varieties have been raised which flower very quickly from seed, and can be grown as annuals and for bedding. The 'Non-stop' series can be grown from seed as well as tubers.

'Pin-up' A single-flowered picotee variety, grown from seed to flower the same year. Stems to 30cm; flowers to 12cm across. Sow indoors from March onwards. There is a new variety 'Pin-up Flame' with yellow, orange and red picotees.

Semperflorens begonia 'Victory White'

Tuberous begonias in Eccleston Square

Semperflorens begonia 'Excel' mixed

Begonia × tuberhybrida 'Pin-up'

145

Impatiens balfourii

Impatiens glandulifera

Specimens from Eccleston Square, August 3rd, ½ life size

Impatiens textori in Japan in October

Impatiens c.f. *monbeigii* near Zhongdian

Balsam Of the 900 or so species of *Impatiens*, in the family *Balsaminaceae*, most are tropical or subtropical perennials, and only a few are annuals and suitable for temperate conditions. Most species are found in E Africa, India and the Himalayas, with one or two species in Europe and North America. Of these hardly any are cultivated, though a few, notably *I. glandulifera*, the Himalayan balsam, and the weedy *I. parviflora*, have become naturalised outside their native range. The commonly grown annual busy lizzies are derived from the African perennial species *I. walleriana*, and the so-called New Guinea hybrids from *I. hawkeri* from New Guinea. Because the seeds of most species have short viability, and die if they dry out, it is difficult to introduce new species from distant areas. Keep the seeds moist and as cool as possible, and sow them at the earliest opportunity. Some will germinate immediately; some need chilling, and will not germinate until spring. In the *Impatiens* flower the lower sepal is elaborated into a spur. Of the 5 petals, the lateral pairs are always fused, and the lower lobes of these laterals may form a lip. The capsules of all species explode if touched, even while the seeds are still green.

Impatiens balfourii Hook. fil. A hairless summer annual with alternate leaves and 3–9 pink and white flowers, in branching racemes, held well above the leaves, native of the W Himalayas, growing in light forest or damp places in the open, flowering in June–September. Stems to 50cm. Leaves stalked, the blade ovate to ovate-oblong, 2–13cm long. Flowers 2–4cm, the spur 7–12mm long, slender, straight or curved. Petals white, the lower laterals large, bright pink. Upper petal hooded. Capsule narrowly club-shaped. Easily grown in sun or light shade, but not good in deep shade. The seed may germinate early in spring and be damaged by late frost.

Impatiens balsamina L. An often hairy summer annual with alternate leaves and 1–3 white, pink, violet, crimson or orange flowers on very short stalks among the leaves, native of C and S India, but widely naturalised elsewhere in the tropics, growing in damp, open places, flowering in July–September. Stems to 60cm. Leaves very short-stalked, the blade lanceolate to oblanceolate, 2.5–9cm long. Flowers sometimes double in cultivated varieties, 3–5cm, the spur 1.6–2.1cm long, slender, curved. Upper petal hooded. Capsule hairy, spindle-shaped, hanging down. Requires heat, humidity and rich soil to grow and flower well. 'Topknot' is a dwarf variety to 20cm, with double flowers in all colours. 'Camellia-flowered' have double flowers on stems around 60cm. To grow the tall varieties outside, pinch the main shoot to make the plants branch at around 10cm.

Impatiens capensis Meerburgh **Jewelweed** A hairless summer annual with alternate leaves and 2–3 orange flowers on short stalks, held a little above the leaves, native of North America from Newfoundland to Florida, westwards to Saskatchewan and Nebraska, and naturalised in Europe, including England as far north as SW Yorkshire, growing in wet places by streams, often in shallow water, flowering in June–September. Stems to 1.5m. Leaves stalked, the blade ovate to ovate-oblong, 3–8cm long, with shallow teeth. Flowers 2–3cm, the spur 2cm long, saccate, pointing backwards, with a thin spur strongly curved forwards. Petals orange, blotched or spotted with reddish-brown. Upper petal hooded. Easily grown in sun in wet soil. Common in the Thames valley and along the chalk streams of Hampshire.

Impatiens glandulifera Royle, syn. *I. roylei* Walp. **Himalayan Balsam, Policeman's Helmet** A very large, fleshy, scented summer annual with whorled leaves and several white, pink or crimson flowers on short stalks, held above the leaves, native of the Himalayas from Pakistan to Uttar Pradesh, growing in scrub and damp meadows at 1800–4000m, and naturalised in Europe by streams and rivers, flowering in July–September. Stems to 2.5m. Leaves stalked, with red, scented glands near the base, the blade lanceolate to lanceolate-elliptic, 6–20cm long, with sharp, gland-tipped teeth. Flowers 3–4cm, the spur 2cm long, very wide, pointing backwards, with a short, thin appendage strongly curved forewards. Lower lobes of lateral petals forming a lip; upper petal hooded. Easily grown in sun in moist soil, or in drier spots in the shade. A powerful and invasive annual, but easily controlled by pulling up the seedlings at around 30cm tall.

Impatiens textori Miq. A summer annual with alternate leaves and purplish-pink flowers in an umbel-like group, held above the leaves on stalks with red, fleshy hairs, native of Japan, growing in damp places in open woods, flowering in July–September. Stems to 80cm, often reddish. Leaves short-stalked, the blade ovate to narrowly ovate, 6–15cm long, cuneate at the base. Flowers around 3cm, the spur around 1.2cm long, curled. Petals with a white throat, spotted with crimson, with 2 yellow blotches. Upper petal hooded. Capsule oblanceolate, 1–2cm long. Easily grown in sun or light shade, in damp soil. The seed may germinate early in spring and be damaged by late frost.

Impatiens c.f. monbeigii A delicate, branching summer annual with alternate leaves and deep purplish flowers in pairs beneath the leaves, native of SW China, in Yunnan, growing in damp places in open woods and among rocks, at 2500–3000m, flowering in August–November. Stems to 60cm. Leaves short-stalked or sessile, the blade ovate, 6–10cm long, with wavy edges, cuneate at the base. Flowers 2.5cm, the spur tapering to a long point, downcurved, around 1.5cm long, with a white throat, veined blackish-purple; lateral sepals purple. Upper petal hooded, with a keel. Capsule linear, 2–3cm long.

Impatiens balsamina with *Callistephus chinensis* in Yunnan

Impatiens glandulifera in the Lake District

Impatiens balfourii

Impatiens capensis

Impatiens glandulifera 'Alba'

Impatiens falcifer Hook. fil. (*Balsaminaceae*)
A tall summer annual with alternate leaves
and flat, yellow, red-spotted flowers among
the leaves, native of the Himalayas from C
Nepal to Sikkim, growing in forest and scrub,
at 2500–3600m, flowering in July–September.
Stems to 1m. Leaves with the blade narrowly
elliptic, 4–8cm long, with sharp teeth, tapered
into a short stalk, or the upper sessile. Flowers
around 2cm, the spur around 2cm long,
abruptly narrowed into a downward- and
foreward-curving point. Lateral petals with
upcurving, falcate spotted lobes. Upper petal
hooded, finely spotted with red, with a keel.
Capsule linear, 3–4cm long, pendulous. Easily
grown and self-seeding in a cool, shady but
not wet position. Often sold as *I. oncidioides*, a
tropical perennial from Malaysia.

Impatiens C.D.& R. 2387 A delicate
summer annual with alternate leaves and
bright yellow flowers with long, pointed
lower petals, held above the leaves, native of
SW China in Sichuan, above Wolong, growing
on rocks and trees in damp, mossy woods, at
around 2000m, flowering in
September–October. Stems to 60cm. Leaves
with the blade broadly ovate, crenate, 4–6cm
long, with the apex rounded, and long-
stalked. Flowers around 1.5cm, with the spur
around 2cm long, red and slender, curving
downwards and forewards. Upper petal small,
hooded and keeled. Lower lobes of lateral
petals ovate, acuminate, forming a wide lip.
Capsule linear, 2–3cm long, pendulous.
A tricky one to grow, as it is late to flower and

seed, and is often damaged by the first frosts
of autumn.

Impatiens C.D.& R. 2490 A tall,
branching summer annual with alternate
leaves and pale yellow flowers with red
blotches in the throat, held among the leaves,
native of SW China in Sichuan near Luding,
growing in damp places in wet forest and
among rocks, at 2500–3000m, flowering in
August–October. Stems to 1m. Leaves often
with a blackish patch near the base of the
blade when young, narrowly elliptic, 4–8cm
long, with blunt teeth, tapered into a short
stalk or the upper sessile, long-acuminate,
base unequal. Flowers around 2cm, the spur
around 2.5cm long, narrowing into a coiled
point. Upper petal hooded, blotched with red,
with a green keel. Capsule clavate, 2–3cm
long. Easily grown and self-seeding in a cool,
shady, damp position.

Impatiens vittata group A tall, branching
summer annual with alternate leaves and pale
cream flowers with red veins in the throat,
held among the leaves, native of SW China in
Sichuan near Luding, growing in damp
places in wet forest and among rocks, at
2500–3000m, flowering in August–October.
Stems to 1m. Leaves with the blade narrowly
elliptic, 5–10cm long, with blunt teeth, sessile,
the base cordate, the apex acuminate. Flowers
around 2cm, the spur around 2.5cm long,
narrowing abruptly into a recurved and forked
point. Upper petal hooded, veined with red,
with a brownish keel. Capsule clavate, 2–3cm

long. Easily grown and self-seeding in a cool,
shady, damp position.

Impatiens dicentra Franchet A tall,
branching summer annual with alternate leaves
and bright yellow flowers with red veins in the
throat, held among the leaves, native of SW
China in Sichuan near Luding and Wolong,
growing in damp places among rocks and on
cottage roof tops, at 2000–2500m, flowering
in August–October. Stems to 80cm. Leaves
with the blade ovate-lanceolate, 5–8cm long,
with sharp teeth, sessile or tapering into a
short stalk, the apex acuminate. Flowers
around 2cm, the spur around 2.5cm long,
narrowing abruptly into a recurved and forked
point. Upper petal hooded, veined with red,
pointed and keeled. Capsule clavate, 2–3cm
long. Easily grown and self-seeding in a cool
shady, damp position. The seed may
germinate early in spring and be damaged
by late frost.

Impatiens parviflora DC. A summer
annual with alternate leaves and small, pale
yellow flowers held above the terminal rosette
of leaves, native of Central Asia in most of the
mountain ranges, growing in shady places,
flowering in May–July. Stems to 80cm. Leaves
with the blade ovate-elliptic, 4–20cm long,
with sharp teeth, stalked. Flowers 6–18mm,
the spur 2–5mm long, almost straight. Upper
petal hooded. Capsule narrowly clavate.
Often naturalised in dry, shady places in
Europe, especially in eastern England, where
it is usually regarded as a weed.

Impatiens C.D.& R. 2387, from Wolong

Impatiens C.D.& R. 2490 in wet woods on Gonga Shan

Impatiens dicentra on a roof in Wolong, Sichuan

Impatiens parviflora

Impatiens dicentra

Impatiens C.D.& R. 2490

Impatiens vittata
group

Impatiens C.D.& R. 2387

Impatiens falcifer

Specimens from Quince House, August 3rd, ½ life size

Impatiens delavayi in wet woods above Lijiang

Impatiens conchorifolia above Lijiang

Impatiens cristata in cultivation

Impatiens cristata

Impatiens species in the Zhongdian river gorge

Impatiens delavayi Franch. (*Balsaminaceae*)
A delicate summer annual with alternate leaves and bright yellow flowers with purple veins and blotches in the throat, held among the leaves. Native of SW China in Yunnan, above Lijiang, growing on rocks and trees in damp, mossy woods, at 2400–3200m, flowering in August–October. Stems to 30cm. Leaves with the blade ovate, 5–8cm long, crenate, stalked, the apex rounded. Flowers around 2cm, the spur around 2.5cm long, narrowing into a recurved and forked point. Upper petal hooded, veined with red, pointed and keeled. Lower lobes of lateral petals forming a wide lip. Capsule linear, 2–3cm long, pendulous.

Impatiens conchorifolia Franchet
A much-branched summer annual with alternate leaves and bright yellow, solitary flowers with a swollen, downward- and forward-curving spur, held beneath the leaves. Native of SW China in Yunnan, above Lijiang, growing on damp screes and by rocky streams, at around 2400m, flowering in August–October. Stems to 30cm, reddish. Leaves with the blade lanceolate-hastate, 5–10cm long, finely toothed, almost sessile, the apex acuminate. Flowers around 2cm, with the spur around 2.5cm long, swollen, with a curled appendage. Upper petal hooded, pointed and keeled. Lower lobes of lateral petals forming a lip. Capsule clavate, 2–3cm long, pendulous.

Impatiens aristulata Hook. fil. group
A summer annual with a rosette of leaves and a raceme of bright yellow flowers held above the leaves, native of SW China in Yunnan, above Dali, growing on rocks by streams and in ditches, at around 2500m, flowering in August–October. Stems to 30cm, reddish-purple. Leaves with the blade lanceolate, 4–8cm long, crenate, the lower stalked, the upper sessile with an acuminate apex. Flowers around 2cm, the spur around 2.5cm long, pointing upwards and narrowing into a recurved point. Upper petal hooded and keeled. Lower lobes of lateral petals forming a wide lip. Capsule not seen.

Impatiens cristata Wall. syn. *I. scabrida* Hara non DC.   A robust, branching summer annual with alternate leaves and pale cream to yellow flowers with brownish spots in the throat, held among the leaves, native of the Himalayas from Kashmir to Bhutan, growing in woods and scrub, at 1200–3600m, flowering in May–October. Stems 20–120cm, pubescent. Leaves with the blade ovate to elliptic or elliptic-lanceolate, 4–15cm long, with sharp teeth, stalked, the apex acuminate. Flowers around 2.5–4cm, the spur around 2.5cm long, narrowing abruptly into a recurved appendage. Upper petal hooded, keeled. Capsule cylindrical, around 4cm. Easily grown, but not as persistent as some other species.

Impatiens pallida Nutt.   A branching summer annual with bluish-green leaves and yellow flowers with reddish-brown spots, native of eastern North America from Nova Scotia and Saskatchewan southwards to Georgia and Kansas, growing in woods and damp places, flowering in July–September. Stems 20–150cm, glabrous. Leaves alternate, stalked, the blade 1.5–10cm long, oblong to ovate-elliptic, shallowly crenate. Flowers 1–3 together, 2.5–3cm long, the spur petal broad,

Impatiens aristulata group, in a stream above Dali in September

narrowing abruptly into a recurved point about 1cm long. Capsule around 4cm, narrowly ovate. Touch-me-not, *I. noli-tangere* L. from Europe eastwards to Central Asia, Japan, and northwestern North America, is similar but has flowers around 3.5cm long, a more tapering spur and more deeply crenate leaves.

Impatiens potaninii Maxim.   A spreading, branching summer annual or perhaps perennial, with alternate leaves forming a rosette and pale yellow flowers with a short, fat, curling spur, held just above the leaves, native of SW China in the Wolong valley, growing in wet places among rocks, at 2000–2500m, flowering in August–October. Stems to 80cm. Leaves with the blade ovate, 5–8cm long, shallowly crenate, stalked, the apex acute. Flowers solitary or paired, around 2cm, the spur around 2.5cm long, fat and tightly curled forewards. Upper petal rounded, hooded, pointed and keeled. Capsule not seen.

Impatiens unidentified species   A tall, branching summer annual with alternate leaves and pale yellow flowers with groups of red spots in the throat, held among the leaves, native of SW China in the Zhongdian river gorge, growing in damp places among rocks, at 2000–2500m, flowering in August–October. Stems to 80cm, glaucous and with fine hairs. Leaves with the blade ovate-lanceolate, 5–8cm long, with sharp teeth, sessile or tapering into a short stalk, the apex acuminate. Flowers around 2cm, the spur around 2.5cm long, narrowing abruptly into a recurved and forked point. Upper petal hooded, pointed and keeled. Capsule not seen.

Impatiens potaninii, in wet woods above Wolong

Impatiens unidentified species, in the gorge of the Zhongdian river

Impatiens pallida in North America

Impatiens hawkeri

Impatiens walleriana in the Botanical Garden in Pietermaritzburg, Natal

Impatiens walleriana 'Dark Plum Variegated'

Impatiens walleriana 'Accent Coral'

Impatiens hawkeri Bull (*Balsaminaceae*) A perennial, sometimes hairy, with whorled leaves and large, flat flowers with all the petals equal, native of New Guinea eastwards to the Solomon Islands, flowering much of the year. Stems much-branched, to 1m. Leaves linear-lanceolate to elliptic and ovate, often marked with cream along the mid-vein. Flowers 4–6cm across, with a narrow spur to 7.5cm long, curving backwards and downwards. Capsule thickest around the middle. Commonly grown from cuttings as well as from seed; a selection of the named clones can be seen in *Conservatory and Indoor Plants* volume 1. At present, seed-raised strains of New Guinea *Impatiens* in mixed colours include 'Safari' F_2 and 'Spectra' F_1 with stems 30–45cm, and often with the leaves marked with cream. 'Tango' has bronze leaves and orange flowers.

***Impatiens* 'Seashells' hybrids** A group of recently produced hybrids, now available in **'Apricot'**, 'Yellow', 'Tangerine' and 'Papaya'. These are tender perennials, grown from cuttings or micropropagated and sold as young plants. Perhaps derived from the yellow-flowered *I. auricoma* Baill. from the Comoro Islands, off the north coast of Madagascar; this grows best in a greenhouse, but will do outside in humid, partial shade in warm areas.

Impatiens walleriana Hook. fil. **Busy Lizzie** A branching perennial with ovate to broadly elliptic, pale green leaves and white, pink, purple, red or orange, flat flowers, with all the petals equal, native of E Africa from S Kenya to Malawi and Mozambique, flowering much of the year. Stems much-branched, to 50cm. Flowers 2.4–4cm across, with a narrow spur to 4.5cm long, curving backwards. Capsule thickest around the middle.

The seed should be sown at 20–25°C in early spring, and the young plants put out when the soil has warmed and all danger of frost has passed. *Impatiens* are good summer bedding plants for shade.

There are several seed-raised strains in mixed and single colours available at present, mostly F_1 hybrids, but new ones are frequently introduced, and old ones dropped: 'Bruno' mixed is a new tetraploid with large flowers (said to be up to 6cm across), of excellent substance; 'Firefly', on the other hand, has masses of small flowers, around 2cm across. Both are available as young plants, and 'Bruno' also as seed. Forms with variegated leaves are available both from seed and as young plants, with flowers in a variety of colours.

'Accent Coral' The 'Accent' series is available in a range of colours, with stems 15–25cm. Some have a white star.

'Dark Plum Variegated' Leaves edged with white. Flowers purplish, double or single. Available as small plants.

'Dazzler Violet Star' Flowers purplish, with a white centre to each petal.

'Double Rosebud Pale Pink' Available as small plants.

'Double Rosebud Peach' Available as small plants. 'Double Confection' mixed, raised from seed, has most of the flowers double or semi-double.

'Mega Orange Star' Large, orange flowers with a white star.

Mixed *Impatiens walleriana* in Southsea

Impatiens walleriana 'Mega Orange Star'

Impatiens 'Seashells Apricot'

Impatiens walleriana 'Dazzler Violet Star'

Impatiens walleriana 'Double Rosebud Pale Pink'

Impatiens walleriana 'Double Rosebud Peach'

Smyrnium perfoliatum

Smyrnium olusatrum

Bupleurum croceum near Isparta, Turkey in May

Bupleurum rotundifolium

Anethum graveolens L. (*Umbelliferae*) **Dill**
A spring or summer annual with hair-like leaf
segments and umbels of yellow flowers, native
of Asia, but widely grown and naturalised
elsewhere in open ground, flowering in
June–July. Stems to around 60cm, little-
branched, glaucous. Basal leaves 3–5-pinnate.
Umbels with 15–30 rays, 8–10cm across;
without bracts or bracteoles. Fruits ellipsoid,
flattened, 3–4.5mm long. Easily grown and
very like fennel, which is a tough perennial.
Dill is quicker to flower and easier to remove
if it seeds itself. Sow the seed in late spring.

Bupleurum croceum Fenzl (*Umbelliferae*)
A winter or spring annual with almost round
leaves and small umbels of yellow flowers
surrounded by petal-like bracts, native of most
of Turkey and Syria, growing in cornfields and
dry, grassy places, at 400–1850m, flowering in
May–July. Stems 25–65cm, not glaucous.
Upper leaves perfoliate, yellowish. Umbels
with 8–17 rays, around 5cm across; the outer
3 bracteoles larger than the 2 inner, apiculate.
Fruits 3.5–4mm long, smooth.

Bupleurum rotundifolium L. **Hare's Ear**
or **Thorow-wax** A winter or spring annual
with almost round leaves and small umbels
of greenish-yellow flowers surrounded by
petal-like bracts, found wild in much of
Europe and Asia, and possibly originating in
Turkey, growing as a weed in cornfields and
dry, grassy places, at up to 2000m, flowering
in June–July. Stems 25–80cm, glaucous.
Upper leaves perfoliate, green. Umbels with
4–8 rays, around 5cm across; the outer
5 bracteoles more or less equal. Fruits
3–3.5mm long, smooth. Formerly a frequent
weed in cornfields, but becoming very rare;
almost extinct in England.

Smyrnium olusatrum L. (*Umbelliferae*)
Alexanders A biennial with shining, bright
green leaves and umbels of yellowish-green
flowers without bracts, found wild in much of
Europe, W Turkey and Algeria, growing on
roadsides and in stony and rocky scrub near
the sea, at up to 300m, flowering in
March–May. Stems 30–150cm. Upper leaves
with three leaflets, green. Umbels with 7–17
rays, around 10cm across. Fruits 5–7mm long,
smooth, black. Formerly grown as a pot herb,
and useful as its leaves emerge in early spring.
In England and S Scotland at least, it is
usually found near towns which were
important in Roman or Medieval times.

Smyrnium perfoliatum L. A biennial
with shining, dark green leaves, the upper
surrounding the stem and appearing perfoliate,
and with umbels of yellowish-green flowers
without bracts, found wild in S and C Europe,
W Turkey and the Crimea, growing in rocky
scrub and on the margins of woods, at
250–2000m, flowering in May–June. Stems
20–25cm. Lower leaves with sharply toothed
leaflets, upper alternate, yellowish-green.
Umbels with 7–14 rays, around 7cm across.
Fruits 4mm long, smooth, dark brown. An
attractive plant, which will sow itself in well-
drained places under trees. Other species, such
as *S. connatum* Boiss. & Kotschy, from Turkey
southwards to Israel, have opposite stem
leaves which are connate and truly perfoliate.

Smyrnium olusatrum in Dover, Kent

Anethum graveolens in a kitchen garden

Heracleum mantegazzianum by the river Don in Aberdeenshire

Angelica gigas Nakai (*Umbelliferae*) A huge biennial with umbels of deep maroon flowers, native of Japan in Shikoku and Kyushu, of Korea and N China in Heilonjiang, growing in openings in damp woods, flowering in August–September. Stems blackish, to 2m or more, from a thick root. Leaves with lanceolate divisions. Umbels 12–15cm across. Fruits 8mm long, 5mm wide, flattened. This fine plant often takes more than one year to build up to flowering size, and the young plants are very vulnerable to slugs. The flowers are much visited by wasps. Sow the seed immediately it is ripe, which is only a few weeks after flowering. The best plants are grown in rich, moist soil in slight shade.

Heracleum mantegazzianum Somm. & Lev. (*Umbelliferae*) **Giant Hogweed** A huge biennial or monocarpic perennial with thick, hollow stems and flat umbels of white flowers, native of the Caucasus, and often naturalised in other parts of Europe, growing in damp places by streams and rivers, flowering in June–July. Stems to 5m, up to 10cm in diameter. Leaves with very jagged divisions. Umbels to 1.5m across. This plant has a bad reputation because contact causes skin to become sensitive to sunlight and burn, and it is not legal to plant it. However, should it appear, it is wonderful for the wild garden with other giants like *Gunnera* and tall grasses.

Orlaya grandiflora (L.) Hoffm. (*Umbelliferae*) A winter or spring annual with finely divided leaf segments and umbels of white flowers with the outer petals much enlarged, native of Europe from Belgium southwards to Spain, and of Algeria, Central Asia, Turkey and Israel, growing in dry, stony places and on screes, at below 650m, flowering in June–July. Stems branched, to around 40cm. Umbels with 5–12 rays, 6–8cm across; outer petals enlarged, 9–14mm long. Fruits spiny, 1–1.1cm long. Easily grown in a sunny position in well-drained soil.

Artedia squamata L. (*Umbelliferae*) An annual with hair-like leaf segments and umbels of white flowers, with the central ones sterile and forming a tuft of black or purplish bristles. Native of the E Mediterranean area from Turkey to Syria and Israel, eastwards to Iran and N Iraq, growing on dry hills and in stony places, at below 1500m, flowering in April–July. Stems branched, to around 40cm. Umbels around 6cm across; outer petals enlarged, 8–12mm long. Fruits 6–8mm long, strongly flattened, with scarious projections

Angelica gigas at Harry Hay's

Orlaya grandiflora

Tordylium aegaeum near the ruins of Termessos, near Antalya, Turkey

forming an interrupted wing. An attractive, dainty plant for a dry spot.

Coriandrum sativum L. **Coriander**
(*Umbelliferae*)   A much-branched summer annual with narrow, flat leaf segments and small umbels of white flowers, long-cultivated, and unknown wild, flowering in May–August. Stems to around 50cm. Umbels around 6cm across; outer petals enlarged, around 8mm long. Fruits 3–4mm long, globose. Useful for decoration, as well as for its seeds and leaves.

Tordylium aegaeum Runem. (*Umbelliferae*) A winter annual with broad, flat leaves and umbels of white flowers with the outer petals much enlarged, native of Europe in the Greek islands and Turkey eastwards to Antalya, growing in dry, stony places, below 300m, flowering in May. Stems branched, to around 30cm, softly hairy to scabrous. Basal leaves simple, ovate or pinnate, with 1–2 rounded leaflets, upper leaves simple, lanceolate to basally lobed. Umbels with 5–12 rays, 6–8cm across; outer petals enlarged, around 1.2cm long, divided into 2 very unequal lobes. Fruits ovate to elliptic, with a strongly thickened and ribbed margin and scattered hairs on the face, around 5mm long. For a dry, sunny position, in well-drained soil.

I am uncertain of the identification of this picture without ripe fruit; *Ainsworthia trachycarpa* Boiss., from Turkey to the hills above the Dead Sea, is very similar but differs in having fruit with a smooth margin, and with long bracteoles. Whatever its name, it would be worth introducing by anyone visiting Aspendos in June or July.

Tordylium aegaeum

Artedia squamata at Termessos

Coriandrum sativum

Trachymene coerulea wild near Perth in Western Australia

Trachymene coerulea

Trachymene coerulea, pink form at Suttons

Eryngium campestre L. (*Umbelliferae*)
A much-branched and very spiny biennial or
short-lived perennial, with bluish-green or
yellowish-green heads of small flowers
surrounded by spiny bracts, native of Europe
from SE England to North Africa and
eastwards to Afghanistan, growing in dry,
grassy places and open woodland, at up to
1800m, flowering in July–September. Stems to
60cm. Basal leaves triangular-ovate in outline,
ternate, with deeply divided segments. Heads
ovoid-globose, 7–13mm across. Bracts 5–6.
Two varieties are recognised: var. *campestre*
with a bluish-green inflorescence, and bracts
linear-lanceolate, 2–4mm broad, is the more
common variety in NW Europe, and in damper
areas; var. *virens* Link, with a yellowish-green
inflorescence and linear-subulate bracts
1–2mm broad, is more common in SE Europe
and SW Asia, and in drier areas.

Eryngium carlinae Delar. A small
biennial, or possibly a short-lived perennial,
with a basal rosette of spiny leaves and
branching stems and numerous, small heads
of flowers with 3 spiny bracteoles emerging
from the top. Native of Mexico and Central
America, growing in dry scrub, meadows, and
grassy places in oak or coniferous forest, and
in alpine meadows, at 2300–4000m, flowering
in September–November. A variable species
with stems 5–50cm. Basal leaves oblanceolate,
3–10cm long, with spiny teeth. Heads blue,
violet or white, subglobose, ovoid or ellipsoid,
6–10mm long, 5–7mm in diameter, with 8–12
lanceolate bracts equal to or longer than the
heads. Easily grown, but apparently

monocarpic. Sow seed as soon as it is ripe.
Shown here is C. D. & R. 1346, introduced
in 1991 from near Zacatecas.

Eryngium giganteum M. Bieb. A tall
biennial with upright, candelabra-like stems
and oval heads of small flowers surrounded by
silvery, spiny bracts, native of N Turkey from
Bolu eastwards to the Caucasus, growing in
open places in woods and scrub, and on stony
roadside banks, in rather dry valleys at
800–2300m, flowering in July–August. Stems
to 1.3m. Basal leaves long-stalked, cordate,
not spiny. Stem leaves spiny. Heads ovate to
oblong, 1–2.5cm across, to 4cm long. Bracts
6–9, leafy and spiny, from as long as the head
to twice its length. Easily grown and self-
seeding in good soil in partial shade. Sow
collected seed as soon as it is ripe, so that it
germinates the following spring. Two forms
are grown in England, as opposite.
'Miss Willmott's Ghost' has been long
cultivated, and was introduced in 1820; the
name has in the past been used for the species
in general. It is named after Ellen Willmott of
Warley Place, Essex, a grand lady gardener,
who is said to have dropped seed of this plant
in suitable places when she visited a garden.
The whole plant is very stiff, upright and
greenish, and has broad, silvery bracts about
equalling the head.
'Silver Ghost' was introduced from near
Trabzon in Turkey in 1982 by Dick and Ros
Banks, Jimmy Smart and Martyn Rix. More
silvery than 'Miss Willmott's Ghost', with
longer, more spiny and more deeply cut
bracts, and more flexuous stems forming a

more widely branching, less stiff plant. If the two are grown together, the distinctions will probably disappear.

Eryngium serratum A small biennial, or possibly a short-lived perennial, with a basal rosette of spiny leaves, branching stems and numerous small heads of flowers without spiny bracteoles, native of Mexico, growing in moist, grassy places, and flowering in September–November. Stems erect, 10–50cm. Basal leaves oblanceolate, 3–10cm long, with spiny teeth. Heads silvery, subglobose, ovoid or ellipsoid, 6–10mm long, 5–7mm in diameter, with 12–15 toothed, broadly lanceolate bracts, shorter than the heads. Easily grown, but apparently monocarpic. Sow seed as soon as it is ripe. Shown here is C. D. & R. introduced in 1991 from El Salto, Durango. *E. lemmoni* Coult. & Rose, from SE Arizona and N Mexico, is very similar.

Trachymene coerulea (DC.) Graham, syn. *Didiscus caeruleus* DC. (*Umbelliferae*) **Blue Lace Flower** A winter or spring annual with broad, flat leaflets and tight umbels of pale blue, pink or white flowers, native of Western Australia, growing in dry, sandy places in scrub, flowering in spring. Stems to 60cm, hairy. Upper leaves with linear, almost undivided leaflets. Umbels around 5cm across, simple, with numerous rays, the flowers all equal or the outer a little larger. Easily grown, but in cool areas best started in heat in early spring. As this is one of the very few blue *Umbelliferae*, it is ironic that pink and white forms are commonly offered by the seed suppliers.

Eryngium carlinae, from Mexico

Eryngium serratum near Durango, Mexico

Eryngium giganteum 'Silver Ghost', collected from near Trabzon, at Sellindge

Eryngium campestre in France

Eryngium giganteum 'Miss Willmott's Ghost'

Anagallis monellii, in central Spain north of Salamanca in May

Anagallis monellii on the coast near Cadiz

Anagallis arvensis var. *caerulea*

Primula sinensis in a trial at Wisley in 1995, photographed by Michael Warren

Anagallis arvensis L. var. *arvensis*
(*Primulaceae*) **Scarlet Pimpernel**
A sprawling winter or spring annual with
small, bright orange, rarely flesh-pink or lilac
flowers, native of Europe and Asia eastwards
to Iraq and Afghanistan, and naturalised
elsewhere, growing in waste places and
cornfields and on sand dunes and river banks,
flowering in March–September. Stems
trailing, to 70cm. Leaves around 1.2cm long,
ovate to oblong-ovate. Pedicels 6–30mm,
longer than the leaves. Flowers opening in the
sun, 3.5–5.5mm, or rarely to 7mm across,
bright orange, or blue with a crenate edge in
var. *caerulea* (L.) Gouan. Though they are
thought by many a weed, I am always happy to
have these appearing in the garden. They are
seldom prolific enough to be a nuisance. The
blue-flowered form is rarer in the north. The
flowers open in warm weather in the morning,
and close by mid-afternoon or if the
temperature drops.

Anagallis foemina Mill. A small spring or
summer annual with small, bright blue
flowers, native of S Europe and Asia eastwards
to Iraq and Afghanistan, and naturalised
elsewhere, growing in waste places, cornfields,
rocky limestone slopes and scrub, flowering in
June–October. Stems to 30cm. Leaves around
1.2–1.7cm long, ovate to lanceolate. Pedicels
5–17mm, equalling or shorter than the leaves.
Flowers 4–5.5mm across, bright blue, with a
crenate margin. Very close to blue *A. arvensis*,
but differing in its shorter pedicels.

Anagallis monellii L. A perennial often
grown as an annual, with bright blue, rarely
red or white flowers, native of SW Europe in
Spain, Portugal, Sicily and Sardinia, and of
North Africa, growing on coastal dunes and
in sandy places inland, flowering in
March–September. Stems sprawling, to 50cm.
Leaves around 1–1.5cm long, 2–4mm wide,
lanceolate to linear-lanceolate. Pedicels
2–5cm, longer than the leaves. Flowers
1.5–2.5cm across. Though said to be perennial
in the wild, it is best grown as an annual in
northern Europe and North America, as it
cannot survive either much cold or excessive
wet in winter. 'Blue Light' and 'Skylover' are
selections with large flowers. 'Sunrise' has red
flowers. Subspecies *linifolia* (L.) Maire is the
name given to forms with narrow leaves. Red-
flowered forms are found mainly on the coast.

Primula forbesii Franch. (*Primulaceae*)
A graceful, hairy annual, with stalked leaves
with rounded blades and pinkish-purple to
white flowers, native of W China in Yunnan,
from Kunming to Dali, and of SW Sichuan,
growing in marshes by ricefields and canals,
and cultivated in village and temple gardens in
the Lijiang valley, flowering in January–April.
Leaves with blades 2–5cm long. Stems
10–30cm, with 1–3 whorls of 4–8 flowers, each
around 1cm across. Calyx lobes acute,
somewhat spreading.

Primula malacoides Franch. A hairy
annual, with stalked leaves with a rounded
blade and pinkish-purple to white flowers,
native of W China in Guizhou and Yunnan,
and of N Burma, growing on shady banks and
as a weed in bean fields, especially in the Dali
valley, flowering in January–April. Leaves with
blades 3–10cm long. Stems 10–40cm, with 1–6
whorls of 4–20 flowers, each 5–15mm across.
The blunt, somewhat reflexed calyx lobes
distinguish it from *P. forbesii*. The species was

introduced by George Forrest from the Dali area in 1906. Dwarf strains such as 'Lilac Queen' have lost much of the grace of the wild plant.

Primula obconica Hance   A short-lived perennial, usually grown as an annual, with stalked leaves with a rounded blade, and flowers from red to pink, lavender-blue and white, native of W China from Hubei to Guizhou and Yunnan, growing on shady rocks and in woods, flowering in March–May. In the wild, the flowers are 1.5–2.5cm across, but in cultivated forms they may be up to 5cm. The species was introduced in 1879 from the Ichang gorges by Charles Maries collecting for Messrs Veitch, who soon realised the potential of the species as a winter-flowering plant for the cool conservatory. Easily grown from seed

sown in a cold frame in June or July; the young plants should be potted up and brought indoors in September. Single-coloured strains include **'Salmon'**, with flowers opening white, becoming salmon, and **'Blue Agate'**, 'Cantata Apricot', from the 'Cantata' series, 'Queen of the Market' which has large, deep red flowers, and 'Red Agate', which flowers red and white.

Primula sinensis Lindl.   A softly hairy perennial with deeply-lobed leaf blades and an umbel of rounded flowers to 7.5cm across, with a very large calyx, long cultivated in China. Introduced to Europe from the Canton region by John Potts in 1821. Augustine Henry found the wild form of this, *P. rupestris* Balf. fil. & Forrest, flowering in December and January on the sides of the

San-yu-tung glen, "the cave of the three pilgrims", the site of a temple near the junction of the narrow ravine, which enters the Yangtze from the north.

It is sad that this attractive plant has almost entirely disappeared from cultivation. Its cultivation reached a peak in the late 19th century, and even in 1933 Carters listed 13 varieties, including doubles and those with fern-leaved foliage; they boasted, quoting the *Gardener's Chronicle*, that one of their greenhouses at Forest Hill "containing upwards of three thousand plants of selected varieties of *Primula sinensis* is worth travelling a long distance to see." Sow seed in May, June or July, at 15°C, and then grow in cool but light conditions until bringing the plants under cover in September, or before the first frost, for flowering through the winter.

Primula obconica 'Salmon'

Primula obconica 'Blue Agate'

Primula malacoides in the Temperate House at Kew

Anagallis foemina in South Africa

Anagallis arvensis var. *arvensis*

Primula forbesii in an old temple near Lijiang

Limonium sinuatum in South Africa

Limonium sinuatum

Limonium sinuatum 'Supreme Chamois'

Psylliostachys suworowii, with *Linaria* 'Fairy Bouquet'

Limonium sinuatum 'Heavenly Blue'

Sea Lavender or **Statice** The genus *Limonium* in the family *Plumbaginaceae* contains around 350 species of perennials and subshrubs, with a few annuals, found throughout the world in dry, open habitats and particularly in salt marshes and on cliffs. In Spain, 107 species are recognised in the latest flora, many very similar to one another and restricted to small areas of cliff or mountain, differing in small but recognisable characteristics. They set seed without fertilisation, so all these small differences are preserved. The annual cultivars are derived from both perennial and annual species.

Limonium sinuatum (L.) Mill., syn. *Statice sinuata* L. A perennial often grown as an annual, with winged stems and papery, usually blue calyces and creamy white corollas. Native of S Portugal, the Mediterranean area, and Georgia near Batumi, and now found wild in other parts of the world, growing on cliffs and dunes and in sandy places near the sea, flowering in April–August. Stems to 40cm. Leaves wavy-edged to pinnatifid, 3–15cm long. Calyx 1.15–1.45cm long. Petals 1.2–1.5cm long. If they are grown in very well-drained, sandy soil, the plants might survive a mild winter.

Statice cultivars Over 50 cultivated varieties are grown, both for garden ornament and for use as dried flowers. The papery calyces keep their colour when dried, the whitish corollas soon fade. In addition to the perennial *L. sinuatum*, the cultivars are derived from the annual *L. lobatum* (L. fil.) Chaz., syn. *Statice thouinii* Viv. from S Spain, North Africa and SW Asia, with pale blue calyces and yellow corollas, and *L. bonduellei* (Lestib.) O. Kuntze, from North Africa, with unwinged stems and yellow calyces. All the cultivars are easily grown in well-drained, sandy soil in full sun and air. Shown here are:

'Blue Peter' A compact variety with tight, deep blue flowerheads.
'Forever Gold' Tall, to 65cm, with large, tightly packed flowerheads on branching stalks; other colours in this series are blue, lavender, rose and white. 'Moonlight' is a creamy lemon.
'Gold Coast' Flowers yellow; stems to 60cm.
'Heavenly Blue' Tall, to 65cm, with large, tightly packed flowerheads on widely branching stalks.
'Iceberg' A pure white variety.
'Petite Bouquet' A dwarf, bushy, compact series with stems to 30cm; available in **White, Blue, Salmon** and **Yellow**.
'Roselight' Stems tall, to 60cm. Flowers pink and white.
'Sunset' Stems tall, to 60cm. Flowers in pastel shades of pink, orange and apricot.
'Supreme Chamois' An attractive shade of orange-buff. Stems around 45cm.

Psylliostachys suworowii (Regel) Roshk., syn. *Limonium suworowii* Regel (*Plumbaginaceae*) An upright summer annual with wavy-edged leaves and long, narrow, branching spikes of bright pink or purplish-pink flowers, native of Iran, Afghanistan and Central Asia, growing in dry, sandy places, flowering in early summer. Stems to 1.5m, though usually around 45cm. Leaves glabrous, oblanceolate, mostly in a basal rosette. Flowers minute, in sessile, 2–4-flowered spikelets. Easily grown in a warm, sheltered position in full sun, in deep sandy soil. In cool areas, such as Britain and northwestern North America, it is best sown indoors and put out as young plants. *P. spicata* (Willd.) Nevski, has stems to 40cm, pale rose-pink flowers and pubescent, deeply cut leaves. It is found around the Caspian and into Central Asia, growing in sandy areas and on salty clay soils.

'Heavenly Blue'

'Iceberg'

'Sunset'

'Gold Coast'

'Blue Peter'

'Roselight'

'Forever Gold'

'Petite Bouquet White'

'Petite Bouquet Salmon'

'Petite Bouquet Blue'

'Petite Bouquet Yellow'

Specimens from Thompson and Morgan, July 15th, ⅖ life size

Gentianella species by the Zhongdian river in NW Yunnan

Gentianella campestris in St Luc, Switzerland

Centaurium erythraea

far south as Mexico, growing in grassy places, in England generally on dry chalk downland and on sand dunes, in California in damp places in the mountains, flowering in June–September. Stems to 30cm, usually around 10cm, branching. Flowers 5-merous, 1.6–2cm long. Calyx lobes slightly unequal. Corolla with fine hairs in the throat. Easily grown in well-drained, sandy soil in full sun.

Gentianella campestris (L.) Börner
A dwarf biennial with small, purplish flowers, native of most of Europe except the far south, growing in grassy, heathy places, in England generally on acidic grassland, flowering in June–August. Stems to 35cm, usually around 10cm, branching. Flowers 4-merous, 1.5–3cm long. Calyx lobes very unequal, the outer pair enclosing the inner. Corolla with fine hairs in the throat. Easily grown in well-drained, sandy soil in full sun.

Gentianella ciliata (L.) Borkh. A slender biennial with narrow leaves and blue flowers, native of most of Europe except the north, Siberia, Morocco, the Caucasus, N Turkey and NW Iran, growing on grassy slopes and in open woods, usually on limestone, flowering in August–October. Stems 5–30cm. Leaves lanceolate to linear-lanceolate. Calyx lobes equal. Corolla 3.5–5cm long, usually with 4 lobes with a long-fimbriate margin. This and the next two species are often put in the genus *Gentianopsis* Ma.

Gentianella detonsa (Rottb.) G. Don fil.
A slender annual or biennial with narrow leaves and blue flowers, native of Arctic areas of Europe, Asia and North America, and of NE California southwards to Tuolumne Co. (subsp. *holopetala* J. Gillett), growing in damp meadows, bogs and wet prairies, mainly in the mountains, flowering in July–September. Stems to 60cm. Leaves linear to lanceolate. Calyx lobes unequal. Corolla 3.5–4cm long, the 4 lobes short-fringed, pale blue to purplish-blue. The emblem of the Yellowstone National Park, where it is sometimes called *G. thermalis* Kuntze.
    Gentianella crinita Froel. has broadly lanceolate leaves and long fringes on the lobes; found from Ontario to Georgia, in moist woods and meadows.

***Gentianella* species** A very slender annual or biennial with deep purplish-blue flowers, native of SW China in Yunnan, growing in grassy places and by streams in scrub and open forest, flowering in September–October. Stems around 20cm. Leaves linear. Flowers around 4cm long. An attractive species photographed in the Zhongdian valley.

Lomatogonium carinthiacum (Wulfen) Reichenb. (*Gentianaceae*) A dwarf, many-stemmed annual with pale blue, starry flowers, native of the Alps from Switzerland to Romania, of SE Turkey, of Central Asia and of the Himalayas from Afghanistan to SW China, growing in dry mountain meadows, at 2000–4800m, flowering in August–October. Stems to 15cm. Basal leaves elliptic, usually faded by flowering time. Flowers around 3cm across, with 5 corolla lobes. Calyx lobes ovate. Style and stamens blue. An attractive small plant for late flowering. *L. rotatum* (L.) Fries ex Fernald is found in Iceland, in Arctic Asia and in North America in the Arctic and the Rockies. It has linear calyx lobes longer than the corolla.

Centaurium erythraea Rafn. (*Gentianaceae*)
Centaury A glabrous biennial with opposite leaves and flat-topped heads of starry, pink flowers, native of all Europe except the far north, growing in open, sandy or grassy places, flowering in June–September. Stems to 50cm. Basal leaves ovate to elliptical; stem leaves smaller and narrower. Flowers 1–2cm across. A variable species, very attractive in a wild garden or meadow. The largest flowers are found in subsp. *majus* (Hoffmans & Link) Melderis, from the mountains of SW Europe. The attractive dwarf form shown here, from exposed cliff tops in W Europe, has been called *C. capitatum* Willd. Other species are found in western North America, especially *C. venustum* (Gray) Rob., which is found in the Sierra foothills and along the coast of S California.

Gentianella amarella (L.) Börner
(*Gentianaceae*) A dwarf winter or spring annual with small, purplish flowers, native of most of Europe, N Asia and North America as

Gentianella detonsa in Montana

Gentianella ciliata in S France above Grasse

Gentianella amarella

Lomatogonium carinthiacum, above Wolong in Sichuan

Gentianella amarella on chalk downland at Chilbolton, Hampshire

Exacum affine Balf. fil. ex Regel
(*Gentianaceae*) **Persian Violet** A much-
branched glabrous annual or short-lived
perennial, with, usually pale mauve, starry,
lightly scented flowers, native of Socotra and
S Arabian Peninsula, growing near streams on
limestone and other soils, flowering in summer
and autumn. Stems to 60cm. Leaves opposite,
ovate to elliptic, to 4cm. Flowers also dark
lavender, pink and white, to 2.5cm across.
Capsule subglobose. A popular pot plant.
Propagate from seed sown in late summer or
cuttings in autumn, keeping the plants above
10°C through the winter. 'Midget' and 'White
Midget' have stems 15–20cm long.

Of the 65 species of *Exacum*, 38 are found
in Madagascar, 2 in Africa and 21 in Asia.
E. trinervium (L.) Druce, is a tall perennial
with handsome purple flowers, found in the
high mountains of Sri Lanka.

Eustoma grandiflorum (Raf.) Schinn., syn.
E. russellianum (Hook.) G. Don ex Sweet
(*Gentianaceae*) **Prairie Gentian** A tall,
upright winter annual or perennial, with
cup-shaped flowers, purplish in the wild,
native of North America from Nebraska and
Colorado to Texas, growing on prairies,
flowering in May–August. Stems to 75cm.
Leaves stiff and fleshy, bluish-green, opposite.
Flowers 5–7.5cm across. **'Echo Pink'** is a
short-stemmed double. Other cultivars have
single and double flowers in shades of white,
blue, purple, pink, red and yellow. They are
valuable and long-lasting as cut flowers. Sow
seed in autumn, and pot up 3 or more in deep
pots to encourage the tap root. Keep as light,
cool and airy as possible, and avoid disturbing
the roots when planting out in spring.

Halenia elliptica D. Don (*Gentianaceae*)
An upright summer annual with branching
stems and small, long-spurred, bluish flowers,
native of the Himalayas from Kashmir to
SW China in Yunnan, growing in open forest,
bushy and grassy places, at 1800-4500m,
flowering in July–October. Stems to 60cm.
Leaves opposite, narrowly elliptic, to 5cm
long. Flowers around 8mm across, with spurs
to 7mm long, pointing outwards or
downwards in flower, erect in fruit.

Halenia elliptica, with *Anaphalis triplinervis* in the mountains above Dali, Yunnan in September

Jaeschkea canaliculata in Kashmir

Halenia elliptica

Halenia elliptica var. *grandiflora* in Lijiang

Halenia deflexa (Sm.) Griseb. is found in moist woods in E North America, and several other species occur in the Andes.

Halenia elliptica D. Don var. **grandiflora** Hemsl.   This variety was described as having larger flowers. This striking, bicoloured form was common in limestone alpine meadows above Lijiang. The flowers have white corolla lobes and very long, blue, recurving spurs.

Jaeschkea canaliculata (Royle) Knobloch (*Gentianaceae*)   An erect summer annual with globular flowers and enlarged calyx lobes, native of the Himalayas from Pakistan to Kashmir, where it is common, growing in grassy alpine meadows and scrub, flowering in July–September. Stems to 50cm. Leaves oblong, acuminate, opposite. Flowers 6mm long, elongating to 1.3cm. The capsule is unusual in that it divides into 2 in fruit, each with half a style. A small genus of two species.

Halenia elliptica var. *grandiflora* in limestone pastures on the pass above Lijiang

Eustoma grandiflorum

Exacum affine

Eustoma grandiflorum

Eustoma grandiflorum 'Echo Pink'

Salpiglossis sinuata 'Kew Blue'

Salpiglossis sinuata 'Triumph' mixed

Salpiglossis sinuata 'Festival' mixed at Suttons Seeds

Salpiglossis sinuata 'Diablo' mixed

Salpiglossis sinuata, wild form from Chile at the Chelsea Physic Garden

Salpiglossis sinuata Ruiz & Pavon (*Solanaceae*) A sticky summer annual with trumpet-shaped, heavily veined flowers, native of Chile, S Peru and N Argentina, growing in the 3 Andes, flowering in October–December (late spring and summer). These are some of the most beautiful of all annuals, with flowers similar to the unrelated *Alstroemeria* in the *Amaryllidaceae*, another native of the same areas of South America. Stems with glandular hairs, much-branched, to 60cm. Leaves elliptic to oblong, sinuate, toothed or pinnatifid. Flowers to 6cm long, ranging from yellow to maroon or bluish-purple, with dark veins and a flare on the upper lobes. Capsules dry; seeds very small. Introduced in 1820. 'Yellow Chilli' (not shown) is similar to the wild type.

There are several cultivars and mixed strains available commercially, in a wide

Salpiglossis sinuata 'Casino' mixed, well grown in the cold conservatory at Wisley

variety of colours, mostly derived from *S. sinuata*. They will only do well outside in sheltered, warm gardens where they are protected from the wind and rain; unless you are prepared to stake them, choose compact varieties such as 'Ingrid'. Seed is best sown under glass during late March, and kept at a temperature of about 15°C, before pricking out the seedlings and potting on. Once all danger of frost has passed they can be planted out, preferably into light but fertile soil, which should be well-drained without drying out completely. Earlier flowering as pot plants under glass can be achieved by sowing seed at the beginning of autumn and overwintering plants in a warm greenhouse, but this method requires considerable care, as the plants are susceptible to damping off caused by overwatering during the winter. Because of their dislike of excessive moisture, salpiglossis often do best when planted in pots and kept in a semi-sheltered position in the garden. Illustrated here are:

'Casino' mixed F_I Height to 45–60cm.
'Diablo' mixed Height to 35cm.
'Festival' mixed Height to 30cm. An F_I variety.
'Ingrid' Height to 30cm. An F_I variety.
'Kew Blue' Height to 75cm.
'Triumph' mixed Height to 60cm, an old variety, raised and introduced by Suttons in the 1950s.

Salpiglossis sinuata 'Ingrid'

Schizanthus hookeri from Chile

Schizanthus grahamii, P.&W. 6440A

Schizanthus grahamii at Harry Hay's

Schizanthus pinnatus 'Angel's Wings'

Schizanthus hookeri Gillies (*Solanaceae*)
A sticky-stemmed annual, up to 50cm, with deeply divided, pale green leaves, to 8cm. Flowers in shades of pink: the lower lip with acute lateral divisions, the upper lip, to only 20mm, with a yellow, subrhombic central lobe; stamens short. Corolla tube much longer than the calyx. A very elegant species, collected in Chile at La Campana, at an altitude of 1500m.

Schizanthus grahamii Gillies, syn. *S. retusus* Hook. An upright summer annual, native of Chile and Argentina, with sticky, hairy stems to 80cm. Leaves very finely divided, to 8cm. Flowers varying in colour from pink to violet and purple, with a deep yellow blotch on the central lobe. Corolla tube as long as or a little longer than the calyx. Capsule ovoid, to 1cm. The red form shown here is P. &W. 6440A, from the Argentinian Andes, which was called *S. retusus* Hook. in the past.

Schizanthus cultivars There are a number of cultivars, most of which have a more compact habit and larger flowers in a wider range of colours than the species. They are beautiful plants for the cool greenhouse, for cutting, or for bedding out in sheltered spots in warm, sunny gardens. For summer flowering outdoors, seed is best sown at around 15°C under glass in early spring; once germinated, the plants can be pricked out and potted on. To encourage a bushy habit, pinch out the growing tips once the plants reach about 9cm. Harden off gradually, and plant out into light, well-drained but fertile soil once the weather has warmed up. Water freely once growth is under way, and be prepared to stake the taller cultivars.

For spring-flowering greenhouse plants, sow seed in a cold frame in late summer, prick out the seedlings, and grow on in a cool (min.10°C) greenhouse throughout the winter. Water sparingly to begin with, increasing the amount as the days lengthen, and pinch out the growing tips once they are about 10cm long.

The cultivars are based on the following species and group of hybrids.

Schizanthus pinnatus Ruiz & Pavon
A species with fern-like, pale green leaves and clusters of exotic-looking flowers, native of Chile, flowering from summer to autumn. Stems erect, branched, to 50cm. Leaves lanceolate to oblanceolate, finely divided, to 12cm. Flowers showy, to 4cm across, in panicles, pinkish-violet, with a yellow throat; corolla tube shorter than calyx, and exserted stamens prominent. Capsules ovoid-globose, to 5mm.
'Angel's Wings' A good, compact, bushy plant to 45cm, suitable for growing outdoors.
'Giant Hybrids' Derived from this or the following hybrid, with stems to 1.2m, best suited to growing in an airy greenhouse.

Schizanthus × wisetonensis hort. (not illustrated) This is a garden hybrid between *S. grahamii* and *S. pinnatus*, and is similar in habit and foliage to *S. pinnatus*. The flowers are white, pink, lilac or maroon, with the central lobe of the upper lip often flushed yellow. Many named strains were available.

Schizanthus pinnatus 'Angel's Wings'

Schizanthus pinnatus 'Giant Hybrids'

Petunia axillaris, pink form

Petunia axillaris, white form at Kew

Petunias The genus *Petunia* Juss., in the family *Solanaceae*, contains around 35 species of perennials and annuals native of tropical South America, but the hybrids commercially available are mostly descended from *P. axillaris*, *P. violacea* and *P. integrifolia*. Cultivated petunias are now available in a wide range of flower types and colours, and have been the subject of much – perhaps too much – attention from plant breeders in recent years. Compared with the species, described below, most of the modern F_1 hybrids have larger, more showy flowers, and, with the exception of Surfinias and varieties raised for hanging baskets, a more compact habit of growth. The downside of this breeding is that sometimes the colours have become so virulent and the flowers so large, that their resistance to wind and rain is feeble.

Petunia 'Primetime White'

Petunia 'Blue Vein'

An elegant planting of petunias in Regent's Park, with white *Salvia farinacea*

Petunias originate from South America, where they usually grow in the pampas. The name is derived from the Brazilian *petun*, meaning tobacco, to which petunias are very closely related (see *Nicotiana*, p.178–183).

Amongst the different groups of cultivars available are the Grandifloras (large trumpet-shaped flowers, up to about 12cm across), Multifloras (numerous smaller flowers to about 8cm across), Millifloras (many small flowers, less than 8cm across) and the newer Surfinias, which have become popular for their free-flowering and trailing habit, making them excellent plants for containers.

Petunias are not particularly easy to grow from seed as they need warmth (15–20°C) to germinate, followed by very careful watering, and growing on at a cooler temperature to encourage bushiness, and they can be susceptible to damping off if the compost is too wet, but will die if allowed to dry out; for this reason many seed companies now offer young plants as well as seed for sale. Propagation by cuttings taken in the autumn is also possible, and is usually successful, provided the young plants are overwintered in a warm greenhouse, and hardened off outside. Once planted out, petunias do well in full sun, preferably in a light soil, and will tolerate reasonably dry conditions; cool, wet weather will not produce good results, and the flowers of some of the larger-flowered varieties are spoilt by rain. It is worth dead-heading if you have the time, as the spent flowers look unattractive, and have a habit of staying on the plant. The good news for gardeners is that, unlike some other annuals, there are a number of named colour forms available, which makes planning a colour scheme simpler; we illustrate some currently available ones here (grouped by colour, rather than by type).

Petunia axillaris (Lam.) Britton, Sterns & Pogg., syn. *P. inflata* R. E. Fries   A spreading or erect annual species, to 60cm tall, with flowers of dull white or pink, scented at night, native of S Argentina, Brazil and Uruguay, growing in open places, flowering in summer. Leaves to 10cm, ovate, entire, covered with fine, sticky hairs. Flowers to 5cm across, dull white, buff-white or pink, with a slender tube 5–6cm long. Introduced to Britain in 1823, from near the mouth of the Rio de la Plata.

***Petunia* 'Blue Vein'**   A Surfinia petunia, with a trailing habit that makes it particularly suitable for pots and hanging baskets, or for use as a ground-cover plant, due to its capacity for spreading over a large area. The flowers are pale blue with darker blue veining, and are produced over many weeks.

***Petunia* 'Million Bells White'**   A small-flowered type, particularly suitable for planting in containers.

***Petunia* 'Primetime White'**   An F_1 hybrid with white, green-throated flowers, introduced by Colegrave in 1994.

***Petunia* 'Prism Sunshine'**   A compact F_1 hybrid, to 25cm high, with large, yellow flowers that soon fade to cream, with green veining.

***Petunia* 'Summer Sun'**   This new Multiflora F_1 hybrid grows up to about 22cm high, and has creamy yellow flowers up to about 8cm across.

A potful of blue and white Surfinia petunias and *Convolvulus sabatius*

Petunia 'Prism Sunshine' with *Malva* 'Primley Blue'

Petunia 'Million Bells White'

Petunia 'Summer Sun'

Petunia 'Rainbow' mixed at Thompson and Morgan's trial grounds

Petunia 'Pink Morn'

Petunia 'Chiffon Morn'   A later-flowering F_1 hybrid, to 30cm tall, with flowerheads to about 7cm across. Flowers pale pink with a greenish-yellow throat.

Petunia 'Horizon Pastel Throat'
An attractive new variety with deep pink, white-throated flowers, being tested by Suttons.

Petunia 'Pearly Wave'   A low-growing F_1 hybrid, to only about 15cm high, but capable of spreading to 1m across. Some of the pale pink petals have distinctive white markings. The trailing habit makes it suitable for use in baskets and containers.

Petunia 'Peppermint Tart'   A new variety from Suttons, this double, pink variety seems able to withstand hot, dry conditions well.

Petunia 'Pink Morn'   One of the 'Fantasy' series of Milliflora petunias, this grows up to about 30cm tall. The small, slightly trumpet-shaped flowers appear throughout the summer, and are pale pink with a yellow throat.

Petunia 'Pink Wave'   An F_1 hybrid, with a trailing habit and deep pink flowers produced along the length of the stems. Low-growing, to only about 15cm high, but capable of spreading to 1m across. Suitable for use in baskets and containers.

Petunia 'Rainbow' mixed   These F_2 hybrids grow to about 30cm high and have flowers in a blend of white, blue, light and dark pink and red shades.

Petunia 'Satin and Silk'   A mixed blend of white, pale blue, and light and dark pink shades, some veined. Plants to about 30cm high.

Petunia 'Chiffon Morn'

An old-fashioned pink petunia, seen in a garden in northern Spain

Petunia 'Satin and Silk'

Petunia 'Horizon Pastel Throat'

Petunia 'Pink Wave'

Petunia 'Pearly Wave'

Petunia 'Peppermint Tart'

Petunia 'Primetime Red Frost'

Petunia 'Velvet Picotee'

Petunia 'Purple Wave'

Petunia 'Crystal Red'

Petunia 'Purple Pirouette'

Petunia integrifolia (Hook.) Schinz & Thell., syn. *Petunia violacea* Lindl. (*Solanaceae*)   A spreading annual species, occasionally a short-lived perennial, to 60cm tall, with violet flowers, native of Argentina along the banks of the Uruguay River, from where it was introduced to Britain, flowering for the first time in Glasgow Botanic garden in 1831. Stems branched, covered with fine, sticky hairs. Leaves to 5cm, elliptic to lanceolate, entire. Flowers solitary, violet on inside, violet tinged rose-red on outside, with a slender tube to 4cm long.

'Blue Daddy'   An F$_1$ hybrid, to about 30cm tall. The flowers are light lilac-blue with darker violet veins.

'Fantasy Blue'   An F$_1$ Milliflora hybrid, with masses of small, dark purple-blue, trumpet-shaped flowers over a long season. A compact variety, growing to no more than 30cm, and so good for use in pots and containers. **'Crystal Red'** is another colour form of this type.

'Primetime Red Frost'   Large flowers with red centres and broad white margins, and some resistance to bad weather. One of the earlier varieties to flower.

'Purple Pirouette'   An unusual, bushy F$_1$ hybrid, with carnation-like, double, purple or rose-pink flowers, edged with frilled bands of white.

'Purple Wave'   A bright magenta, free-flowering variety, with trailing stems and a spreading habit, making it suitable for hanging baskets, containers or ground cover.

'Trailing Million Bells'   A new cultivar, derived from 'Million Bells' (see p.173), this has a trailing habit, making it good for pots and hanging baskets. Available in white, pink and violet-blue.

'Ultra Star' Series   A group of compact F$_1$ hybrids, to about 30cm high. The large flowers are available in 3 colours: purplish-blue, crimson and red, each with white, star-shaped markings.

'Velvet Picotee'   An experimental F$_1$ hybrid Multiflora, with striking magenta flowers edged with white.

Climbing petunias   These were grown from cuttings received from Belgium, and are possibly a selection of the old variety known as 'Leviathan'. Seen here at Wisley.

Petunia integrifolia at Suttons Seeds, compared with a white modern cultivar

Petunia 'Blue Daddy'

Climbing petunias at Wisley

Petunia 'Ultra Star' Series

Petunia 'Fantasy Blue'

Petunia 'Trailing Million Bells'

Nicotiana rustica

Nicotiana alata at Quince House

Nicotiana knightiana

Nicotiana glutinosa from Silene Nursery,
Belgium

Tobacco The genus *Nicotiana* L., in the family *Solanaceae*, is named after Jean Nicot, a French consul in Portugal during the 16th century, who is credited with introducing tobacco to France. There are more than 60 species, from Australia, Namibia and Califonia southwards in the Americas, some of which are grown for ornament, whilst *N. tabacum* produces most of the leaves used in commercial tobacco production. There are also many garden hybrids available, in various colours, although the forms with white or pale green flowers usually have the best scent.

Tobaccos like a sunny position in good, deep, rich, but well-drained soil. Most are perennial, but are usually treated as annuals in the northern hemisphere; in a mild year some, such as *N. alata*, will often sprout again from the previous year's rootstock, and will also self-sow with abandon. Nicotianas have better resistance to the vagaries of the British weather than the closely related petunias, and are well able to withstand wet and windy conditions.

Tobaccos are grown from seed sown in gentle heat, about 18°C, under glass in early spring; the fine seed is best sown on the surface of the compost, and left uncovered. The young plants are then pricked out and potted on, before being hardened-off and planted out once the danger of frost is past. As some tobacco flowers do not open until late in the day, and therefore the scent is at its best at that time, they are often planted near paths or seats or below windows, so that the smell can be enjoyed to full advantage in the evening air.

All species of *Nicotiana* are poisonous, the nicotine contained in *N. tabacum* and *N. rustica* particularly so.

Nicotiana alata Link & Otto., syn. *N. affinis* hort. A bushy perennial with loose heads of large, very fragrant, greenish-white flowers, native of South America from NE Argentina to S Brazil, flowering in summer. Stems sticky to 1m or more. Leaves spathulate-ovate, to 25cm. Flowers with funnel-shaped corolla to 10cm, greenish-white outside, white inside, scented at night. This is the species from which most of the ornamental cultivars derive.

Nicotiana glutinosa L., syn. *N. attenuata* hort. non. Torr A summer annual with very sticky, hairy leaves and brownish-pink flowers, native of Peru and Bolivia, flowering in summer. Stems around 60cm. Leaves ovate-cordate. Flowers with the tube narrow at the base, widening abruptly to a short, open, campanulate mouth with acuminate lobes.

Nicotiana knightiana Goodspeed An upright summer annual, with tubular green flowers, native of Peru around Arequipa, flowering in summer. Stems erect, to 2m. Leaves ovate. The flowers are distinguished from those of *N. langsdorfii* in their straight-sided tubes

Nicotiana langsdorffii J.A.Weinm. A tall summer annual with small, bright green flowers, native of Brazil, flowering in summer. Stems erect, branched, sticky, to 1.5m or more. Upper leaves lanceolate, lower leaves ovate, undulate. Flowers trumpet-shaped, green, to 2.5cm, in pendent panicles. Attractive for the unusual shape of its flowers.

Nicotiana rustica L. A summer annual to 1.5m high, with clusters of greenish-yellow flowers, native of Mexico and much of the South American Andes, from Bolivia northwards to Ecuador, flowering in summer. Stems sticky and slightly hairy. Leaves ovate or elliptic, hairy, to 30cm or more. Flowers opening early in the day, greenish-yellow, trumpet-shaped, to 2cm long, in panicles.

This was the original tobacco cultivated in Virginia by the Indians, and later by British colonists. It was superseded as a commercial crop by *N. tabacum*, but has lately regained some importance as a source of nicotine sulphate for use in insecticides, for which it was grown in kitchen gardens in the 18th century.

Nicotiana × sanderae hort. Sander ex W.Wats. (not illustrated). A garden hybrid of *N.alata* and *N.forgetiana*, a species from Brazil. Used to produce compact, annual cultivars (see pp.182–183). *N. × sanderae* grows up to 75cm tall and has ovate, mid-green leaves and pale yellow, tubular flowers tinged with pink.

Nicotiana alata with phlox and *Lavatera* 'Barnsley' at Cockermouth Castle, Cumbria

Nicotiana langsdorffii at Ventnor Botanic Garden, Isle of Wight

Nicotiana sylvestris at Wave Hill

Nicotiana sylvestris

Nicotiana sylvestris Speg. & Comes.
A perennial or biennial species, often grown as
an annual in cooler climates, to 2m tall, with
flat-topped heads of very fragrant, white,
tubular flowers in summer, native of the
Andean foothills of NW Argentina, flowering
in summer. Stems stout, branching, with a
woody base. Leaves lyre-shaped, rough,
sessile, to 30cm. Flowers tubular, to 8cm,
white, fragrant, in short, racemose panicles.
Introduced to Britain in 1898.

Nicotiana sylvestris makes a very striking
plant for the back of a border, and, despite its
height, has such strong stems that it rarely
needs staking. As its specific name suggests,
its natural habitat is in woods, so it will do
well in a partially shaded position. It has a
particularly strong and delicious scent when
the flowers are open – during the day if
cloudy, or in the evening in hot dry weather.

Nicotiana tabacum L. A tall annual or
biennial species, with greenish-white or pink
flowers in summer, native of NE Argentina
and Bolivia. Stems sticky, sometimes woody at
base, to 1.2m. Leaves ovate to elliptic or
lanceolate, to 25cm. Flowers tubular, to 6cm,
greenish-white or pale pink, open during the
day, in pendent clusters.

This is the species grown commercially for
tobacco production, and it has been of great
economic importance to the many countries
where it is cultivated, amongst them parts of
South America, Cuba, and South Africa, and
in particular, Zimbabwe. The North American
Indians chewed tobacco and used it as snuff,
and pipes have been found dating back to
AD 700.

Popular theory has it that Sir Walter Raleigh
(1552–1618) was responsible for introducing
both "the weed" and potatoes to Britain,
although this is not proved beyond a doubt.
A.L. Rowse, however, in his very readable
book, *Raleigh and the Throckmortons* (1962)
refers to Raleigh's practice of supplying
tobacco and pipes to the rich and famous, a
habit that did not endear him to King James I,
who even in those days could see the dangers
of smoking, describing it as a filthy habit
"neither brought in by king, great conqueror,
nor learned doctor of physic...but by a father
so generally hated."

In *Plant Hunters in the Andes*, published in
the 1940s, the American botanist T. Harper
Goodspeed describes his travels throughout
South America in search of tobacco plants,
which he hoped would lead to an
understanding of the way in which the
different species of one genus of flowering
plants developed. He proved that the
commercial tobacco plant is a hybrid
produced in the possibly distant past, by the
natural crossing of different ancestral species
of *Nicotiana* growing throughout the Andes.

Nicotiana trigonophylla Dunal
A biennial or short-lived perennial with
greenish-white, tubular flowers, native of
Mexico, Texas and California in the Mojave
and Colorado deserts northwards to Mono
Co., growing in rocks, desert and creosote
bush scrub, below about 1200m, flowering
from March–June. Stems sticky, erect,
sparsely branched, to 80cm. Leaves petiolate
at base, sessile and oblong-lanceolate to
lanceolate further up, to 8cm long.
Inlorescence lax, paniculate-racemose.
Flowers to 25mm long, and 1cm across at top.

Nicotiana tabacum

Nicotiana trigonophylla above Palm Springs

Nicotiana 'Evening Fragrance'

Nicotiana 'Domino Salmon Pink'

Nicotiana 'Havana Appleblossom'

Nicotiana 'Domino Rose Picotee'

Nicotiana 'Domino Lime Green'

Nicotiana 'Domino Red'

Nicotiana 'Havana Lime'

Nicotiana **'Domino' strain**   The 'Domino' F_1 hybrid strain was created in the 1980s by Mike Hough of the Floranova company, using the garden hybrid *N. × sanderae*, and was bred to produce plants with good resistance to extreme weather conditions. The resulting plants are stronger, with stouter stems and more flowers; they are also shorter (to about 30cm) to avoid wind damage, with the result that these are plants for the front of the border rather than the back. There are 10 different shades available mixed or separately, which is useful for the gardener planning a colour scheme. The downside is that, as so often happens, the scent is not as strong as in some of the species.

Shown here are; **'Domino Red'**, red, **'Domino Lime Green'**, very pale green, **'Domino Rose Picotee'**, pale pink edged with deeper pink, and **'Domino Salmon Pink'**, soft pink.

'Evening Fragrance'   Introduced by Suttons in 1967.

'Fragrant Cloud'   A strong-stemmed *N. × sanderae* hybrid, to 90cm, with large, white flowers, scented in the evening.

'Havana Appleblossom'   An F_1 hybrid of *N. × sanderae*, to 40cm, with flowers that are white on the upper side, rose-pink on the underside.

'Havana Lime'   Very pale green flowers on stems to 40cm.

Nicotiana 'Fragrant Cloud' in the Trials at Wisley in 1998

183

Solanum rostratum in Montana

Datura discolor in the semi-desert, east of Durango, Mexico

Solanum rostratum fruit

Capsicum annuum 'Black Prince'

Capsicum annuum L. **'Black Prince'**
(*Solanaceae*)   An ornamental variety of the
well-known chilli and sweet peppers, native of
Mexico and Central America. Stems around
90cm, purple, branched. Leaves ovate to
lanceolate, to around 10cm. Flowers solitary,
small, purple. Fruit deep purple.

Peppers are fast-growing annuals and do
well in warm, sunny conditions. Seed should
be sown under glass in early spring, and the
young plants grown on and hardened off
before planting out, which should only be
done once all danger of frost has passed.

Datura   The genus *Datura* in the family
Solanaceae consists of about 8 annual or
perennial species of shrubby herbs, with
luxuriant foliage and large, erect, trumpet-
shaped flowers from summer to early autumn;
these are moth-pollinated and therefore often
scented, particularly at night. The flowers tend
to open in the evenings and stay open during
the night and morning, but close in the
middle of the day if exposed to hot sun; sadly,
they are of little use for cutting as they flop in
water. All daturas contain extremely
poisonous, narcotic alkaloids and should be
handled with care; ingestion can be fatal.

Daturas are best grown from seed sown
in situ in spring, or raised earlier under glass
and set outside once the danger of frost has
passed. They do best in deep, well-drained but
moisture-retentive soils.

The shrubby species of *Datura* are now
known as *Brugmansia* – see our *Conservatory
and Indoor Plants* vol. 2, pp.138–139.

Datura ceratocaula Ortega   An annual
with erect, fragrant, white flowers, native of
Mexico, growing in seasonally wet, open
places, flowering in summer to autumn. Bushy
annual to 90cm tall, young stems and foliage
grey-haired. Leaves to 20cm long, ovate, with
a few triangular lobes on each side, grey-
haired beneath. Flowers to 18cm long,
trumpet-shaped, with 5 shallow lobes
alternating with 5 small teeth, white with
reddish-purple marks in the throat. Fruit a
smooth, fleshy, nodding capsule. Recognised
by its boldly lobed leaves.

Datura discolor Bernh.   An erect annual
with upward-facing white flowers, native of
the Colorado Desert and other parts of
S Arizona, Mexico and SE California, where
it grows in scrub on roadsides and waste
ground, usually at altitudes below 700m,
flowering from summer to autumn. Stems to
50cm, with broadly ovate, wavy-edged,
toothed leaves, to around 12cm long; calyx
prismatic, to 6cm long. Corolla white, tinged
pale purple in the throat, to 14cm long;
anthers white. Seeds black. This plant was
wrongly named *D. inoxia* subsp. *quinquecuspida*
in *Conservatory and Indoor Plants* vol. 2, p.139.

Datura inoxia Mill. subsp. ***inoxia***   A finely
downy annual with upward-facing, fragrant,
white or violet-tinted flowers, native of southwestern North America and Mexico, growing
in open, scrubby or waste areas, flowering in
summer. Bushy annual to 90cm tall, the stems
purplish. Leaves to 25cm, ovate, entire or
wavy-margined, dark or greyish-green. Flowers
funnel-shaped, to 20cm long, about 10cm
across the rounded, 5-toothed rim, solitary, in
the axils of the branches. Fruit a nodding,
spiny capsule. Like all species of *Datura*, all
parts are toxic. The name is sometimes,
apparently incorrectly, spelt *innoxia*.

Datura inoxia subsp. *quinquecuspida* in the Sierra Madre Occidental, NW Mexico

Datura ceratocaula in Copala, Mazatlan, W Mexico in late October

Datura inoxia subsp. *inoxia* in Kent

Datura inoxia Mill. subsp. **quinquecuspida** (Torr.) A.S. Barcl., syn. *D. wrightii* Regel An annual or short-lived perennial of spreading habit, with grey foliage and erect, fragrant, white or pale violet flowers, native of southwestern North America and N Mexico, growing in open, scrubby or waste places, flowering in summer. Stems to 1m. Leaves to 25cm long, ovate, like the stems, covered with fine, grey hairs. Flowers up to 20cm long, erect, tubular with a spreading, shallowly 5-lobed rim, each borne in the axil of a branch and lasting only one night. Fruit a spiny, nodding capsule. Hardy to −5°C.

Datura stramonium L. An erect annual, with fragrant, white, tubular flowers, native of most of the temperate and subtropical regions of the northern hemisphere and naturalised in Britain, growing in waste places and amongst old buildings, flowering in summer. Stems erect, stout, branched, to 1m. Leaves ovate, coarsely toothed, acute or acuminate, to about 20cm. Flowers 6–8cm long, erect,

solitary; calyx tubular, light green; corolla funnel-shaped, white or occasionally purple. Fruit a many-seeded, green, spiny capsule.

Solanum rostratum Dunal (*Solanaceae*) **Buffalo Burr** A spiny annual, with golden-yellow, star-shaped flowers, native of North Dakota and Wyoming to Arizona and Mexico, growing on plains and roadsides and in waste places, at 300–2000m, flowering in summer. Naturalised elsewhere, including Europe, as a result of burrs caught in wool and fabrics. Stems to 80cm tall, with yellow prickles. Leaves green, to 12cm long, divided into pinnate lobes, with prickles on the undersides of the veins. Flowers golden-yellow, with prickly calyx; corolla to 2.5 cm wide, 5-pointed; anthers unequal in length. Fruits round, green, spiny, to about 1cm in diameter.

All parts of this plant are poisonous if eaten. This species is suspected to have been the original host of the Colorado beetle before it attached itself to cultivated potatoes.

Datura stramonium, purple-flowered form

Nierembergia hippomanica var. *violacea* at Ventnor

Nolana paradoxa subsp. *paradoxa* 'Blue Bird'

Nicandra physalodes 'Violacea' at Rosemoor

Nicandra physalodes (L.) Gaertn.
(*Solanaceae*) **Shoo Fly**   A hardy annual, the
only species in the genus, with blue, bell-
shaped flowers, native of Peru, where it grows
in waste places, flowering in late summer.
Stems erect, much branched, to 1.2m. Leaves
ovate, to 10cm long, and half as wide at base,
with wavy margins. Flowers opening in the
middle of the day, solitary, to 4cm across, pale
mauve with white throat and corolla. Fruit a
brown berry.

'**Violacea**' is a form with deeper purple
flowers and fruit surrounded by attractive,
papery, purple calyces like a Chinese lantern.

Nicandras can be grown from seed, sown
under glass in spring at a temperature of 15°C
and hardened off before planting outside.
Once all danger of frost has passed, it may also
be sown *in situ* in good, deep, moist but
well-drained soil in a sunny place.

Nierembergia hippomanica Miers var.
violacea Millán., syn. *N. caerulea* Sealy
(*Solanaceae*)   A half-hardy perennial or
subshrub, usually grown as an annual, with
pale lavender flowers in summer, native of
Argentina. Stems slender, erect, branching, to
25cm, forming a clump. Leaves green, hairy,
very narrow, longer than those of the species,
to 2cm long. Flowers to 2.5cm across, pale
lavender with a yellow throat. Nierembergias
do well in moist but well-drained soil,
preferably in a sunny, sheltered place, as the
flowers are liable to be damaged by excessive
wind and rain. *N. hippomanica* will often
survive outside in a mild winter; it should be
cut right down to ground level in mid-
autumn, and given some form of protection.
Seed should be sown under glass at 15°C in
early spring, and the young seedlings pricked
out and potted on before hardening off and
planting outside. Can also be increased by
cuttings with a heel, taken in summer.

Nicandra physalodes showing fruit

Nicandra physalodes 'Violacea'

Nicandra physalodes near Volcan Collima Mexico

Nolana humifusa (Gouan) Johnst. (*Nolanaceae*) **'Shooting Star'** A trailing, perennial herb often grown as an annual, with pale lilac flowers, native of South America from Chile to Peru and the Galapagos Islands, flowering in summer. Stems trailing, to 15cm or more. Basal leaves to 2.5cm long, elliptic or spathulate; other leaves smaller, stalkless, and oblanceolate. Flowers with scalloped edges, pale lilac, with central blotch and streaks of dark purple.

Nolana paradoxa Lindl. subsp. **paradoxa** A trailing annual or perennial, with funnel-shaped, blue flowers, native of Chile and Peru, flowering in summer. Stems to 25cm, usually trailing; leaves slightly sticky and succulent, in rosettes at the base but opposite, ovate-elliptic further up the stem. Flowers trumpet-shaped, to 5cm wide, deep blue with a white centre and yellow throat. **'Blue Bird'** has numerous deep sky-blue flowers with white throats; **'Snowbird'** has trailing stems to about 60cm, and white flowers with yellow centres.

Nolanas are easily grown from seed sown *in situ* in any reasonable soil in full sun, and they are usually remarkably tolerant of heat and drought.

Nolana paradoxa subsp. *paradoxa* 'Snowbird'

Nolana humifusa 'Shooting Star'

Ipomoea lobata at Wisley

Ipomoea hederifolia in Mexico

Ipomoea quamoclit

Convolvulus tricolor L. (*Convolvulaceae*)
A non-climbing annual or short-lived
perennial with broad, stemless leaves and
flowers with blue, white and yellow bands,
native of Portugal and the Mediterranean
region, growing in dry, open, grassy places,
flowering in April–June. Stems to 60cm,
usually much-branched. Leaves obovate to
oblanceolate. Flowers 1.5–4cm long. Capsule
pubescent. Other annual Mediterranean
species have smaller flowers. Cultivated strains
of *C. tricolor* include **'Royal Ensign'**, with
particularly deep blue flowers, and the
'Ensign' series, which is available separately
in white, red, pink and blue flowers as well
as mixed.

Convolvulus sabatius Viv., syn.
C. mauritanicus Boiss. A perennial often
grown as an annual for pots and baskets, with
silky leaves and sky-blue flowers, growing on
dry limestone rocks on the coasts of NW Italy,
Sicily and NW Africa, flowering in
April–October. Stems to 50cm. Leaves
orbicular to oblong. Flowers 1.5–2.2cm,
sometimes pink. A lovely but tender plant,
which may survive a few degrees of frost over
winter if the plants are pushed into a dry
crevice in a wall. Young basal shoots root easily
in spring or autumn.

Ipomoea hederifolia L. (*Convolvulaceae*)
(section *Quamoclit*) A climbing annual with
small, bright scarlet flowers with a curved tube
and exserted style and stamens, native of
Mexico to South America, but now found
throughout the tropics, flowering in summer
and autumn. Stems to 2m; leaves heart-shaped
or shallowly 5–7-lobed, to 10cm across.
Flowers tubular, 2.5–4.5cm long, to 2.5cm
across, with exserted style and stamens. Easily
grown in warm seasons, best started indoors
in cool areas. This and other members of
section *Quamoclit* are typical hummingbird-
pollinated flowers.

Convolvulus tricolor near Cadiz in southern Spain

Convolvulus tricolor with *Hedysarum coronarium* in S Spain, near Seville

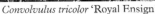

Convolvulus tricolor 'Royal Ensign'

Convolvulus sabatius

Ipomoea lobata (Cerv.) Thell., syn. *Mina lobata* Cerv., *Quamoclit lobata* (Cerv.) House A climbing perennial, often grown as an annual, with a forked, upright inflorescence of many small flowers, red in bud, becoming orange and yellow before opening nearly white, native of Mexico to South America, flowering in summer and autumn. Stems climbing to 5m; leaves deeply lobed, somewhat maple-like. Flowers tubular, 1.8–2.2cm long, with exserted style and stamens. Easily grown in warm seasons, best started indoors in cool areas.

Ipomoea quamoclit L., syn. *Quamoclit pennata* Boj. A climbing annual with finely divided leaves and small, bright scarlet flowers with a straight tube and 5-lobed mouth, native from Mexico to South America, but now found throughout the tropics, flowering in summer and autumn. Stems climbing to 2m; leaves pinnate, with linear lobes. Flowers tubular, 2.5cm long, to 1.5cm across; there is a rare white form. Easily grown in warm seasons, best started indoors in cool areas.

Convolvulus tricolor mixed at Suttons

Ipomoea purpurea

Ipomoea hederacea

Ipomoea purpurea var. *diversifolia* at Kew

Ipomoea alba L. syn. *Calonyction aculeatum*
House (*Convolvulaceae*) **Moonflower**
A rampant, climbing annual or perennial with
long-stalked, heart-shaped leaves and large,
white flowers with a long, narrow tube, native
of the tropical Americas, but now widely
cultivated and naturalised throughout the
tropics. Stems climbing to 5m, with tubercules
on the stem; leaves 6–20cm long, usually
entire, but sometimes deeply 3-lobed. Outer
sepals awned. Flowers opening in early
evening, scented, 11–16cm across, with the
tube 7–12cm long. Capsule with 4 large seeds
of various colours. A lovely plant in a tropical
climate, but not easy in a greenhouse, as it
needs a long period of growth to reach
flowering size. Sow early in heat and keep
humid. Watch especially for attack by red
spider mite, which seems to love all Ipomoeas.

Ipomoea hederacea (L.) Jacq.   A hairy
annual climber with 3-lobed leaves and pale
blue flowers, native from Mexico to
Argentina, and naturalised in North America
from Maine southwards to Florida, growing in
scrub and waste places. Climber to 2m, with
bristly and hairy stems; leaves hairy, 2–10cm,
deeply 3-lobed. Sepals acuminate, bristly-
hairy at the base. Flowers to 2.5–3cm across,
blue with a white tube, 1–3 in a loose head. A
more modest plant than some of the other
morning glories.

Ipomoea × imperialis hort. **'Early Call'**
mixed   A group of hybrids between *I. nil* and
other species. They need heat and humidity to
grow and flower satisfactorily. 'Early Call' is
one of the first to flower from seed. In 'Scarlet
O'Hara' the flowers are bright purple. *I. nil*
(L.) Roth. has very narrow sepals, 2.2–2.5cm
long, and a flower similar to *I. purpurea*.

Ipomoea purpurea (L.) Roth. (section
Ipomoea)   A hairy annual climber with deep
purplish-blue flowers, native of Mexico and
the West Indies, and but now found further
north in North America and throughout the
tropics, growing in scrub and waste places.
Climbs to 3m, with bristly and hairy stems;
leaves hairy, 2–10cm, ovate. Sepals lanceolate,
bristly-hairy. Flowers to 3–5cm across, blue or
purplish, becoming pinker through the day,
red, pink, white or striped in cultivars, with up
to 7 flowers in a loose head.
    In var. **diversifolia** (Lindl.) Don the leaves
are often ovate and 3-lobed on the same plant.

Ipomoea tricolor Cav. (section *Leiocalyx*)
Morning Glory   An annual climber, native
of Mexico and the West Indies to tropical
South America, growing in scrub and waste
places, flowering in late summer to winter.
Climbs to 3m, with glabrous stems; leaves
hairless, 4–10cm, ovate, cordate. Sepals
lanceolate, smooth at the base. Flowers to
6–10cm across, pale sky-blue, greenish or
blue-and-white striped, becoming pinker as
they fade during the day. This annual
morning glory is the easiest in temperate
climates, the most commonly grown form is
'Heavenly Blue'. The leaves are very prone
to attack by red spider mite, so the plants
should be kept very humid and warm while
they are growing up, and cooler while they are
in flower in late summer and autumn. The
seeds were used as a hallucinogen by the
Aztecs, and at one point in the 1960s all
morning glory seed was withdrawn from sale
in case hippies should make the same use of it.

Ipomoea tricolor near Lake Chapala, SW Mexico in late October

Ipomoea in Regents Park

Ipomoea tricolor 'Heavenly Blue'

Ipomoea alba at Le Clos du Peyronnet, Menton

Ipomoea tricolor mixed colours in the wild in Mexico

Ipomoea × imperialis 'Early Call' mixed

Cobaea scandens at Tapeley Park, Devon

Collomia grandiflora

Collomia biflora

Phlox drummondii 'African Sunset'

Phlox drummondii 'Twinkle' mixed

Cobaea scandens Cav. (*Polemoniaceae*)
A perennial climber, usually grown as a
summer annual, with green flowers becoming
purple as they mature, rarely white or deep
indigo blue, native of S Mexico around
Puebla, and naturalised in parts of South
America, flowering in summer and autumn.
Stems to 8m, even in one season. Leaves with
3 pairs of ovate leaflets, each around 8cm long.
Flowers held horizontally, around 8cm long.
Fruit a green, ovate capsule. Seeds need heat
(20–25°C) to germinate and grow on until the
weather has warmed up, when the plants can
be put out on a warm wall.

Collomia biflora Dougl. ex Lindl.
(*Polemoniaceae*) A winter or spring annual
with narrow leaves and heads of red or orange
flowers, native of Chile, flowering in spring
and summer. Stems 30–45cm. Leaves
linear-lanceolate, sometimes forked or divided
towards the tip. Corolla around 1cm long.
Easily grown in good soil in a sunny position.

Collomia grandiflora Dougl. ex Lindl.
A winter or spring annual with dark green
leaves and heads of pale salmon-orange or
creamy flowers, native of much of California
below 2500m, eastwards to the Rockies and
northwards to British Columbia, growing in
open ground and scrub, flowering in
April–July. Stems 10–100cm. Leaves lanceolate
to linear, the lower with a few teeth. Corollas
1.5–3cm long, produced in succession from a

Phlox drummondii 'Brilliant' at Suttons Seeds

head of sticky, glandular calyx lobes. Easily grown in good soil in a sunny position, and self-seeding in a suitable position.

Phlox drummondii Hook. (*Polemoniaceae*) A densely glandular summer annual with mainly red to purple flowers, native of Texas in the middle of the coastal plain, growing in open oak woodland and sandy grassland, flowering in February–May. Stems to 50cm, usually around 15cm in the modern strains. Leaves linear to ovate-lanceolate, opposite below, alternate above. Flowers around 2.5cm across.

Seed is best sown in gentle heat in early spring, and seedlings put out after all frost is past, or it may be sown directly outside in late spring to flower in late summer and autumn.

The wild plant was introduced in 1835, and has tall stems around 45cm, with flowers mainly red, crimson, pink or white. Something similar is still available from Chiltern Seeds under the name 'Choice Mixture'. The other group with tall stems are the 'Grandiflora' series. 'Chanal' is salmon-pink with double flowers, in which the beauty of the singles is lost.

'African Sunset' Bright red, with stems to 10cm.

'Brilliant' A tall variety with stems around 30cm and large, mainly red and pink flowers.

'Tapestry Mixture' Attractive soft colours with contrasting stars and eyes.

'Twinkle' mixed A dwarf *cuspidata* or *stellata* type with starry flowers with pinked edges. Stems 15–20cm.

Phlox drummondii 'Tapestry Mixture' at Suttons Seeds

Linanthus 'French Hybrids' at Suttons Seeds Trials

Navarretia minima, with woolly buns of Evax canescens

A dried vernal pool in northern California, habitat of Navarretia minima

Langloisia schottii (Torr.) Greene (*Polemoniaceae*) A small, wiry desert annual with prickly leaves and 2-lipped, pale mauve, white, pinkish or yellowish flowers, native of S California, to Utah, Arizona and Baja California, growing on dry, sandy or gravelly hills, flowering in March–June. Stems 2–10cm. Leaves 1–3cm long, linear to linear-oblanceolate, pinnate, with bristle-tipped teeth. Flowers 8–12mm long, with the lower lip 2-lobed, the upper 3-lobed, spotted near the base. *L. matthewsii* (Gray) Greene has larger flowers with rounded lobes, the upper marked with white and small, red spots. It is often common in the S Californian deserts.

Langloisia setosissima (Torr. & Gray) Greene A dwarf desert annual with prickly leaves and regular, pale mauve, unspotted flowers, native of Oregon and California, to Idaho, Utah, Arizona and Baja California, growing on dry, sandy or gravelly deserts below 1100m, flowering in March–June. Stems 2–7cm. Leaves 1–2cm long, with 3 large, bristle-tipped teeth. Flowers 1.2–1.6cm long. *L. punctata* (Cov.) Goodd. has larger flowers with many small spots around the edges of the petals.

Leptosiphon Of the 40 species of *Linanthus*, in the family *Polemoniaceae*, in western North America and Chile, 34 are in California; all save 1, *L. nuttallii* (Gray) Greene, are annuals. The dwarf hybrids commonly cultivated are often found under the old name *Leptosiphon*.

Linanthus aureus (Nutt.) Greene A small winter annual with mossy leaves and pale to deep yellow flowers, native of S California, Nevada, New Mexico and Baja California, growing in sandy places in Joshua tree woodland, below 1800m in the Mojave and Colorado deserts, flowering in March–June. Stems 5–16cm. Leaves deeply divided into 3–7 narrow lobes 3–6mm long. Flowers short-tubed, 6–13mm long, yellow with an orange or brownish-purple throat, or whitish with a dark throat in var. *decorus* (Gray) Jeps., which is found in the same areas. A very attractive dwarf desert annual, sometimes very plentiful over small areas.

Linanthus ciliatus (Benth.) Greene A small winter annual with mossy leaves and pale rose to white flowers, native of Oregon, California and Nevada, growing in dry, open places in scrub and grassland, below 2000m, flowering in April–July. Stems 5–30cm. Leaves deeply divided into 5–11 narrow, ciliate lobes 5–20mm long. Flowers long-tubed, 1.2–2.5cm long, with a yellow throat, the outside of the tube pubescent.

Linanthus dianthiflorus (Benth.) Greene **Ground Pink** A small winter annual with mossy leaves and white to pink or lilac flowers with pinked edges, native of S California from Santa Barbara Co. to the W edge of the Colorado desert and Baja California, growing in sandy places in coastal scrub, chaparral or grassland, below 1300m, flowering in February–April. Stems 5–12cm. Leaves linear, filiform, mostly opposite, 1–2cm long. Flowers short-tubed, 1–2.5cm long, with dark spots and a yellow throat. A particularly pretty dwarf annual for warm, sandy soil.

Linanthus 'French Hybrids' syn. *Leptosiphon* 'French Hybrids' A small winter or spring annual with mossy leaves and white, pink, lilac or red flowers with rounded lobes, probably derived from *L. androsaceus* (Benth.) Greene, a native of most of California, from Humbolt and Shasta Cos southwards to Santa Barbara Co. and the W edge of the Mojave desert and Baja California, growing in open, grassy places in oak woodland, chaparral or grassland, below 1500m, flowering in April–June. Stems 5–30cm. Leaves opposite, divided into 5–9 narrow lobes 1–3cm long, so appearing whorled. Flowers with a long tube, 1–2.5cm long, often with dark spots and a yellow throat. I have found these charming annuals easy to grow and quick to flower from seed sown in late spring, but vulnerable to damage by slugs and snails in wet summers.

Navarretia minima Nutt. (*Polemoniaceae*) A dwarf annual with small, white flowers, native of Washington and Idaho to N California, growing in vernal pools, at below 1600m, and flowering as they dry out in June–August. Stems 3–10cm. Lower leaves linear or dissected, upper wider, 1–2.5cm long. Flowers 4–6mm long. Of the 29 species of *Navarretia*, several are members of the specialised flora which are adapted to this environment: they must live underwater in winter, and flower in summer as the pools dry out. The white, fluffy plants seen here among the *Navarretia* are dwarf specimens of *Evax caulescens* (Benth.) Gray.

Langloisia schottii in the desert mountains above Anza-Borrego

Linanthus ciliatus near Benbow, N California

Langloisia setosissima in the desert mountains above Anza-Borrego

Linanthus aureus in the Joshua Tree National Monument

Linanthus dianthiflorus on the hills above Malibu Beach

Gilia tricolor in Devon

Ipomopsis aggregata on dry limestone hills near Saltillo, north-eastern Mexico

Gilia achilleaefolia Benth. (*Polemoniaceae*)
A winter or spring annual with divided leaves
and heads of blue flowers, native of California
from Marin Co. southwards to Santa Barbara
Co., growing in open soil on the coastal strand
and in the Coast Ranges, flowering in
May–June. Stems to 70cm, often floccose
below, glandular above. Leaves 2-pinnate, the
segments falcate. Corolla 1–2cm long, with
oval lobes. Distinguished from the more
common and very variable *G. capitata* by
having fewer flowers with larger corollas and
broader lobes.

Gilia capitata Sims   A winter or spring
annual with divided leaves and fluffy heads of
blue flowers, native of California from Marin
Co. northwards to British Columbia and
Idaho, growing on open slopes below 1800m,
in the Coast Ranges, flowering in May–July.
Stems to 80cm, often floccose below, glandular
above. Leaves 2-pinnate, the segments
straight, to 1mm wide. Flowers 50–100 in the
head; corollas 6–8mm long, with linear lobes
to 1mm wide. Easily grown; often self-seeds
after warm, dry summers. Subsp. *abrotanifolia*
(Nutt. ex Greene) V. Grant has 25–50 larger
flowers, often white, with lobes 1.5–3mm
wide. It is found mainly in the Sierra foothills
from Madera Co. southwards to Baja
California, especially after fires.

Gilia tricolor Benth. **Bird's Eyes**
A spreading annual with usually pale lavender
flowers with a dark eye, native of N California
inland from Tulare Co. northwards, and from
San Benito Co. northwards in the Coast
Ranges, growing in grassy places below 800m,
flowering in March–May. Stems 10–40cm.
Leaves pinnate. Flowers solitary or in heads of
2–5; corolla 1.1–1.6cm long, around 1.5cm
across when fully open, with dark spots and an
orange or yellow throat; occasionally deep
blue-violet in the wild. A very easily grown and
lovely annual with a long flowering season in a
cool summer from a spring sowing directly
sown where it is wanted.

Gilia capitata on a sunny, rocky bank in Devon

Gilia achilleaefolia

Ipomopsis aggregata (Pursh) V. Grant, syn. *Gilia aggregata* (Pursh) Spreng. **Skyrocket** (*Polemoniaceae*)   An upright annual with a rosette of feathery leaves and spikes of bright red flowers, native of California in the Sierras from Inyo Co. northwards to Idaho, and in the Coast Ranges from Trinity Co. to British Columbia, growing in open, stony places and on rocky ridges at 1000–3000m, flowering in June–September. Stems 30–80cm. Leaves pinnate. Flowers in an elongated panicle; corolla 2–3.5cm long, with yellow spots on a red ground, but in other subspecies pink, white or yellowish. Not easy to grow, as it hates winter wet, though it tolerates cold if dry.

Ipomopsis rubra (L.) Wherry, syn. *Gilia rubra* L. **Texas Plume**   A tall, upright biennial or short-lived perennial with a rosette of pinnate basal leaves and a narrow panicle of red flowers, native of S Carolina to Florida and Texas, growing in dry, stony places, flowering in July–September. Stems to 2m, usually around 1m, not glandular. Flowers 2 2.5cm long, the lobes around 9mm, sometimes yellowish.

'Presidio' is a cultivar with yellowish flowers. Except in areas with very dry winters, *Ipomopsis* should be sown in late summer and kept as airy and dry as possible under glass for the winter, before planting out in late spring. If the seed is sown in spring, the plants can be brought into flower under glass late in the following winter.

Ipomopsis rubra 'Presidio' at Thompson and Morgan's trial grounds

Ipomopsis rubra

Phacelia parryi after a fire in a canyon above Irvine, S California

Phacelia parryi above Malibu Beach, southern California

Phacelia viscida

Phacelia minor with scentless mayweed at Quince House

Phacelia viscida in the Theodore Payne Foundation, S California

Phacelia There are around 150 species of *Phacelia*, in the family *Hydrophyllaceae*, found only in the Americas, with the greatest concentration, of around 90 species, in California. Most are annuals, and many are low plants with very bright blue or purple flowers. Others have long stamens and are especially attractive to bees; *P. tanacetifolia* is sometimes planted for bees or to attract hoverflies into the garden. Like the closely related family *Boraginaceae*, the flowers of the *Hydrophyllaceae* tend to be in coiled cymes.

Phacelia campanularia Gray **Californian Bluebell** An upright winter annual with bright deep blue, bell-shaped flowers, native of S California in the western part of the Colorado desert, growing in sandy and gravelly places, flowering in February–April. Stems to 60cm, usually around 15cm. Leaves ovate, coarsely toothed, 2–7cm long. Flowers 1.5–3cm long, occasionally white. Stamens dilated and usually glabrous at the base. Subsp. *vasiformis* Gillett, has flowers 2.5–4cm long. The cultivated plant, shown on the next page, has more open flowers.

Phacelia minor (Harv.) Thell., syn. *Phacelia whitlavia* Gray, *Whitlavia minor* Harv. An upright winter annual with bright purplish-blue, bell-shaped flowers, native of S California, from the Santa Monica mountains to the edge of the desert, and to Baja California, growing in dry, open places below 1500m, and most common after fires, flowering in March–June. Stems to 60cm, usually around 20cm. Leaves ovate, coarsely toothed, 2–7cm long. Flowers 1.5–4cm long, occasionally white, narrowed at the throat. Stamens dilated and usually hairy at the base. An attractive plant for a warm winter climate, flowering in spring, or in summer if sown in late spring.

Phacelia parryi Torr. An upright winter annual with open, bright purple flowers with 2 white spots at the base of each lobe, native of S California, from Monterey Co. in the Coast Ranges to the edge of the Colorado desert and to Baja California, growing in dry, open and grassy places below 1200m, and most common after fires, flowering in March–May. Stems to 50cm, usually around 20cm, pubescent and glandular. Leaves ovate, coarsely toothed, 1.5–5cm long. Flowers 1–2cm long, open bell-shaped to almost flat. Stamens winged and usually pubescent at the base. Very striking when growing in quantity, especially when contrasting with orange Californian poppies.

Phacelia viscida (Benth.) Torr. An upright winter annual with open, bright blue flowers with a white centre, native of S California, from Monterey Co. to San Diego Co., growing in dry, open and sandy places near the coast below 600m, and most common after fires, flowering in March–May. Stems to 70cm, usually around 30cm, very glandular. Leaves oblong-ovate to rounded, double-toothed, 4–9cm long. Flowers 8–18mm long, almost flat, with a white or purplish centre. Stamens slender and pilose at the base. The exceptional deep blue of the flowers is set off by the white centre. In cultivation, this species is sometimes sold as 'Tropical Surf'.

Phacelia campanularia in the Mojave desert, California

Phacelia minor above Palm Springs

Phacelia campanularia

Phacelia divaricata in Devon

Phacelia campanularia, white form

Cultivated *Phacelia campanularia*

Emmenanthe penduliflora in San Andreas
Canyon, near Palm Springs

Phacelia campanularia Gray
(*Hydrophyllaceae*) An upright winter annual
with bright, deep blue, bell-shaped flowers,
native of the deserts of S California. The
cultivated plant, shown here, has more open
flowers than the wild species, shown on the
previous page. There is also a rare white form.
P. campanularia is easily grown in well-drained
soil in full sun. It does best with ample water
in spring, followed by a dry, sunny summer, or
can be sown in autumn and kept frost-free
and to flower in early spring.

Phacelia crenulata Torr. An upright winter
annual with open, purplish-blue flowers with a
white centre, native of S California in the
Mojave and Colorado deserts eastwards to
Utah, Nevada and Arizona, growing in sandy
places in the desert below 1500m, flowering in
February–June. Stems to 40cm, very glandular,
and smelling of onions. Leaves oblong, pinnate
or lobed, 4–12cm long. Flowers 6–10mm long,
in dense cymes grouped into flattish panicles.
Stamens glabrous, 1–1.4cm long. Very
common in desert areas, and very variable.
Var. *funerea* J. Voss ex Munz, with purplish
stems and the inflorescence not flat-topped, is
found in the mountains around Death Valley.

Phacelia distans Benth. **Wild Heliotrope**
An upright winter annual with fern-like leaves
and open, bluish flowers, native of California
from Mendocino and Tehama Cos,
southwards to Baja California, and in the
Mojave and Colorado deserts eastwards to
Nevada, Arizona, in the Grand Canyon, and
N Mexico, growing in fields and open slopes
below 1300m, flowering in February–June.
Stems 20–80cm, glandular above. Leaves
ovate in outline, 1–2-pinnate, 2–10cm long.
Flowers 6–8mm long, in simple or branched
cymes. Stamens glabrous, as long as the
corolla, or shortly exserted. A very common
plant in dry areas, disappearing as soon as the
soil dries out in early summer.

Phacelia divaricata (Benth.) Gray
A spreading annual with open, pale lavender-
blue flowers with darker veins, native of

N California from Mendocino to Monterey
and San Benito Cos in the Coast Ranges,
growing in dry, open and grassy places and
clearings below 600m, flowering in
March–May. Stems to 30cm, usually around
20cm, pubescent, but rarely glandular. Leaves
elliptic to narrowly ovate, not toothed, rarely
lobed, 1.5–5cm long. Flowers 1–1.2cm long,
open, bell-shaped to almost flat. Stamens
glandular and sometimes hairy. A modest
annual, easy to grow and flowering
throughout a cool, moist summer.

The phacelia sold as 'Sea Seventeen' seems
to belong to this species.

Phacelia tanacetifolia Benth. **Fern-leaf
Phacelia** A robust winter annual with
fern-like leaves and small, bluish flowers with
long stamens, native of California from Lake
and Butte Cos southwards to Baja California,
and in the Mojave and Colorado deserts
eastwards to Nevada, and widely naturalised
on roadsides in Europe, growing in fields and
on open slopes below 1300m, flowering in
March–May. Stems 20–120cm, hairy and
glandular above. Leaves ovate in outline,
1–2-pinnate, 2–10cm long. Flowers 6–8mm
long, in simple or branched cymes. Stamens
glabrous, 1.5–2 times as long as the corolla,
long-exserted. Commonly and easily
cultivated and often planted for bees, but
larger and coarser than most other species.

Emmenanthe penduliflora Benth.
(*Hydrophyllaceae*) **Whispering Bells** A
winter annual with small, narrow, bell-shaped,
yellow flowers, native from C California to
Baja California and eastwards to Utah and
Arizona, growing in dry, rocky places where it
is especially common after fires, flowering in
April–July. Stems 10–50cm, sticky, with
minute glands, and pleasantly scented. Leaves
linear-oblong, 3–10cm long. Flowers 8–12mm
long, the corolla remaining after the flower has
faded. On the inner side of the Coast Ranges
from Santa Clara Co. to Ventura Co. there is
var. *rosea* Brand., with pink flowers. Called
Whispering bells because the dry, persistant
corollas rustle in the desert wind.

Phacelia tanacetifolia

Phacelia crenulata in San Andreas Canyon above Palm Springs

Phacelia distans in the hills above Malibu Beach

Nemophila menziesii in sage bush scrub in the mountains above Anza-Borrego, in late March

Nemophila menziesii in cultivation

Nemophila menziesii, white form

Nama demissum Gray (*Hydrophyllaceae*) A creeping winter annual with greyish, hairy stems and purple flowers, native of California in the E Mojave and Colorado deserts, southwards to Baja California and eastwards to Utah and Arizona, growing on dry slopes at up to 1500m, in sandy flats and washes, flowering in February–May. Stems to 15cm long. Leaves 1–4cm long, 1–5mm wide, narrowly spathulate to obovate. Flowers 9–12mm long, tubular to campanulate. Var. *deserti* Brand., with rhombic-obovate leaves, is the common variety in S California and Arizona. A very attractive dwarf desert annual, often covering large areas. The genus *Nama* L. consists of around 45 species, mostly annuals, from south-western North America to South America and Hawaii.

Nemophila maculata Benth. ex Lindl. (*Hydrophyllaceae*) **Five-spot** A spreading winter annual with pinnate leaves and cup-shaped flowers with a purple blotch on the tip of each lobe, native of California on the lower slopes of the Sierra Nevada from Plumas Co. to Kern Co., growing on moist slopes and grassy flats at up to 2000m, flowering in April–July. Stems to 30cm long, with scattered hairs. Leaves 1–3cm long, 5–9-lobed. Flowers 1.5–4.5cm across. One of the easiest annuals for general garden use, best planted in a cool position in partial shade in warm areas.

Nemophila menziesii Hook. & Arn., syn. *N. insignis* Dougl. ex Benth. **Baby Blue-eyes** A spreading winter annual with pinnate leaves

Nama demissum in the Mojave desert in late March

and shallow, cup-shaped, pale blue flowers with a white centre, native of California from Tehama and Butte Cos southwards to San Diego Co., growing on moist slopes and grassy flats at up to 1500m, flowering in February–July. Stems succulent, pubescent, to 30cm long. Leaves 2–5cm long, with 9–11 rounded lobes. Flowers 1.5–4cm across, usually bright blue with a pale centre, but sometimes white. Var. *venosa* (Jepson) Brand., from the S Napa range, has a large, purple blotch on each lobe and in the throat, and blue lobes with dark purple veins in the upper part. Var. *intermedia* (Billioti) Brand, from the outer Coast Ranges from Mendocino Co. southwards to Santa Clara Co., has pale blue flowers with purple or dark blue veins. In subsp. *integrifolia* (Parish) Munz and its varieties, the upper leaves are less divided than the lower; these are found mostly in S California, from the inner side of the Coast Ranges to the edge of the desert. One of the prettiest and easiest of all the dwarf Californian annuals, best in a cool, partly shaded position in hot areas, and good for planting in autumn to overwinter and flower in spring.

Nemophila menziesii subsp. **atomaria** (F. & M.) Brand.   In this subspecies, the flowers are 1.5–3cm across, white, with small, black spots radiating from the centre. Found in moist places in redwood forest and oak woodland near the coast from Santa Clara Co. northwards to Oregon, flowering in March–June. I have found this exceptionally tolerant of frost, wind and rain; from a late-summer planting it has flowered on and off all through the winter, and in early spring is covered with flowers again.

Nemophila menziesii 'Penny Black'
An unusual variety, in which the small flowers are black with a white rim. This is also grown under the name var. *discoidalis*.

Nemophila maculata

Nemophila menziesii 'Penny Black'

Nemophila menziesii subsp. *atomaria*

Echium flavum Desf. (*Boraginaceae*)
A softly hairy biennial with, usually, several tall, unbranched stems and pinkish flowers, native of mountain meadows and screes in S, C and E Spain, flowering in May–July. Stems to 1.5m. Flowers with corolla 1.3–1.6cm, with 5 long-exserted stamens with red filaments. *E. boissieri* Steudel, growing by roadsides and on rocky slopes in S Portugal and S Spain, is an even more striking plant with tall, spire-like, bristly-hairy stems to 2.5m bearing similar pinkish flowers.

Echium lusitanicum L. subsp. *polycaulon* (Boiss.) P. Gibbs   A biennial or possibly a perennial with upright, unbranched stems and small, dull blue flowers, native of WC Spain, growing on roadsides and open ground, flowering in May–July. Stems to 1m or more. Flowers with corolla of 7–10mm, wide open, with the stamens exserted with red filaments. This species is a striking sight on the plains around Valladolid.

Echium sabulicola Pomel   A creeping or spreading biennial or short-lived perennial, with reddish-purple or dark bluish flowers, native of Spain and North Africa eastwards to Italy and Sicily, growing on roadsides and open, sandy ground near the sea, flowering in March–June. Stems to 50cm. Flowers with corolla of 1.2–2.2cm, wide open, with 1 or 2 stamens exserted. Calyx enlarging and white-bristly in fruit. The large, reddish flowers of this species are very showy.

Echium simplex DC.   An upright, monocarpic subshrub with narrow, silvery leaves and dense spikes of small, white flowers, native of NE Tenerife on the Sierra Anaga, at up to 350m, growing in rocky places near the coast, flowering in April–July. Stems unbranched, to 2m. Flowers around 8mm, the stamens exserted. A spectacular plant, seen here naturalised on the coast in South Africa.

Echium pininana Webb & Berth.
A monocarpic shrub with a large rosette on a stout stalk, developing into a massive spike of bluish flowers in its third or fourth year, native of La Palma, growing at around 600m, in laurel forests in the NE part of the island, where it is very rare, flowering in April–July. Stem to 4m; leaves elliptic-lanceolate, rough, green. A spectacular plant for a mild garden, preferring partial shade in hot areas. It grows well in coastal gardens in California and W Europe, as well as along the Mediterranean and in sheltered gardens in London, where it will survive a few degrees of frost. The hybrid between this species and *E. wildpretii* has rich purple flowers on a spike to around 3m.

Echium wildpretii Pearson ex Hook. fil.
A spectacular biennial, forming a large rosette of narrow, silver leaves in the first year and a tall spike of small, crimson flowers in the second, native of Tenerife, growing in dry, rocky places in the subalpine zone at around 2000m, and in the mountains of La Palma, at 1600–1800m, flowering in May–June. Flowering stem to 2m. Leaves linear, with long, dense setae. For a dry, very sunny climate; easy to grow and will tolerate overnight frost, but when grown under glass it tends to go mouldy, especially in warm, damp winters. On bare, dry ground near the Parador at Las Cañadas on Tenerife I found the young rosettes coated with ice in the early morning, before being scorched by the sun all day.

Echium simplex naturalised at Hermanus, South Africa

Echium simplex

Echium lusitanicum subsp. *polycaulon*
S of Valladolid, with an adobe dovecote

Echium sabulicola near Algeciras, SW Spain

Echium wildpretii on Tresco

Echium pininana in the garden at Tresco Abbey, Isles of Scilly

Echium wildpretii in Tenerife

Echium flavum in the Sierra de Gredos in late May

Echium plantagineum near Cnidos in south-western Turkey

Echium vulgare

Anchusa undulata subsp. *undulata* with yellow wood and silver *Onopordum* on the edge of a rye field near Valladolid, western Spain

Echium plantagineum L. (*Boraginaceae*)
A biennial or spring annual with branching, spreading stems 20–60cm, and trumpet-shaped flowers opening blue, becoming purple, then pinkish, native of most of Europe from S England southwards to the Caucasus and S Turkey, growing in open ground, on roadsides and in grassy places, at up to 2400m in Turkey, flowering in March–September. Stems to 65cm. Flowers with corolla 1.8–3cm long, hairless or with a few long hairs on the veins and margins, usually with 2 exserted stamens. Most cultivated annual echiums belong to this species.

'Blue Bedder' is a very floriferous old variety, a good light blue, with stems to around 40cm. It was generally listed under *E. vulgare*. 'Dwarf Brilliant' mixed contains flowers of red, pink, purple and white as well as blue.

Echium vulgare L. **Viper's Bugloss**
A biennial or possibly perennial with upright, unbranched stems and deep blue or purplish flowers, native of most of Europe eastwards to Central Asia and NW China, growing on roadsides, dunes, shingle beaches and open ground, often on chalk or limestone, flowering in May–September. Stems to 90cm or more. Flowers with corolla of 1–1.9cm, wide open, with rounded lobes and 4–5 long-exserted stamens with red filaments. A very beautiful species for well-drained, sandy soil.

Echium vulgare on coastal shingle at Dungerness, Kent

Echium plantagineum 'Blue Bedder' in the trials fields of Kees Sahin in Holland

Anchusa undulata L. subsp. *undulata*
(*Boraginaceae*)   A biennial or short-lived
perennial with hairs and bristles, and blue or
purple flowers, native of Spain and Portugal,
growing in open ground and on roadsides,
flowering in May–July. Stems 10–50cm.
Leaves usually wavy-edged, the bristles
without swollen bases. Bracts lanceolate to
ovate-lanceolate. Flowers 6–8mm across;
corolla tube 8–13mm long, with the stamens
at the top. Subsp. *hybrida* (Ten.) Coutinho,
from the Mediterranean excluding Spain and
Portugal, has broader bracts, flowers only
3–5mm across, and stamens in the middle of
the tube.

Anchusa capensis Thunb.   A perennial,
usually grown as an annual, with deep blue,
white-centred flowers, native of South Africa
from Namaqualand to the Eastern Cape,
growing on roadsides and sandy plains,
flowering in August–November. Stems
roughly hairy, branching from the base to 1m.
Leaves lanceolate. Flowers 6–8mm across,
with conspicuous white scales in the throat.
The original annual or biennial strain is
cultivated under the name 'Blue Bird'; it has
stems to 45cm tall. The modern **'Blue Angel'**
has bright blue flowers and stems to 25cm.
'Dawn' mixed, also to 25cm, has blue, white
and pink flowers. To grow these as biennials,
sow seed in late summer, and overwinter in
frost-free conditions. To grow as annuals, sow
the seed at 15°C in early spring, and plant out
in early summer.

Anchusa capensis 'Blue Angel' at Sutton's
Seeds trial grounds

Anchusa capensis 'Dawn' mixed

207

Heliotropium arborescens at Tapeley Park

Heliotropium arborescens 'Marine'

Cynoglossum amabile

Cryptantha intermedia (Gray) Greene (*Boraginaceae*)   A forget-me-not-like winter annual with hairy stems and small, white flowers, native of California from W Siskyou Co. southwards to Baja California, growing in open, grassy places from the coast to the edge of the desert, at up to 1800m, flowering in March–July. Stems to 50cm, usually around 20cm, usually very hairy, frequently with bristly hairs. Leaves lanceolate to linear, 1.5–5cm long. Inflorescences branching. Flowers 3–7mm across. This species is common in California, especially in areas which have recently been burnt. The genus *Cryptantha* consists of around 65 species of annuals and perennials with white, yellow or orange, usually small flowers. The similar genus *Plagiobothrys*, with around 100 species, always has white flowers; *P. nothofulvus* (Gray) Greene, is very like *C. intermedia* but is less leafy, and usually has brownish hairs and flowers 6–8mm across.

Cynoglossum amabile Stapf & Drummond (*Boraginaceae*)   A biennial or spring annual with sky-blue flowers, native of SW China, in Yunnan and Sichuan, growing in open ground and on banks between paddy-fields, flowering in May–August. Stems 30–70cm. Leaves lanceolate, with distinct lateral nerves. Flowers around 5mm across. The seeds form burrs, and stick in your socks if you walk through the plants. Several different varieties are now available, including 'Avalanche', with white flowers, 'Firmament', with sky-blue flowers and silvery stems to 40cm, and 'Mystery Rose', with pink flowers.

Cynoglossum cheirifolium L.   A silvery biennial with small, purplish or deep blue flowers, native of SW Europe from Portugal to Sicily and North Africa, growing in dry, grassy and rocky places, flowering in March–May. Stems 25–40cm. Flowers around 8mm across. Nutlets burr-like, with a thickened border. A very attractive plant, common in SE Spain. Seed should be sown in mid- or late summer for flowering the following spring.

Heliotropium arborescens L. syn. *H. peruvianum* L. (*Boraginaceae*) **Cherry Pie**, **Common Heliotrope**   A shrubby perennial with hairy leaves and masses of small, sweetly scented, white flowers, becoming purple as they age, native of Peru, flowering most of the year. Stems to 2m; leaves to 8cm; flowers to 5mm across, varying in different cultivars from white to dark blue and purple. This was a very popular plant in Victorian conservatories, the plants being trained and pinched to shape, and brought indoors for their sweet, rich scent. It is also commonly planted as an annual in summer bedding schemes.

Most named cultivars, such as the mauve and strongly-scented 'Chatsworth', are grown from cuttings, but **'Marine'**, a spreading variety around 40cm across with fine, deep lavender-blue flowers, can be raised from seed. It should be sown at around 20°C in late winter or early spring, and planted out when danger of frost is past.

Several white-flowered annual species of *Heliotropium* are found in E Europe, Turkey and SW Asia. They mostly germinate in spring and flower through the summer.

Forget-me-not, *Myosotis sylvatica*, with tulips, wallflowers and white *Muscari*

Cryptantha intermedia in the hills above
Malibu Beach, California

Myosotis sylvatica Ehrh. ex Hoffm.
(*Boraginaceae*) **Forget-me-not**   A biennial
or short-lived perennial with softly hairy leaves
and deep blue flowers, with a yellow eye when
fresh. Native of most of Europe, excluding
Spain and Portugal, with subspecies in
Turkey, the Caucasus and N Iran, growing in
open woods, flowering in March–September.
Stems much-branched, to 50cm. Flowers to
1cm across, but often less. This is one of the
most popular of garden flowers. More compact
varieties have been raised for bedding, and
there are also white- and pink-flowered forms.
If blue-flowered plants are moved while in
flower, they often turn pink. Forget-me-nots
do best in rich, moist soil and a partially
shaded position. If too dry, the plants die
down prematurely and suffer from powdery
mildew. Pull out the old plants when they have
finished flowering, as they are unattractive in
seed, and lay them where you want them to
come up next year. Seedlings will appear with
the first cool rains of autumn, and flower the
following spring.

Cynoglossum cheirifolium in the mountains south of Granada

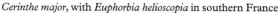
Cerinthe major, with *Euphorbia helioscopia* in southern France

Cerinthe major 'Purpurascens' in cultivation

Arnebia cornuta on dry hills near Samarkhand

Nonea lutea in the order beds at Kew

Arnebia cornuta auct. (*Boraginaceae*)
An upright winter annual with narrow, hairy leaves and yellow flowers, which have dark spots when they open, native of Central Asia, growing in dry, gravelly places, flowering in March–May. Stems 20–40cm. Flowers 1.8cm across, the dark spots fading as the flower ages. Although it was cultivated from its introduction in 1888 until around 1915, this attractive plant does not seem to be in cultivation at present. The name is uncertain, as *A. cornuta* (Ledeb.) Fisch. & Mey. is now considered a synonym of *A. decumbens* (Vent.) Cosson & Kralik, which has unspotted flowers.

Cerinthe major L. (*Boraginaceae*)
An upright or spreading winter annual with leaves that are white-blotched when young, followed by striking, often blue-green bracts that almost hide the tubular flowers. It is native of Portugal and the Mediterranean area, growing in grassy places below 100m, flowering in March–May. Stems to 60cm.

Flowers 1.5–3cm long, 5–8mm in diameter, either yellow, reddish or purplish.

Sow the seed in autumn in mild areas, otherwise in spring. Self-sown seedlings will survive mild winters.

'Purpurascens' This very fine, dark, cultivated variety seems to have arrived back in Europe having been popularized in Australia or New Zealand. If it is kept well watered, it will flower until killed by hard frosts. Similar forms with ultramarine-blue bracts are common in S Spain; the greener-bracted forms are more common in S France and Italy.

Nonea lutea (Descr.) DC. (*Boraginaceae*)
A bristly winter annual with yellow flowers, native of NE Turkey, the Caucasus, S Russia and N Iran, and naturalised elsewhere in Europe, growing in open ground and on rocky slopes, flowering in April–June. Stems to 60cm. Leaves oblong-lanceolate to linear-lanceolate. Flowers 1.1–1.8cm, the lobes spreading, with a ring of hairs and small scales

in the throat. Easily grown, and with flowers like a yellow *Pulmonaria*, but distinguished by the scales in the throat.

Omphalodes linifolia (L.) Moench (*Boraginaceae*) A pale blue-green winter annual with white flowers, native of SW Europe from Portugal to S France, and of North Africa, growing in dry, open places, usually on limestone, flowering in April–June. Stems to 40cm, usually around 20cm, with lanceolate to linear leaves. Inflorescence without bracts. Flowers 5–10mm across, rarely bluish. Nutlets with an incurved, irregularly toothed wing. An easily grown but rather short-lived annual, attractive and valuable for its very pale leaves. Other annual species include *O. littoralis* Lehm., with small, white flowers, from the Atlantic coast of France, *O. brassicifolia* (Lag.) Sweet, with white flowers and broad, amplexicaul leaves, from S Spain and North Africa, and *O. kuzinskyanae* Willk., with blue flowers, from NW Spain and Portugal.

Cerinthe major with purple flowers, wild near Ronda in southern Spain

Omphalodes linifolia with catmint

Verbena bonariensis with *Callistemon* and *Perovskia* at Tapeley Park, Devon

Verbena bonariensis at Quince House

Verbena tenuisecta 'Imagination' at Wisley

Verbena   Although they are mostly perennials or shrubs, many of the ornamental species of *Verbena*, in the *Verbenaceae*, are treated as annuals and will flower in the first year from seed. The genus contains around 200 species, of which 2 or 3 are found in Europe, and the remainder in North and South America.

Verbena bonariensis L.   A tall, stiff, upright perennial with purple flowers, native of South America in Argentina, S Brazil, Uruguay and Paraguay, growing in wet fields and open ground, flowering in late summer and autumn.

Plants often flower in the first year from seed. Stems square, to 1.5m. Leaves linear, sessile, amplexicaul. Inflorescence branched, flat-topped, with small, purple flowers around 1mm across. This will survive a few degrees of frost in a well-drained soil. Easily grown and most effective if planted in a mass. The plants often seed themselves. Adored by bees and butterflies, especially, in England, red admirals and small tortoiseshells in late summer.

Verbena tenuisecta Briq.   A prostrate perennial with usually reddish-purple flowers, native of South America, and now widely

naturalised on road verges in California, Arizona and N Mexico, flowering in summer and autumn. Stems to 30cm or more, creeping and rooting. Leaves triangular in outline and divided many times into linear segments. Inflorescence elongating in fruit. Flowers around 1cm across. Calyx hairs ascending-spreading, not glandular. Often confused, as in our *Perennials* vol. 2, with *V. tenera* Spreng., which has calyx hairs adpressed.

   'Imagination'   A seed-raised variety, close to *V. tenuisecta*, or perhaps a hybrid of it, with deeply divided leaves and creeping stems with numerous, small heads of blue-purple flowers.

Verbena 'Lipstick' (See page 214)

Verbena 'Adonis Light Blue' (See page 214)

Verbena bonariensis with *Crocosmia* 'Lucifer', cardoons and tamarix at Bressingham, Norfolk

Verbena 'Violette' (See page 214)

Verbena with silver-leaved *Lotus berthelotii* and *Plechostachys serpyllifolia* in the Dutch Garden at Hestercombe, Somerset

Verbena 'Silver Anne' (See page 214)

Verbena 'Romance Lavender'

Verbena 'Pink Parfait'

Verbena 'Romance Pink'

Verbena 'Peaches and Cream'

Verbena 'Rasberry Crush'

Verbena 'Sissinghurst'

Verbena ×hybrida hort., syn. *V. ×hortensis* hort. (*Verbenaceae*) **Common Garden Verbena** A complex race of hybrids derived from the South American species *V. incisa, V. peruviana, V. phlogiflora* and *V. teucrioides,* grown since 1837; hundreds of varieties were raised in the 19th century. Stems generally spreading and rooting. Flowers 1–2cm across, in flattish heads 6–8cm across. Many of the modern strains can be raised from seed to flower the same year. Other named varieties need to be bought as young plants, then overwintered as rooted cuttings in a frost-free greenhouse. Sow seed in heat (21–24°C) in early spring and put out young plants when all danger of frost is past and the soil has begun to warm up. Illustrated here are:

'Adonis Light Blue' A seed-raised variety with flowers of a good bright blue and stems around 20cm. (Illustrated on page 213.)

'Arrow' series: 'Pink', 'Rose', 'Scarlet with Eye' and **'White'**.

'Blue Lagoon' A seed-raised variety with flowers of a good clear blue and stems to around 25cm.

'Derby' mixed A seed-raised variety with stems to 20cm; many of the flowers have white eyes.

'Garden Party' A mixture of colours, usually with a white eye.

'Lipstick' A cutting-raised variety with stems trailing to 30cm. (Illustrated on page 213.)

'Novalis' series A seed-raised series with fairly upright stems to 30cm, and rather large flowers. Shown here are the colour forms: **'Bright Scarlet', Brilliant Rose', 'Deep Blue with Eye', 'Rose Pink with Eye', 'Rose Red with Eye', 'Scarlet with Eye'** and **'White'**.

'Peaches and Cream' A seed-raised variety with stems to 25cm.

'Pink Parfait' A cutting-raised variety with trailing stems to 45cm and very striking, bicoloured flowers.

'Rasberry Crush' A seed-raised variety with stems to 30cm tall.

'Romance Pink' and **'Romance Lavender'** From a seed-raised series with dwarf plants to 15cm tall, available as some single colours or as a mixture.

'Sparkle' series A seed-raised series with dwarf plants to 15cm, available as some single colours or as a mixture. Shown here is **'Scarlet'**, sometimes called **'Sandy Scarlet'**.

'Silver Anne' A cutting-raised variety with trailing stems to 45cm. (Illustrated page 213.)

'Sissinghurst' A cutting-raised variety with trailing stems to 45cm.

'Violette' (Illustrated on page 213) A seed-raised variety close to, and probably a hybrid of, *V. rigida* Sprengel, syn. *V. venosa* Gillies, from Argentina and S Brazil; a tuberous-rooted perennial often grown as an annual, with coarse, upright stems and flat heads of purplish flowers. Stems leaves narrowly ovate, shallowly toothed. Apart from the normal purple-flowered *V. rigida* there is a lovely pale blue variety **'Polaris'**.

COMMON GARDEN VERBENA

'Garden Party'

'Sparkle Scarlet'

'Blue Lagoon'

'Derby'
mixed

'Novalis Scarlet
with Eye'

'Novalis
Brilliant Rose'

'Novalis Rose Pink with Eye'

'Arrow Rose'

'Peaches and
Cream'

'Arrow White'

'Novalis Rose Red
with Eye'

'Arrow Scarlet
with Eye'

'Novalis Bright Scarlet'

'Novalis Deep Blue with Eye'

'Novalis White'

'Arrow Pink'

Specimens from Colegrave Seeds, July 23rd, ½ life-size

Molucella laevis on dry hills near Tuz Gölu south of Ankara in September

Molucella laevis L. (*Labiatae*) **Bells of Ireland** A spring annual with the light green calyx much enlarging in fruit to form rather papery, green bells, native of SW Asia from Turkey and Cyprus to Caucasia, Syria and Iraq, growing in cornfields and vineyards, flowering in April–June. Stems erect, to 75cm. Leaves opposite, ovate, crenate. Inflorescence of many axillary whorls; calyx with white, reticulate veins. Flowers small, white or pinkish-mauve and fragrant. Flowering and fruiting in late summer and useful for cut flowers when dry.

Salvia argentea L. (*Labiatae*) A densely hairy biennial or short-lived perennial, usually grown as a half-hardy annual or for its overwintering rosette of silver leaves, native of the S Mediterranean and North Africa, growing on rocky hillsides, flowering in early summer. Stems in the second year to 1m tall, bearing a large, many-branched panicle. Leaves simple, ovate to oblong-ovate, upper surface rugose and pubescent, lower surface densely pubescent. Inflorescence with many whorls of 4–10 white or yellowish flowers flecked with pink or violet, widely spaced. Calyces with long, mucronate teeth. Upper lip of flowers strongly sickle-shaped.

Salvia carduacea Benth., syn. *S. gossypina* Benth. A woolly winter annual resembling the thistle genus *Carduus* in leaf shape and spines, native of California and Baja California, growing on open desert plains and among rocks, flowering in July–September. Stems 10–50cm, four angled. Leaves pinnatifid, lobed and spiny. Flowers in clusters, bracts spine-tipped. Calyx densely clad in long hair. Flowers violet, tube with a ring of hair within, middle lobe of lower lip with lacerated margin.

Salvia columbariae Benth. An attractive winter annual with clear blue flowers, found growing in similar situations to *S. carduacea*, flowering throughout summer. Stems 10–50cm, erect. Leaves 3–7cm long, pinnatifid, lobes rounded, coarsely hairy on both surfaces, upper surface finely blistered. Inflorescences clustered, bracts rounded, apices notched and spinose. Flowers smooth within, lips entire. It produces a mucilage around the seed coats when wet, which is used as a valuable herbal medicine for coughs known as *chia* in Mexico.

Salvia viridis L., syn. *S. horminum* L. A tall summer annual with small, violet flowers, distributed all round the Mediterranean, flowering during late summer and autumn. Stems in gardens to 65cm, although wild plants may be very short, usually branched; in cultivation the flowers are topped by a coloured tuft of bracts, although in wild plants these may be insignificant. Leaves oblong-ovate, both surfaces rough and coarsely hairy. Inflorescence whorls fairly congested. Bracts to 2.5cm across, broadly ovate, persistent, usually violet in wild plants but can be pink, purple, red or white in cultivation and often with noticeably reticulate veins. Flowers rather small, sometimes white.

Plants in cultivation with prominent coloured bracts are distinguished as *S. viridis* var. *comata* Held. The var. *viridis* is not showy and therefore of little garden merit.

Molucella laevis

Salvia viridis wild form in SW Turkey

Salvia viridis mixed colours

Salvia viridis white form with white Veronica

Salvia columbariae

Salvia argentea in the gravel garden at the old Vicarage, Edington

Salvia columbariae in the Joshua Tree National Monument, Mojave Desert in late March

Salvia carduacea at the Theodore Payne Foundation

Salvia farinacea 'Alba' with shrubby *Argyranthemum* and cosmos in Paris

Monarda citriodora Cerv. ex Lag. (*Labiatae*)
An aromatic spring annual, strongly
lemon-scented, native of southern USA and
N Mexico, growing in meadows, flowering in
late summer and autumn. Stems to 60cm,
erect, sometimes branching, softly pubescent.
Leaves simple, lanceolate to oblong-lanceolate,
finely hairy throughout. Inflorescence of
capitate glomerules above pinkish or purplish,
leaf-like bracts. Flowers white or pink, dotted
with purple within.

Perilla frutescens (L.)Britton var. **crispa**
(Benth.) Deane ex Bailey, syn. *P. ocymoides*
var. *crispa*; *Dentidia nankinensis*; *Perilla
frutescens* var. *nankinensis* (*Labiatae*)
An aromatic summer annual, always with
purple leaves, native of E Asia, particularly
China, growing in field margins and
roadsides, flowering in late summer. Stems
branched, to 1m. Leaves ovate or broadly
ovate, apex acuminate, margins deeply serrate
or laciniate, sometimes crispate. Flowers
small, white or pinkish. Grown as an
ornamental for its foliage. 'Atropurpurea' has
uncrispate, deep reddish-purple leaves.
Var. *frutescens* is not in cultivation in Britain.
It has larger calyces and leaves which are
usually green and more circular with coarsely
serrate margins. It is cultivated in China
where the leaves are used as a flavouring and
the oil from the seeds is used to make paint
and to waterproof paper. Another variety,
var. *purpurascens,* has short calyces and leaves
with coarsely serrated margins, but these are
purple above and green beneath.

Salvia coccinea Murray, syn. *S. pseudococcinea*
Jacq., *S. rosea* Vahl (*Labiatae*)   A short- lived
perennial usually grown as a half-hardy
annual, with narrow, scarlet flowers, originally
most probably a native of Brazil but now very
widely naturalised and occurring as a wayside
weed in Mexico and many other subtropical
and tropical countries, flowering throughout
summer and autumn. Stems branched,
30–60cm with a few bristly hairs. Leaves
entire, triangular-ovate, more or less softly
hairy on both surfaces and serrate. Flowers in
3–6 flowered whorls, tube 1.3–1.7cm long,
straight. Stamens red, long-exserted. Cultivars
include 'Cherry Blossom', with bright pink
flowers, **'Coral Nymph'**, with salmon-pink
flowers, 'Lactea', with white flowers and **'Lady
in Red'**, with rather large, scarlet flowers.

Salvia farinacea Benth.   An upright
perennial, usually cultivated as a half-hardy
annual, with deep blue flowers, native of
Mexico, growing in the understorey of dry

Salvia splendens, a deep purple variety

Salvia coccinea 'Coral Nymph' at Suttons

Monarda citriodora

Perilla frutescens var. *crispa*

Salvia farinacea 'Strata'

Salvia coccinea 'Lady in Red'

Salvia splendens 'Splendidissima' at Villa Pallavicino, Lago Maggiore

pine forests, flowering from midsummer to autumn. Stems 20–100cm, arising from a woody base, grey-haired. Leaves ovate-lanceolate to oblong-lanceolate, entire to widely serrate. Inflorescences densely spicate, erect, covered in mealy hairs, with whorls of 12 or more flowers. Calyx densely covered with soft, fine, blue hairs. Flowers sometimes white. Cultivars include: 'Victoria' and **'Strata'**, flowers very dark blue, **'Alba'** and 'Cirrus', flowers white.

'Indigo Spires' is of hybrid origin, probably between *S. farinacea* and *S. mexicana*. It is a showy plant 80–140cm tall, with striking, deep blue, densely flowered spikes covered in mealy hairs.

Salvia splendens Roemer & Schultes
A much-branched shrub with tubular, scarlet flowers, usually grown as a half-hardy annual, native of Brazil, growing on forest margins, flowering throughout summer and autumn. Stems 20–120cm. Leaves ovate, surfaces hairless. Inflorescences in 1–3 flowered whorls. Bracts ovate, 1–2cm long, showy, deciduous, scarlet. Calyx membranaceous, inflated in fruit, scarlet. Flowers scarlet in wild plants. Many cultivars are grown with a wide range of flower colours, including salmon-pink, lilac, lavender, purple, white and dark red; some newer cultivars have different coloured bracts and flowers and many cultivars are listed by seed suppliers as series. 'Blaze of Fire' grows 20–30cm tall and has bright scarlet bracts, crimson calyces and scarlet corollas. **'Splendidissima'** is also around 30cm. 'Van-Houttei', a tall cultivar 80–100cm, is near to the wild species with very dark red calyces and large scarlet flowers.

Satureja seleriana Loes., syn.
S. guatemalensis Standl. ex Epling & Jativa (*Labiatae*)   An aromatic, sprawling, half-hardy subshrub, often grown as an annual in cultivation, native of Guatemala, growing among rocks in the wild, flowering throughout summer. Stems loosely spreading to 45cm. Leaves glabrous, strongly aromatic, ovate. Flowers crimson, calyx with teeth more than 2mm long, corolla tube inflated, without a ring of hairs within, to 3cm long, borne in the leaf axils on long pedicels.

Salvia coccinea

Satureja seleriana

Bellardia trixago on the island of Kos in April

Parentucellia viscosa near Cadiz in SW Spain

Castilleja minor in Colorado

Rhinanthus minor with a pink Centaurea
in NW Spain

Bellardia trixago (L.) All. (*Scrophulariaceae*)
A sticky, upright, semi-parasitic annual with
pink-and-white, or plain-yellow flowers, native
of the Mediterranean area, eastwards to the
Caucasus and Iran, southwards to Ethiopia
and E Africa in South Africa, flowering in
March–June. Naturalised in the Americas and
Australia, growing in grassy, rocky places on
limestone, wet meadows and cornfields.
Stems to 70cm. Leaves 3–9cm, linear to
linear-oblong. Flowers 1.7–2.3cm long, the
two colour forms sometimes growing
together. An attractive plant, which needs the
presence of other annuals to grow into a good
specimen.

Castilleja minor (Gray) Gray
(*Scrophulariaceae*)   An erect, hairy annual
with linear to lanceolate leaves and red-tipped
bracts, native of North America in the
Rockies, from Nebraska to New Mexico, and
westwards to Nevada and Arizona, growing in
sage-bush scrub in moist places, flowering in
May–September. Stems to 1m. Leaves 4–8cm
long. Flowers greenish-yellow, the upper lip
1.2–2cm, much longer than the lower.
Castilleja, of which there are around 200
mainly perennial species in North and South
America, are partial parasites; their
combination of red bracts and green or yellow
flowers is typical of flowers pollinated by
hummingbirds.

Digitalis lanata Ehrh. (*Scrophulariaceae*)
A tall, slender, biennial or short-lived
perennial with small, white, brown-veined
flowers, native of SE Europe from Hungary
south-eastwards to NW Turkey, growing in
scrub and open woods, flowering in May–July.
Stems to 80cm or more, often purplish, hairy.
Leaves oblong-lanceolate to oblanceolate.
Flowers crowded on the spike, 1.8–2.5cm
long, with the middle lobe of the lower lip
1–1.3cm. Easily grown in rather dry partial
shade.

Digitalis purpurea L.   A tall biennial or
short-lived perennial with purplish, pink or
white, tubular flowers, native of W Europe
from Ireland south-eastwards to Sardinia,
growing in scrub and open woods and on
hillsides, flowering in June–August. Stems to

2m or more. Leaves ovate to lanceolate.
Flowers loose on the spike, 4–5.5cm long,
usually spotted inside. Easily grown in rather
dry partial shade.
  Two subspecies from Spain and Portugal
have white-woolly leaves and stems, and tend
to be more perennial, with several stems from
the base: subsp. *mariana* (Boiss.) Rivas Goday
has purplish flowers, and subsp. *heywoodii*
P. & M. Silva has white flowers. *D. thapsi* L.,
which is common in rocky areas in C Spain
and E Portugal, has stems and leaves covered
with yellowish, sticky hairs. It is usually
perennial.

Melampyrum arvense L. (*Scrophulariaceae*)
Field Cow Wheat   An upright, semi-
parasitic annual with green or pinkish, deeply
divided bracts and small purplish flowers,
native of much of Europe, growing in grassy
meadows and on banks, flowering in
May-August. Stems 15-50cm. Leaves
lanceolate, entire or toothed. Flowers 2–2.5cm
long.An attractive plant for a meadow garden,
conspicuous by roadsides in C France.

Parentucellia viscosa (L.) (*Scrophulariaceae*)
Caruel   A sticky, upright, semi-parasitic
annual with pale yellow flowers, native of
W Europe including S England and the
Mediterranean area, eastwards to N Iran, and
naturalised in South Africa, the Americas and
Australia, growing in damp, grassy places,
flowering in April–July. Stems to 70cm. Leaves
1–4.5cm, oblong to lanceolate. Flowers
1.5–2.5cm long. This probably needs the
presence of other annuals to grow into a good
specimen, and is an attractive addition to a
wildflower meadow.

Rhinanthus minor L. (*Scrophulariaceae*)
Yellow Rattle   An upright, semi-parasitic
annual with yellow flowers, native of much
of Europe except the Mediterranean area,
growing in grassy meadows and on dunes,
flowering in May-August. Stems to 50cm.
Leaves 3–9cm, linear to linear-oblong.
Flowers 1.3–1.5cm long, the calyx becoming
papery in fruit, and rattling in the wind.
An attractive plant for a meadow garden,
which is said to have the useful property of
suppressing the growth of grass.

Digitalis lanata

Melampyrum arvense in the Massif Centrale

Digitalis purpurea, white form, with ox-eye daisies and *Sanguisorba armena* at Quince House

Verbascum pulverulentum in the university Botanic Garden, Cambridge

Verbascum lychnitis, wild on a sandy bank near Leeds, Kent

Verbascum sinuatum on the ruins of Phaselis near Antalya, SW Turkey

Mullein The genus *Verbascum* in the family *Scrophulariaceae* contains around 360 species, of which 228 are recorded from Turkey and 87 from Europe. Most are tall biennials with hairy leaves and yellow flowers. To be at all confident of the identification, it is necessary to have the flowers, especially the stamens, the fruit, the basal leaves, and a portion of the stem with its leaves, as well as a note of the size and habit of the plant. *V. thapsus* L. is the most common species in NW Europe in gardens and waste places; it is often attacked by the colourful yellow and black caterpillars of the mullein shark, *Cucullia verbasci*, which overwinter in a cocoon in the earth to emerge in May and June.

Verbascum bombyciferum Boiss. A very large biennial with woolly stems and leaves and yellow flowers, native of NW Turkey on Ulu Dag (Bithynian Mount Olympus) and around Bursa, growing in oak scrub and pine forest and among limestone rocks and ancient walls, at up to 550m, flowering in May–June. Stems to 1.5m, or to 2.4m in gardens, usually unbranched. Flowers 3–4cm across, in dense clusters of 3–7, their bracts and calyces embedded in the wool. Stamens 5, unequal, the filaments with whitish-yellow hairs, those of the 2 lower stamens glabrous near apex.

This is possibly the most handsome of the mulleins for garden use. Sow the seed in early spring, and put the young plants into their final places in late summer. In wet areas, protect the rosettes from excessive rain in winter. This species is sometimes called 'Broussa', an old spelling for Bursa.

Verbascum lychnitis L. **White Mullein**
A sparsely hairy biennial with branched stems of small, white flowers, native of most of Europe except the Mediterranean region, growing on sandy banks and hills, flowering in June–August. Basal leaves greenish above, white beneath. Stems to 1.5m. Flowers sometimes yellow, 1.2–2cm across, on pedicels 6–11mm long. Stamens 5, equal, the filaments with whitish or yellow hairs.

Verbascum pulverulentum Vill. **Hoary Mullein** A floccose biennial with branched stems of small, yellow flowers, native of most of W Europe eastwards to Greece and Romania, growing on roadsides and hills, flowering in June–August. Basal leaves often wavy-edged or crenate, greenish when mature. Stems to 1.2m. Flowers 1.8–2.5cm across, on pedicels 2–5mm long. Stamens 5, equal, the filaments with whitish hairs.

Verbascum sinuatum L.   A densely greyish- or yellowish-haired biennial, with wavy or lobed leaves and branched stems of yellow flowers, native of most of S Europe eastwards to Iran and Turkmenia, growing on roadsides, hills, and dunes by the sea, flowering in May–October. Basal leaves incised-lobed or pinnatifid. Stems to 1m, with long branches from the base. Flowers 1.5–3cm across, on pedicels to 4mm long, in widely spaced clusters of 1–7. Stamens 5, equal, the filaments with purple hairs, those of the 2 lower stamens glabrous near apex. An attractive plant, common near the Mediterranean coast.

Verbascum thapsus L. **Aaron's Rod**
A woolly biennial with usually unbranched stems and yellow flowers, native of most of Europe and Asia eastwards to the W Himalayas and China, growing on chalky hills and dunes and in dry waste places, open forest and scrub, flowering in June–August. Basal leaves woolly. Stems to 2m. Flowers 1.2–3cm across, on pedicels 1–5mm long. Stamens 5, unequal, the filaments of the 3 upper with whitish or yellow hairs, of the 2 lower glabrous or sparsely hairy with decurrent anthers. This plant usually seeds itself in gardens once it is established; it has fine rosettes in spring, but tends to become tatty around flowering time.

Verbascum thapsus

Verbascum bombyciferum at West Dean Gardens, Sussex

Verbascum sinuatum at Phaselis

A bed of antirrhinums at Glenbervie with scarlet *Tropaeolum speciosum* on the yew behind

Snapdragon   Most of the 20 or so species of *Antirrhinum*, in the family *Scrophulariaceae*, are perennials, found growing on cliffs and rocky places in the SW Mediterranean area from Portugal to Sicily, but there is a group of small-flowered, mostly annual species in western North America. Most of the cultivars that are grown as annuals are derived from the European *A. majus* (see page 226) and related species. The trailing varieties bred for hanging baskets are shrubby perennials, available as young plants, although the variety 'Chinese Lanterns' (not shown), is grown from seed; these varieties are bred from *A. hispanicum* (see page 226) and related species.

In Britain seed of the annual varieties is generally sown indoors at around 15°C in early February and the young plants grown slowly and planted out in mid-May to flower in July and August. Light, but fertile chalky soil is best. In mild areas, seed may be sown in late summer, and the plants grown slowly through the winter in a cold frame or nursery bed and planted out in early spring. Seed sown outdoors in late March will flower in late summer and autumn. Particularly beautiful plants will have a good chance of surviving for a second year if seeding is prevented and the plant is put in a hole in an old wall or crevice between rocks.

Some cultivars are peloric (the flowers are not snapdragon-like, but are radially symmetrical), others are double, with twisted petals in the centre of the flower. Varieties vary in height from 'Giant Forcing', raised especially for cutting, with stems to 1.25m, to 'Floral Showers', with trailing stems to 20cm.

'Apple Blossom'   Stems much-branched, to 90cm. Flowers large, pale pink, in a rather loose spike. Usually behaves as a biennial or perennial.

'Corona' mixed   An F_2 hybrid. Stems to 45cm. Flowers of several colours, available as a mixture.

'Coronette' series   Raised by Sluis & Groot N.V., Enkhuizen, Holland. F_1 hybrids. Plants 50–75cm, upright and branched, with dense spikes of large, single flowers, available in 9 separate colours or as a mixture. Flowering in early July, after planting out in mid-May.

'Candyman' mixed   An unusual variety with striped and stippled flowers. Plants to 40cm.

'Liberty' series F_1 hybrids. Plants 60–75cm, upright and branched, with a long, dense spike of single flowers; available in 9 separate colours or as a mixture.

'Mme Butterfly' mixed F_1 hybrids. Plants 60–75cm, upright and branched, with a dense spike of double flowers, in shades of white, yellow, orange, pink and crimson.

'Little Darling' mixed   Raised by Goldsmith Seeds Inc., Gilroy, California. F_1 hybrids. Plants around 55cm, upright and branched, with a dense spike of double flowers, in shades of white, yellow, orange, pink and crimson. Very quick to flower, by early June after planting out in mid-May.

'Princess'   An F_1 hybrid. Stems much-branched, around 30cm. Flowers white with a purple eye.

Antirrhinum 'Apple Blossom'

Antirrhinum 'Candyman' mixed

SNAPDRAGON

'Liberty Pink'

'Liberty Rose'

'Liberty Bronze

'Liberty White'

'Liberty Crimson'

'Liberty Yellow'

'Liberty Cherry'

'Liberty Lavender'

'Coronette Yellow'

'Coronette Rose'

'Coronette Pink'

'Coronette Orchid'

'Coronette Bronze'

'Coronette Cherry'

'Coronette White'

'Coronette Crimson'

'Coronette Scarlet'

'Mme Butterfly' mixed

'Corona' mixed

'Little Darling' mixed

'Princess'

Specimens from Colegrave Seeds, July 23rd, ⅔ life-size

Antirrhinum latifolium in the limestone hills above Grasse, in France

Antirrhinum hispanicum subsp. *mollissimum* on a dry wall at Quince House

Antirrhinum hispanicum Chav.
(*Scrophulariaceae*)   A trailing subshrub with
short spikes of white or pink flowers, native of
SE Spain and North Africa, growing on rocks
and old walls, flowering in April–June. Stems
to 60cm, with glandular hairs. Leaves
lanceolate to orbicular, 5–35mm long. Flowers
2–2.5cm, sometimes with a yellow mouth.
Subsp. *hispanicum*, syn. *A. glutinosum* Boiss. &
Reut., has lanceolate to broadly ovate leaves
and stem hairs less than 0.5mm long.
Subspecies **mollissimum** (Rothm.) D.A.
Webb has broadly ovate to orbicular stem
leaves and longer stem hairs, to 2mm.
'Avalanche' is a white form. *A. hispanicum* is
probably one of the main parents of the
trailing cultivars, which have names such as
'Chandelier' and 'Candalabra', and are
available in pink, lilac and pale yellow, for
training in large urns and hanging baskets.

Antirrhinum latifolium Mill.   A perennial
with long, upright spikes of yellow flowers,
native of NE Spain eastwards to C Italy,
growing on limestone rocks and stony slopes,
flowering in April–November. Stems
glandular-pubescent, little-branched, to 1m.
Leaves 2–7cm long, ovate, obtuse. Flowers
3.3–4.8cm. A handsome plant, common in
S France.

Antirrhinum majus L. **Snapdragon**
A perennial with spikes of pink or purple
flowers, native of the W Mediterranean area
and Portugal, but widely naturalised
elsewhere, growing on old walls, cliffs and
rocky places, flowering in April–November.
Stems to 1.5m, often scrambling, glabrous or

Misopates orontium in South Africa

Antirrhinum majus subsp. *majus* on
La Gomera

Antirrhinum majus subsp. *tortuosum* on Gibraltar

glandular-pubescent. Leaves linear to ovate.
Flowers 3–4.5cm long.

Subsp. **tortuosum** (Bosc) Rouy, with
linear or linear-oblong leaves to 5mm wide
and flowers 3–3.7cm long, is commonly found
wild in S Spain, North Africa and Sicily.

Subsp. **majus**, with elliptic-lanceolate to
linear-oblong leaves and flowers to 4.5cm
long, is native of NE Spain to SC France, and
widely naturalised elsewhere from cultivation
in the past. Seed of these more natural
varieties are available from Chiltern Seeds.

Misopates orontium (L.) Raf.
(*Scrophulariaceae*) **Weasel's Snout**
A slender annual with small, red, snapdragon-
like flowers, native of much of W and S Europe
and SW Asia, and naturalised elsewhere, such
as in North America and South Africa,
growing in cornfields and sandy places,
flowering in April–August. Stems to 50cm.
Leaves 2–5cm, linear to oblong-elliptic.
Flowers 1–1.5cm long. Becoming very rare in
NW Europe, because of agricultural
weedkillers. *M. calycinum* Rothm., from France
and Portugal to Sardinia, Sicily and North
Africa, has white flowers 1.8–2.2cm long.

An antirrhinum self-seeded in an old kitchen garden in France

Linaria amethystea

Linaria viscosa 'Gold' with candytuft

Linaria spartea near Valladolid

Linaria maroccana 'Fairy Bouquet'

Toadflax The genus *Linaria* Mill., in the family *Scrophulariaceae*, consists of around 150 species of annuals and perennials in Europe, North Africa and Asia; they are particularly common and diverse in Spain and Morocco, and it is from this area that the ornamental species have been brought into cultivation. The flowers are all of the snapdragon type, usually with a long, downward-pointing spur. The seeds form a valuable aid to the identification of the species.

The largest flowers in the genus are found in the perennial *L. triornithophora* (L.) Willd., so called because the flowers look like 3 little parrots perched on the stem.

Linaria aeruginea (Gouan) Cav., syn. *L. reticulata* auct., *L. nevadensis* (Boiss.) Boiss. & Reut., and the cultivars 'Gemstones' and 'Crown Jewels' are perennials for the rock garden, sometimes grown as annuals.

Linaria amethystea (Lam.) Hoffmans. & Link, syn. *L. broussonetii* (Poiret) Chav. An upright annual with narrow leaves and usually purplish, rarely cream or yellow, purple-spotted flowers, with a long spur, native of Spain, Portugal and North Africa, growing in open ground and cultivated fields, flowering in April–June. Stems to 35cm, often with purple glandular hairs. Leaves linear to oblanceolate, 4–20mm. Flowers 1–2.2cm, with the spur 4–11mm. Racemes lax in fruit. Seeds blackish, with a tuberculate disc and finely papillose wing. This description covers subsp. *amethystea*, under which the commonly used name *L. broussonetii* is now included. Cultivated *L. broussonetii* has bright yellow, spotted flowers on tall, slender, glandular stems.

Linaria elegans Cav. A slender, upright annual with long spikes of deep purple, purplish-pink or reddish flowers, native of N and C Spain and N Portugal, growing on grassy roadsides and among bracken in open pine forest, flowering in May–July. Stems to 70cm. Leaves to 3.5cm, filiform to linear-lanceolate, alternate. Flowers 1.7–2.5cm long, the spur 1–1.4cm, curved. Seeds 0.6mm, dark grey, finely tuberculate, not winged. A most attractive species, for some reason seldom cultivated, common in the Sierra de Gredos.

Linaria maroccana Hook. fil. An upright annual with linear leaves, and bright purple flowers in the wild, native of Morocco and naturalised here and there in North America, growing in open ground and sandy fields,

Linaria maroccana 'Northern Lights'

Linaria elegans in the Sierra de Gredos above Arenas de San Pedro

Linaria elegans with bracken in pine woods in the Sierra de Gredos

Linaria elegans, reddish form

flowering in April–June. Stems to 45cm. Leaves 2–4cm. Flowers 1.5cm long, with a long, slender spur. Seeds minute, black, coarsely rugose, not winged.

'Fairy Bouquet'   Raised by Bodger Seeds, El Monte, California, this has flowers in mixed, rather delicate colours. Stems to 25cm. 'Excelsior Hybrids' are similar.

'Northern Lights'   Here the flower colours are more intense, with a preponderance of red. Stems to 60cm.

Linaria spartea (L.) Willd.   A very slender, upright annual with few, narrow leaves and yellow, rarely purplish, stalked flowers with a long, straight spur, native of Spain, Portugal and SW France, growing in open, sandy ground and cultivated fields, flowering in April–August. Stems to 60cm, glabrous, or the inflorescence glandular-hairy. Leaves linear, to 4cm long. Flowers 1.8–3cm, with the spur 9–18mm. Seeds blackish, rugose, not winged.

Linaria viscosa (L.) Dum.-Courset, syn. *L. heterophylla* Desf.   An upright or sprawling annual with narrow leaves and yellow or yellow-and-crimson flowers, native of S Italy, Sicily, S Spain, S Portugal and North Africa, growing in open ground and sandy fields, flowering in April–July. Stems to 60cm, sometimes hairy at the base, the inflorescence densely glandular-pubescent. Leaves linear, to 4cm long. Flowers crowded together, 1.8–3cm, with the spur 9–18mm, on short, erect stalks. Seeds blackish, rugose, not winged. The variety 'Elegans', now called **'Gold'**, is commonly cultivated. The flowers are small, but strikingly bicoloured. It is easy and quick to flower from seed.

Linaria elegans, deep purple form

Mimulus bigelovii in a dry, sandy wash in the Joshua Tree National Monument, Mojave desert, California

Mimulus bigelovii

Mimulus layneae

Collinsia heterophylla Buist ex Graham,
syn. *C. bicolor* Benth. non Raf. **Chinese
Houses** (*Scrophulariaceae*) An upright,
branching winter annual with tiers of purple-
and-white or all-white flowers, native of
California from Humboldt and Shasta Cos
southwards to Baja California, growing in
rather shaded places below 800m, flowering in
March–June. Stems 20–50cm. Leaves 1–7cm
long, lanceolate to narrowly oblong, opposite,
the upper sessile. Flowers 1.5–2cm long, in
whorls of 2–7, the lower lip purplish and
horizontal, the upper white or pale purple and
upright. Of around 17 species of *Collinsia*,
16 are found in California.

Monkey Flower The genus *Mimulus* in the
family *Scrophulariaceae* consists of around 150
species of annuals, perennials and subshrubs,
found in most temperate parts of the world.
Of the 77 species found in California, around
15 are perennial, the rest annual; many of
them are small, jewel-like plants found in
sandy places and washes in the deserts. A few
of these annuals are widespread, but most are
rare and local, and differ only in small details.
Some of the perennial species and hybrids
(shown on p238) are grown as bedding plants
for their often spectacularly spotted flowers.

Mimulus bigelovii (Gray) Gray An often
very small, sticky-haired winter annual with
red-purple flowers, native of SE California
eastwards to Nevada and W Arizona, growing
in sandy or gravelly washes in the desert,
flowering in March–June. Stems 5–25cm.
Leaves elliptic to obovate, acute, 1–3cm long.

Mimulus pictus grown by Lieve Adraensens

Mohavea confertiflora on dry hills above
Anza-Borrego

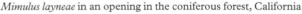

Mimulus layneae in an opening in the coniferous forest, California

Collinsia heterophylla

Flowers 2–3cm long, with a pale yellow throat, finely pubescent outside, mainly clustered near the tops of the stems on very short stalks. Anthers pubescent. Stigmas not exserted. Very common in the Mojave and Colorado deserts and nearby mountains, below 1900m.

Mimulus fremontii (Benth.) Gray, from Monterey and San Benito Cos to Baja California, is superficially similar, but differs in the smooth inner face of the corolla lobes and glabrous anthers. It is found in chaparral, and is especially common in areas that have been recently burnt.

Mimulus laciniatus Gray   An almost glabrous spring annual with divided leaves and yellow flowers with a single large, red spot and several small spots, native of E California from Tuolumne Co. to Tulare Co., growing in damp places and on wet rocks at 1100–3000m, flowering in May–July. Stems 5–30cm. Leaves deeply pinnatifid and lobed, 5–25mm long. Flowers 7–15mm long, on stalks longer than the calyx. Anthers glabrous. Stigmas not exserted.

Mimulus layneae (Greene) Jeps.   An often very small, sticky-haired spring annual with red-purple flowers, native of NE California from Humboldt and Siskiyou Cos southwards to Napa and Fresno Cos, growing in sandy open places, flowering in May–August. Stems 10–20cm. Leaves narrowly oblong to linear, 1–2.5cm long. Flowers 1.3–2cm long, finely pubescent outside, the inner face of the corolla lobes glabrous. Anthers ciliate. Stigmas not exserted.

Mimulus mephiticus Greene   An often very small, sticky-haired spring annual with yellow or red-purple flowers, native of NE California from Plumas to Tulare and Mono Cos, growing in sandy, open places, in coniferous forest at 1500–3000m, flowering in June–August. Stems 2–12cm. Leaves narrowly oblanceolate to broadly linear, 1–2cm long. Flowers 1.2–1.7cm long, finely pubescent outside. Anthers pubescent. Stigmas exserted.

Mimulus pictus (Curran) Gray   A sticky hairy, sprawling winter or spring annual, the flowers veined with red or purple, native of S California in the Tehachapi and Greenhorn mts in Kern Co., growing in dry places in open grassy woodland, at 300–1200m, flowering in Apri–May. Stems 10–30cm. Leaves obovate to oblanceolate, 1–3cm long. Flowers regular, around 1cm across, purple outside, white inside, with T-shaped main veins and thin branching side veins on each truncate lobe.

Mohavea confertiflora (Benth. in DC) Heller (*Scrophulariaceae*) **Ghost Flower** A sticky winter annual with thin, creamy, purple-spotted flowers, native of California and Baja California eastwards to Arizona and Nevada, growing in sandy washes and on gravelly slopes in the desert below 1000m, flowering in March–April. Stems 10–40cm, simple or branched, leafy. Leaves 1–6cm long, linear to ovate-lanceolate. Flowers 2.5–3.5cm long, the lower lip with a hairy palate. A strange-looking plant, often grown in wildflower gardens.

Mimulus mephiticus near Barney Falls

Mimulus laciniatus on Tioga Pass, Yosemite

Nemesia strumosa 'Triumph Red'

Nemesia strumosa, a fine pale yellow form in the trials fields of Kees Sahin in Holland

Nemesia versicolor 'Danish Flag'

Nemesia strumosa a wild yellow-and-white form, at Kirstenbosch

The genus **Nemesia** in the family *Scrophulariaceae* has around 65 species in southern Africa; many of the species in the Cape winter-rainfall area are annuals, whereas most of the species in the summer-rainfall areas of Natal and the Drakensberg are perennials. Most of the cultivated varieties are derived from these two species, *N. strumosa* and *N. versicolor*.

Nemesia strumosa Diels   A winter annual with softly fleshy stems and rounded flowers of red, pink, orange, yellow or white, native of South Africa, in the Western Cape from Piketberg to Malmsbury, growing on sandy flats near the coast, flowering in September–October. Stems 15–30cm. Leaves opposite, lanceolate, toothed. Flowers around 2cm across, with very rounded lobes. This is now very rare in the wild, but commonly cultivated and available in mixed colours, such as 'Carnival', a particularly bright strain, or in separate colours. All are very easy and quick from seed, sown where they are to flower. **'Triumph Red'**   Flowers a particularly intense red, with stems to 20cm.

Nemesia versicolor E. Meyer ex Benth. A winter annual with softly fleshy stems and rounded flowers of blue, blue and white or yellow, native of South Africa, in the Western

Nemesia strumosa yellow form, at Kirstenbosch

Nemesia strumosa pink form, at Kirstenbosch

Nemesia versicolor 'Blue Bird'

Nemesia versicolor 'Blue Bird'

Nemesia versicolor 'Pastel Mixed'

Nemesia versicolor at the Cape of Good Hope

Nemesia versicolor 'KLM'

and Southern Cape from Namaqualand to Knysna, growing on sandy flats, flowering in August–November. Stems 10–50cm. Leaves opposite, lanceolate, toothed. Flowers around 1.5cm across, with the 4 upper lobes narrower than the two lower.

There are several distinctly coloured varieties cultivated:

'KLM' Flowers blue and white; stems 15–20cm.

'Blue Bird' Flowers pale blue with a white throat; stems 15–20cm.

'Danish Flag' and 'National Ensign' Flowers red and white; stems 15–20cm.

'Pastel Mixed' Flowers in a range of soft colours, and has broad upper lobes tending towards *N. strumosa*. Stems to 20cm.

Diascia nana near Sutherland

Diascia namaquensis, east of Kamieskroom

Nemesia leipoldtii purplish form

Nemesia leipoldtii, on the farm Glenlyon, Nieuwoudtville

Nemesia barbata

Nemesia anisocarpa

Diascia Plants in this genus, in the family *Scrophulariaceae*, have recently become very popular as short-lived perennials for pots and raised beds, with flowers in various shades of salmon-pink to white. These perennial species mostly come from the Drakensberg mountains and summer-rainfall areas of South Africa, and prefer cool, moist conditions through the summer. Around 20 of the 50 species in the genus are spring-flowering annuals from the winter-rainfall areas of the Western Cape and Namaqualand, and these include species with orange and deep purple flowers as well as the usual pink. All diascias have 2 conspicuous, often rather baggy spurs, which give them their name, from the Greek *askos*, a wineskin.

Diascia cardiosepala Hiern A small winter annual with mauve-pink flowers with yellow and black markings in the throat, native of South Africa from Namaqualand to the Hex River mountains, growing in sandy places and low scrub, flowering in August–October. Stems to 7cm. Leaves mostly basal, leathery, lobed. Flowers 1.2–1.5cm across. Spurs long, divergent. Fruiting pedicels erect.

Diascia namaquensis Hiern A winter annual with salmon-pink to purple flowers with very long, widely spreading spurs, native of South Africa from Namaqualand to the Calvinia area and southwards to Mamre, growing in sandy places and low scrub, flowering in August–October. Stems to 40cm, branching from the base. Leaves oblanceolate, to 5cm long, variously toothed and lobed. Flowers around 2cm across. Spurs 1.5–2cm long. This is one of the most dramatic species, but generally found only as scattered individual plants.

Diascia nana Schltr. A very small winter annual with pink flowers with yellow and black markings in the throat, native of South Africa in the W Karoo and the Winterberg, growing in damp, gravelly and muddy places, flowering in August–September. Stems to 5cm. Leaves all basal, leathery, lobed. Flowers 8–10mm across. Spurs long, curved and divergent. Fruiting pedicels lying along the ground. Because of the high altitude at which it grows, this species should be hardy as well as quick to grow and flower.

Hemimeris racemosa (Houtt.) Merrill (*Scrophulariaceae*) A diffuse winter annual with masses of small, yellow flowers, native of South Africa in the Cape, from Namaqualand southwards to the Peninsula and eastwards to Knysna, growing on grassy and sandy slopes and flats, flowering in July–October. Stems to 45cm, sparsely hairy. Leaves toothed. Flowers with a pouch at their base, 8–10mm across. *H. sabulosa* L. fil. is a hairier plant with paler flowers 1–1.2cm across, and is found from the Bokkeveld mountains to Caledon.

Nemesia anisocarpa Benth. (*Scrophulariaceae*) A slender, upright winter annual, the flowers with white upper lobes and a yellow lip, native of South Africa in the Western Cape, from Namaqualand to the Cedarberg, growing in sandy places, and flowering in July–September. Stems to 20cm. Leaves mostly basal, shallowly toothed. Flowers 1.5–2cm across, the upper lobes linear and acute, the lip with dark veins and a straight spur.

Diascia cardiosepala at the Tinie Versfeld Reserve

Hemimeris racemosa at the Tinie Versfeld Reserve

Nemesia barbata (Thunb.) Benth.
A small, upright winter annual, the flowers with white upper lobes and a deep blue and white lip, native of South Africa in the Western Cape from Clanwilliam to Swellendam, growing in sandy places, flowering in August–September. Stems to 35cm, branching near the base. Leaves broad and toothed. Flowers 1.2–1.8cm across, the upper lobes short, ovate and rounded, the lip with dark veins and a short, blunt spur.

Nemesia cheiranthos E. Meyer ex Benth.
A slender, upright winter annual, the flowers with long, narrow, white upper lobes and a yellow lip, native of South Africa in the Western Cape, from the Bokkeveldt mountains, Clanwillian and the Piketberg, growing in sandy scrub and rocky slopes, flowering in August–October. Stems to 20cm, branching near the base. Leaves broad and toothed. Flowers 1.8–2.2cm across, the upper lobes long and tapering, mauve at the base, the lip pouched, with a short, straight spur. With its long-horned flowers, this is the most striking of all the species.

Nemesia leipoldtii Hiern   A branching winter annual, the flowers with white upper lobes and a white, 2-lobed lip with a yellow pouch, native of South Africa in the W Karoo, especially around Nieuwoudtville, growing in low scrub on doleritic clay soils, flowering in August–October. Stems to 20cm, branching near the base. Leaves elliptic, shallowly toothed. Flowers 1.5–1.8cm across, sometimes purplish-blue, the upper lobes short, blunt and retuse, the lip pouched with a short, sac-like spur.

Diascia cardiosepala

Nemesia cheiranthos

Nemesia cheiranthos at Padstal farm, Nieuwoudtville

Polycarena batteniana at the Padstal Farm, Nieuwoudtville

Lyperia tristis after a fire near Citrusdal

Polycarena batteniana

Polycarena aurea in the Bidouw Valley

Jamesbrittenia thunbergii (G. Don)
Hilliard, syn. *Sutera tomentosa* Thunb.
(*Scrophulariaceae*) A sticky, glandular winter
annual, with whitish to lilac flowers with a
dark star in the throat, native of South Africa
in S Namibia, Namaqualand and the W and
S Karoo, growing on gravelly slopes and shale,
flowering in July–October. Stems to 60cm,
branching near the base. Leaves elliptic,
toothed. Flowers 1.2–1.5cm across, of
5 more-or-less equal, retuse lobes, with a
long, slender, bent tube.

Lyperia tristis (L. fil.) Benth., syn. *Sutera
tristis* (L. fil.) Hiern (*Scrophulariaceae*)
An upright, glandular winter annual with pale
greenish-yellow flowers, scented like stocks,
native of South Africa, from Namibia to the
Peninsula, growing on gravelly and sandy
soils, flowering in July–October. Stems to
50cm. Leaves elliptic, shallowly toothed.
Flowers 1–1.2cm across, of 5 more-or-less
equal, oblanceolate, rounded lobes.

Polycarena aurea Benth. (*Scrophulariaceae*)
A small, upright winter annual with small
white flowers with buff upper lobes, native of
South Africa from the Bokkeveld mountains
and W Karoo to the Hex River mountains,
growing on clay and sandy soils, flowering in
August–September. Stems to 15cm. Leaves
narrow, shallowly toothed. Flowers 4–6mm
across, of 5 more-or-less equal, blunt lobes,
the upper pair with buff tips and throat.

Polycarena batteniana Hilliard   A small,
upright winter annual with small, white

flowers, scented at night, native of South
Africa from Namaqualand to the Cedarberg,
growing on sandy soils, flowering mainly in
September. Stems glandular, to 15cm. Leaves
linear. Flowers 6–8mm across, with a long
tube and 5 more-or-less equal, rounded lobes,
sometimes with small, orange markings in the
throat.

Zaluzianskya affinis Hilliard
(*Scrophulariaceae*)   A branched, hairy annual
with white to mauve, starry flowers with a
yellow, later purple star in the throat, native of
South Africa from the Richtersveld to the
Olifant's River Valley, growing in sandy and
rocky soils in dry fynbos, flowering in
June–November. Stems with short hairs, to
20cm. Leaves narrow. Flowers 8–10mm
across, with a long tube and 5 equal, forked
lobes.

Zaluzianskya capensis (L.) Walp.
A branched, sticky annual with white flowers
with a purple back, native of South Africa
from Namaqualand to the Eastern Cape,
growing on sand dunes and low slopes,
flowering in April–December. Stems to 40cm.
Leaves linear. Flowers 1–1.5cm across, with a
long, purple tube and 5 equal, forked lobes.
Easily grown and wonderfully scented at
night; the flowers close on bright days, and
look like those of a *Silene* or catchfly.

Zaluzianskya c.f. **gilioides** Schlectr.
A small, sticky annual with bright yellow or
white flowers with rounded lobes, native of
South Africa from Namibia to Clanwilliam

Jamesbrittenia thunbergii in the Karoo Botanic garden, Worcester

Zaluzianskya affinis in a sandy valley near Lambertsbai

Zaluzianskya species in the Knersvlake near Vanrhynsdorp

Zaluzianskya c.f. *gilioides* in a wet seep above Kamieskroom

Zaluzianskya villosa on the Dido Road, Cape Peninsula

eastwards to the Karoo and Lesotho, growing in damp, peaty places among rocks in the mountains, flowering in August–October. Stems to 10cm. Leaves narrow. Flowers 8–10mm across, with a long, purplish-red tube and 5 equal lobes. A very attractive dwarf species, superficially like the American yellow *Linanthus aureus* (page 194).

Zaluzianskya species   A slender, upright annual with starry flowers, the deeply forked lobes with red bases, native of South Africa in the Knersvlake near Vanrhynsdorp, growing in dry, stony, desert soils, flowering in September. Stems to 10cm, with short hairs. Leaves obovate, with short teeth. Flowers 8–10mm across, with a long, greenish tube and 5 equal, forked lobes, with slender bases.

Zaluzianskya villosa (Thunb.) F.W. Schmidt   A branched, hairy annual with starry flowers with a yellow, later purple throat, native of South Africa from Namaqualand to the Peninsula, growing in sandy and rocky soils in dry fynbos, flowering in June–November. Stems to 30cm, with short hairs. Leaves oblanceolate, with scattered teeth. Flowers 8–10mm across, with a long tube and 5 equal, forked lobes.

Zaluzianskya capensis at Cockermouth Castle

Calceolaria 'Cinderella' at Wisley

Calceolaria 'Cinderella'

Mimulus 'Magic Wine'

Mimulus 'Malibu'

Mimulus 'Magnifique' at Wisley

Calceolaria **'Cinderella'** (*Scrophulariaceae*)
A complex group of hybrids between the three
Chilean species *C. crenatiflora* Cav.,
C. corymbosa Ruiz & Pav. and *C. cana* Cav.,
often called the Herbeohybrida group. These
are greenhouse annuals, valuable for winter
and early-spring flowering. Their large flowers
have a characteristic pouch-like lip, around
5cm across, and are often beautifully blotched
and spotted. Seed should be sown in cool
conditions (around 15°C), in June or July,
and the young plants grown on in a cool,
airy frame. Bring into the greenhouse before
the first frost and keep cool and airy, but
frost-free. The softly hairy leaves are prone to
mould and attack by greenfly. The 'Cinderella'
strain has large flowers on compact plants, in
shades of yellow, red and orange.
   Calceolaria mexicana Benth., from Mexico
to Bolivia, is a truly annual species with small,
lemon-yellow flowers with an elongated lip
1cm long. It grows on wet rocks and by
streams in the mountains.

Incarvillea sinensis Lam. **'Cheron'**
(*Bignoniaceae*) An annual or short-lived
perennial with wiry stems, dissected leaves
and red to pink flowers, native of NW China
from Gansu to S Mongolia and Manchuria,
with subsp. *variabilis* (Batalin) Grierson from
Gansu to NW Yunnan. Grows in open ground
by rivers and on old walls and unstable slopes,
at 400–3400m, flowering in April–July.
Stems rather wavy, to around 25cm. Leaves
2- or 3-pinnately lobed. Flowers in a loose
raceme, opening in succession, pale yellow in
'Cheron'. Subspecies *variabilis* differs from
the type in having a woodier and more
branched rootstock, shorter calyx teeth and
paler flowers, usually less than 5.5cm long.
In the *New Plantsman*, vol. 1, part 1,
C. Grey-Wilson mentions the yellow-flowered
var. *farreri* W.W. Sm. from Shensi and Gansu,
but I am not certain that 'Cheron' belongs to
this variety. It is easily grown from seed to
flower the first year and should be perfectly
cold-hardy, but probably requires dry
conditions to survive the winter.

Mimulus **'Magic Wine'** (*Scrophulariaceae*)
The Magic series are F₁ hybrids, available in
separate shades from creamy-white to pink,
orange, yellow, red and crimson, and as
mixtures. Plants will reach around 20cm. All
are essentially perennials, raised from *M. luteus*
L. from Chile, crossed with *M. guttatus* Fisch.
ex DC from northwestern North America and
other species from South America.
   The usual *M. luteus* which is rarely
naturalised by streams in Europe, including
Scotland and N England, has yellow flowers
with large, red blotches and spots. *M. guttatus*
is commonly naturalised, and has smaller
flowers with numerous small spots. Hybrids
between the two are common.
   Mimulus are easily raised from seed sown
in spring at around 15°C. Keep the plants well
watered and watch for greenfly. Plant out in
rich, peaty soil after all danger of frost is past,
and keep watered in dry weather.

Mimulus **'Magnifique'** A perennial
selection with stems to 30cm. Flowers pale
yellow with fine spotting.

Mimulus **'Malibu'** A low-growing strain in
shades of red, orange and cream, with trailing
stems around 15cm, recommended for pots
and hanging baskets. Flowers 4cm across.
Raised by Floranova. The 'Calypso' strain, not

Proboscidea parviflora in Arizona in August

Thunbergia alata

Proboscidea fragrans in Mexico in October

Thunbergia alata white form in Bermuda

shown, also raised by Floranova, has beautifully blotched and spotted flowers.

Proboscidea parviflora (Woot.) Woot. & Standl. (*Pedaliaceae*) **Devil's Claw**
A spreading summer annual with sticky stems and leaves and reddish-purple to nearly white flowers marked with purple and yellow, native of E California, eastwards to W Texas and N Mexico, growing in deserts and waste ground, flowering in April–October. Stems to 80cm. Leaves broadly triangular to ovate, shallowly 5–7 lobed. Flowers 2.5cm across. Fruits, including the horns, 15–20cm long, exceptionally to 30cm!

Proboscidea fragrans (Lindl.) Decne.
A spreading summer annual with sticky stems and leaves and reddish-purple flowers marked with dark purple and yellow, native of Mexico, growing in fields and waste ground, flowering in August–November. Stems to 80cm. Leaves broadly ovate, shallowly 5–lobed. Flowers 3–4cm across. Fruits, including the horns, 12–15cm long.

Thunbergia alata Bojer (*Acanthaceae*)
Black-eyed Susan A perennial climber, often grown as an annual, with orange or pale yellow to white flowers, usually with a dark eye, native of tropical Africa, but widely naturalised elsewhere, growing in rough grassland, flowering in summer. Stems twining, to 2m. Leaves ovate-elliptic, to 7cm. Flowers funnel-shaped, to 4.5cm long and wide, born singly on stalks in the leaf axils. Requires heat, around 25°C, to grow fast and flower well in the first summer.

Incarvillea sinensis 'Cheron'

Centranthus macrosiphon in southern Spain

Asperula orientalis at Quince House

Centranthus calcitrapae near Ronda, southern Spain

Asperula orientalis Boiss. & Hohen., syn. *A. azurea* Jaub. & Spach (*Rubiaceae*)
A slender, upright spring annual with narrow whorls of leaves and long-tubed, sky-blue flowers, native of S and E Turkey, Caucasia, Iran, N Iraq and W Syria, growing in fields, steppe and waste places, at 500–2000m, flowering in April–July. Stems to 30cm. Leaves 7–25mm long, 1.5–5mm wide. Flowers 7–15mm long, lightly scented. Fruits rounded, smooth, around 2.5mm in diameter. A very graceful and easily grown small annual.

Centranthus calcitrapae (L.) Dufresne (*Valerianaceae*) An upright winter annual with divided upper leaves and flat heads of small, pink flowers, native of Portugal and the Mediterranean region and the Crimea, growing on grassy and rocky waste ground, flowering in April–May. Stems to 40cm. Upper leaves lyrate-pinnatifid, lobes often linear. Flowers sometimes white, the tube 1–2mm, with a short, gibbous spur. Superficially very similar to *Valeriana tuberosa* L., but *Centranthus* differs from the closely related *Valeriana* in having a spur or prominent swelling on the corolla tube, and having 1, not 3, stamens.

Centranthus macrosiphon Boiss.
A robust, branching annual with flat heads of pink flowers, red in the throat, native of S and SE Spain and North Africa, growing in rocky places, flowering in April–May. Stems to 50cm. Upper leaves lyrate-pinnatifid with entire or toothed lobes. Flowers with a long tube of 6–8mm, and a spur of around 1mm, which distinguish it from *C. calcitrapae*.

Dipsacus fullonum L. (*Dipsacaceae*)
Wild Teasel A tall, prickly biennial with heads of pale purple flowers, native of most of W and S Europe eastwards to the Ukraine and Turkey, growing in open woods, by streams and in hedges, flowering in July–September. Stems to 2m, branched. Leaves joined at the base to hold water. Bracts linear, very unequal, curving up around the head. Flowers opening in succession from the base. Fruiting heads becoming stiff and dry, remaining into winter. Sometimes appearing as a weed, forming in the first year a rosette of dark green, prickly leaves pressed flat on the ground.

Dipsacus sativus (L.) Honck. **Fuller's Teasel** This differs from the wild teasel in having broader, stiffer and spreading bracts, and the prickly scales on the flower head curving outwards. It was used in the past to raise the nap on woollen cloth.

Fedia cornucopiae (L.) Gaertn. (*Valerianaceae*) A short, fleshy winter annual with small, dark purple flowers with pink markings, native of S Portugal and the Mediterranean region eastwards to Greece and Crete, growing in waste places and olive groves, flowering in March–May. Stems to 30cm, branching. Upper leaves sessile, shallowly toothed. Flowers 8–16mm. Stamens 2, or 3 with 2 joined. Formerly cultivated, but now seldom seen. Several variations from North Africa have received separate names, notably *F. caput-bovis* Pom., which has 2 long calyx teeth.

Scabiosa atropurpurea L. (*Dipsacaceae*) An annual or biennial with pinnatifid upper leaves and large heads of dark red-purple or lilac-pink flowers, native of S Europe from the Azores and Portugal to North Africa and eastwards to Turkey, growing on waste ground, dry fields and dunes, flowering in May–August. Stems to 60cm. Flowerheads 2–3cm across, to 5cm in cultivated strains, sweetly scented. Fruits with long bristles. An easily grown plant, sown where it is to flower; the typical deep purple form is much the most striking. The wild form is sometimes called subsp. *maritima* (L.) Arc., and is much more slender than that usually cultivated.

Scabiosa stellata L. **'Paper Moon'** or **'Drumsticks'** A branching and spreading winter annual with pale blue, flat heads of flowers, which turn into spherical heads of papery fruits, native of SW Europe from Portugal to Sardinia, growing in dry, open ground, flowering in April–July. Stems to 60cm. Upper leaves pinnatifid. Seed heads around 2cm across, the corona to 9.5mm. The two cultivar names are either the same plant or so close as to be indistinguishable. *S. prolifera* L. is sometimes grown for its seed heads, which are on shorter stalks, surrounded by conspicuous bracts. Two eastern Mediterranean annual species, *S. calocephala* Boiss. and *S. rotata* Bieb., have similar, spherical heads with large fruit, the papery corona 6–8mm long.

Morina parviflora Kar. & Kir. (*Morinaceae*) A small, branching annual with spiny leaves and long-tubed flowers, native of Central Asia from Bokhara eastwards to Sinjiang, growing on dunes and in sandy deserts, flowering in April–May. Stems around 10cm. Leaves elliptic, with wide stalks. Flowers around 2cm long. Calyx teeth spiny. An interesting member of this small, usually perennial genus, whose species are found mainly in Central Asia.

Fedia cornucopiae near Cazorla, in southern Spain

Dipsacus sativus at Harry Hay's

Dipsacus fullonum at Wilton, Wiltshire

Dipsacus fullonum, a first year rosette

Scabiosa stellata 'Paper Moon' at Suttons

Morina parviflora in the desert outside Bokara

Scabiosa atropurpurea with *Echinacea purpurea*

241

Campanula incurva on a north-facing wall

Campanula drabifolia at Cnidos

Campanula incurva at Cockermouth Castle

Bellflower The genus *Campanula* (*Campanulaceae*) contains around 300 species found throughout the northern hemisphere, and contains such familiar flowers as the harebell, or bluebell in Scotland (*C. rotundifolia* L.), and Canterbury bells (*C. medium* L.). Around 150 species are recorded in Europe, and 95 in Turkey. A few are annual, several are biennial and most are perennial, growing on rocks and cliffs.

Campanula crispa Lam. A stiff, upright biennial or short-lived perennial, with white or pale blue, rather open flowers, native of E Turkey and Transcaucasia, growing on rocks and cliffs at 1500–2500m, flowering in June–August. Stems to 50cm. Leaves glabrous, shiny. Flowers around 4.5cm across. Stigmas 5. An interesting plant with something of the habit of a *Michauxia* (see page 246); it was discovered by Tournfort and Gundelscheimer and illustrated by Claude Aubriet on their expedition to NE Turkey in 1700.

Campanula drabifolia Sibth. & Sm. A soft, spreading and delicate annual with blue flowers with a white throat, native of S and E Greece, Crete, Cyprus and the Mediterranean coast of Turkey, growing on rocks and cliffs at up to 1000m, flowering in March–May. Stems bristly hairy, to 20cm. Upper leaves 3- to 5-fid. Flowers 1–1.6cm long, tubular with spreading lobes. Stigmas 3.

Campanula incurva Aucher A stiff, usually spreading biennial or short-lived perennial with large, inflated, pale blue flowers, native of E Greece from the lower slopes of Mount Olympus to Euboea, Skopelos and Ikaria, growing on limestone rocks and cliffs at up to 700m, flowering in April–June. Stems greyish-hairy, to 45cm. Upper leaves heart-shaped, shallowly toothed. Flowers 2.5–3.5cm long, incurved at the mouth, with short, blunt, recurved lobes. Stigmas 3. This is one of the best of all species for growing on old walls, where it will naturalise if allowed to seed, or continue flowering into autumn if dead-headed.

Campanula hagielia Boiss. A softly hairy, usually spreading biennial or short-lived perennial with purplish-blue flowers, native of SW Turkey, from near Marmaris eastwards to Antalya, and on Rhodes, growing on limestone rocks, cliffs and old walls at up to 300m, flowering in April–June. Stems

Campanula crispa on Nemrut Da, Tatvan

Campanula sibirica subsp. *elatior,* on the steppes near Stavropol

Campanula medium, wild near Grasse

greyish-hairy, to 45cm. Basal leaves cordate,
with a long, winged and lobed stalk. Flowers
with a tube 2–3cm long, widening at the
mouth with spreading lobes. Stigmas 5. This is
one of the group of showy campanulas found
on classical ruins in the E Mediterranean.

There are many intermediates between this
and *C. lyrata* Lam., the commonest Turkish
member of the group, which is found in
W Turkey, the eastern Aegean islands and
Ikaria; it differs in its stiff, bristly-hairy stems
and leaves and smaller flowers with a tube
1.2–2cm long; *C. lyrata* subsp. *icarica*
Runemark from Samos, Kalimnos and Ikaria
is softly hairy, with larger flowers than
subsp. *lyrata*, up to 2.5cm long.

Campanula medium L. **Canterbury Bells**
An upright, branching biennial with bright,
purplish-blue flowers, native of the foothills of
the Alpes Maritimes in France and Italy, and
naturalised elsewhere, growing on limestone
rocks and stony, grassy slopes, flowering in
May–June. Stems bristly-hairy, to 60cm. Basal
leaves long-stalked, ovate-oblong. Flowers
3–4cm, not nodding. Stigmas 5.

This attractive species is the parent of the
cultivated Canterbury bells. The single,
traditional, cottage-garden variety is still
available in shades of blue, white or pink.
Double and "cup and saucer" varieties have
huge flowers on short stems, and have lost all
the grace of the original. A recent variety,
'Chelsea Pink', with deep pink flowers 5–6cm
long on stems around 30cm tall, is said to
flower in 3 months from seed.

Campanula sibirica L. subsp. *elatior*
(Fomin) Federov   An upright biennial with
single stems and large, bluish flowers, native
of the Ukraine and S Russia, growing on
steppes and open hills, flowering in
June–August. Stems 30–60cm. Basal leaves
obovate, obtuse. Flowers tubular, 2–3cm long,
nodding. Stigmas 3. Subspecies *sibirica* and
other subspecies found from NE Germany to
C Italy and the Caucasus differ in stature and
minor details of the calyx. Subspecies
divergentiformis (Jav.) Domin. has the largest
flowers, 3–4cm long.

Campanula medium, the wild form of Canterbury bells, from above Menton at Quince House

Campanula hagielia near Dalyan, SW Turkey

Campanula hagielia

243

Campanula ramosissima at Harry Hay's

Campanula americana L. (*Campanulaceae*)
A tall, upright biennial with single stems and
starry, bluish flowers, native of North America
from New Brunswick and Ontario southwards
to Arkansas and Florida, but rare near the
E coast, growing in moist scrub and woods,
flowering in July–September. Stems
60–120cm, lightly pubescent. Basal leaves
ovate-oblong or lanceolate, acuminate.
Flowers often nearly white, 2–3cm across,
Stigmas 5, long, protruding. This needs a
sheltered and partially shaded position, and in
cultivation sometimes flowers in the first year
from seed.

Campanula lusitanica L.   A branching
annual with open, starry, blue flowers, usually
with a white throat, native of Spain and
Portugal, growing in bushy places and sandy
fields, flowering in May–June. Stems to 35cm,
often widely branching. Upper leaves oblong
to ovate-lanceolate. Flowers 1–2cm long. This
attractive species is common in parts of the
Picos de Europa, N Spain. *C. patula* L., which
has rather similar flowers, has a taller,
pyramidal and branched inflorescence to
70cm. It is found in open woods throughout
Europe.

Campanula pyramidalis L. **Chimney
Bellflower**   A very tall, upright biennial or
short-lived perennial with many wide-open,
blue or white flowers, native of Italy and along
the coast to Albania, growing on rocks and
walls, flowering in June–August. Stems
normally to 1.5m, branching below to form a
huge, narrow pyramid. Upper leaves sessile,
ovate-lanceolate. Flowers 2–5cm across. In
Victorian times this species was grown to
bring indoors in pots, and there was

competition among head gardeners to grow
the tallest specimens, up to 5m! Detailed
instruction for its cultivation are given in the
Gardeners' Chronicle of 1845, and quoted by
Peter Lewis and Margaret Lynch in
Campanulas (1989). Sow the seeds in early
spring and plant out singly, by stages, into
20cm pots in which the plants grow slowly,
keeping rather dry and away from frost
through the winter. The following spring put
into even larger pots, and slowly bring them
on to flowering. Soil should be rich and well-
drained, with ample limestone and old mortar.

Campanula ramosissima Sibth. & Sm.
A spreading and branching annual with hairy
stems and a violet-blue, starry flowers with a
pale centre, native of SE Europe from Italy
and the Balkans to Greece, growing in grassy
and stony places and olive groves, usually in
the hills, flowering in summer. Stems angular,
20–40cm. Upper leaves spathulate, sessile,
acute. Flowers 1–3cm long. An easy plant
which was cultivated in the past, both in its
violet and its white form.

Campanula spicata L.   An upright
biennial with a spike of many small, narrow,
upward-pointing, blue flowers, native of the
Alps from France to Austria and southwards
to Liguria and Montenegro, growing in
subalpine meadows and open scrub, flowering
in July–August. Stems to 90cm. Leaves
numerous, sessile, lanceolate. Flowers
1.7–2.2cm. A showy species, seldom seen in
cultivation.

Campanula thrysoides L.   An upright
biennial with a spike of many small, narrow,
upward-pointing, yellow flowers, native of the

Alps and Carpathians, and southwards to
Bulgaria, growing in subalpine and alpine
meadows at up to 2500m, flowering in June
and July. Stems sticky below, to 30cm. Leaves
numerous, sessile, linear-lanceolate. Flowers
1.7–2.2cm. Unusual for its yellow flowers.

Symphyandra hoffmannii Pant.
(*Campanulaceae*)   An upright biennial with
creamy-white, tubular flowers, native of
Bosnia, growing in rocky places, flowering in
June–July. Stems pubescent, to 30cm. Leaves
ovate to lanceolate. Flowers 2–3cm. Stigmas 3.
Symphyandra differs from *Campanula* only in
that the anthers are joined around the style
when the flower opens. *S. armena* (Steven)
A. DC., from shady cliffs in NE Turkey, the
S Caucasus and N Iran, is a short-lived
perennial with masses of pale blue flowers
1.5–2cm long.

Symphyandra hoffmannii

Campanula thrysoides at St Luc, Valais

Campanula spicata at St Luc, Valais

Campanula pyramidalis

Campanula americana

Campanula lusitanica in northwestern Spain in May

Michauxia campanuloides, growing on the ruins of Side, southern Turkey

Michauxia campanuloides

Michauxia tchihatchewii on low cliffs near Kayseri

Michauxia tchihatchewii

Michauxia laevigata in the Zab gorge, Hakkari

Jasione montana L. (*Campanulaceae*)
Sheep's-bit A small, tufted biennial,
sometimes an annual or short-lived perennial,
with rosettes of hairy leaves and scabious-like
heads of sky-blue flowers, native of most of
Europe and western North Africa, growing on
banks, stony hills, stable shingle and cliff-tops,
usually on acidic soils, flowering in
May–August. Stems 5–50cm, but usually
around 15cm. Leaves to 5cm long.
Flowerheads 5–35mm across, with ovate to
triangular bracts around the base. Individual
flowers rarely pink or white, around 5mm
long, with 5 narrow lobes. A very variable and
attractive plant, found wild throughout the
British Isles on suitable soils. Some of the
tallest and showiest forms are found in
C Spain.

Legousia pentagonia (L.) Thell., syn.
Specularia pentagonia (L.) A. DC.
(*Campanulaceae*) An upright annual with
starry, violet-blue flowers, native of SE Europe
from Greece to Turkey and Syria, eastwards to
Georgia, NW Iran and N Iraq, growing in
cornfields and on open ground, at up to
2000m, flowering in April–June. Stems
15–30cm, often branching. Leaves obovate to
oblong. Calyx lobes 1–1.6cm, ¼–½ the length
of the ovary at flowering, bristly. Flowers
1.5–2cm long, white at the base, blue in the
middle and violet towards the apex. Capsule
2–3cm. This is the showiest Venus's looking
glass, with larger flowers than *L. speculum-
veneris* (L.) Chaix, in which the flowers are
1–1.5cm and all violet.

Michauxia campanuloides L'Hérit. ex
Aiton (*Campanulaceae*) A tall, upright
biennial with bristly-hairy stems and large
white or pale purple flowers with reflexed
lobes, native of W Syria and SW Turkey from
Antalya to Maras, growing on old walls and
cliffs at up to 1700m, flowering in
May–August. Stems usually branched,
1–1.5m. Basal leaves lyrate-pinnatifid, upper
sessile, oblong to ovate. Pedicels 2–4cm.
Corolla divided to ⅘ its length, the numerous
narrow lobes 2.5–4.5cm. Style 3–4cm. A
striking and variable plant, easy from seed if
planted in stony, dry soil and protected from
excessive winter rain. In cool, wet summers
the seed often does not ripen outdoors.

Michauxia laevigata Vent. A very tall,
upright biennial with prickly-hairy stems and
large, white flowers with curled-back lobes,
native of the Transcaucasus, N and W Iran,
N Iraq and SE Turkey in the Zab gorge and
mountains of Hakkari and Siirt, growing on
cliffs and screes at 1000–1830m, flowering in
June–August. Stems usually unbranched,
70–150cm. Basal leaves double-toothed, upper
sessile, oblong-lanceolate. Pedicels 1cm or
less. Corolla divided to ⅘ its length, the narrow
lobes 1.5–2cm. Style 3–4cm. A striking plant,
easy from seed if planted in stony, dry soil, but
needs even more dry heat than *Michauxia
campanuloides* for the seed to ripen outdoors.

Michauxia tchihatchewii Fisch. & Mey.
A stout, upright biennial with hairy stems and
large, white flowers with spreading lobes,

Legousia pentagonia in cornfields between Anatalya and Isparta in June

Michauxia campanuloides in Kent

Jasione montana Bishops Nympton, Devon

Jasione montana, dwarf form, in Cornwall

native of Turkey in C Anatolia, growing on cliffs and rocks at 500–1800m, flowering in June–August. Stems usually unbranched, 40–140cm. Basal leaves lobed or coarsely toothed, upper sessile, oblong to broadly ovate. Pedicels 1cm or less. Corolla divided to ½ its length, the narrow lobes 7–12mm. Style 1.5–1.7cm. I have not grown this species; the plants and seed usually sold as *M. tchihatchewii* are forms of *M. campanuloides*. *M. thrysoidea* Boiss. & Held. is the rarest of the Turkish species, found only in S Turkey in Konya and Içel provinces, growing on rocks at 900–1900m. It is grey-hairy, with short stems to 40cm, flowering from the base. The corolla is broadly campanulate, divided only to ⅓ its length.

Jasione montana, tall form, in Spain near Salamanca

Laurentia axillaris 'Blue Stars'

Laurentia petraea 'White Stars'

Scaevola aemula wild type

Laurentia anethifolia

Scaevola aemula 'Blue Fan'

Laurentia anethifolia (Summerhayes)
E. Wimmer, syn. *Isotoma anethifolia*
Summerhayes (*Campanulaceae-Lobelioideae*)
A perennial often grown as an annual, with
finely dissected leaves and white, starry
flowers, native of SE Queensland and
NE New South Wales, growing in peaty soil
in granite rock crevices, flowering mainly in
November–February (summer). Plant
20–50cm tall, and as much across. Leaves
smooth, elliptic to ovate in outline, deeply
lobed into hair-like segments to 2mm wide.
Flowers to around 3cm across, the 2 upper
lobes clearly narrower than the lower 3. Easily
raised from seed, and may be overwintered as
cuttings, which will survive a little frost.

Laurentia axillaris (Lindl.) E. Wimmer,
syn. *Isotoma axillaris* Lindl. **'Blue Stars'**
A perennial often grown as an annual, with
dissected leaves and lavender-blue, starry
flowers, native of SE Queensland, E New
South Wales and N Victoria, growing in peaty
and sandy soil among rocks and in mountains,
flowering mainly in September–May (spring
to autumn). Plant 30–60cm tall, and more
across. Leaves smooth, ovate to obovate in
outline, deeply toothed and lobed into linear
segments. Flowers sometimes white, to
around 4cm across, all the lobes more or less
equal. Easily raised from seed, and may be
overwintered by cuttings, which will survive a
little frost.

Laurentia petraea (F. Muell.) E. Wimmer,
syn. *Isotoma petraea* F. Muell. **'White Stars'**
A perennial often grown as an annual, with
toothed or lobed leaves and white, starry

Wahlenbergia androsacea with tree-like *Aloe dichotoma*,
east of Nieuwoudtville

Wahlenbergia prostrata on the Spectakle Pass near Springbok

Wahlenbergia pilosa in a dry sandy area

flowers, native of most of Australia, growing in rock crevices in dry areas, flowering most of the year. Plant 10–50cm tall, and more across. Leaves smooth, lanceolate to ovate in outline, deeply toothed and lobed. Flowers to around 3cm across, all the lobes more or less equal.

Laurentia species syn. *Isotoma* species **'Pink Stars'** A perennial often grown as an annual with dissected leaves and pale pink, starry flowers, with deeper markings. This is often included in mixtures with *L. axillaris*, but we have been unable to find its proper name.

Scaevola aemula R. Br. (*Goodeniaceae*) A rather fleshy perennial, often grown as an annual, with toothed leaves and mauve, fan-shaped flowers, native of Australia from near Sydney to Western Australia and Tasmania, growing mainly near the coast, flowering in spring and summer. Plant creeping, to 1m or more across. Leaves smooth, ovate to lanceolate in outline, deeply toothed and lobed into linear segments. Flowers to around 3cm across, all 5 lobes equal and pointing downwards. 'Blue Wonder' is a selected clone, more floriferous than the wild type. **'Blue Fan'** is an even more robust cultivar, sold in Europe as rooted cuttings for hanging baskets. The family *Goodeniaceae*, found mostly in Australia, differs from *Lobelioideae* mainly in its few, large seeds.

Wahlenbergia (*Campanulaceae*) A genus of around 200 species, with 2 species in Europe,

around 40 in the Cape, and the rest mostly in tropical Africa or Australia; *Campanula*-like, but differs in having apical valves to its capsule.

Wahlenbergia androsacea A. DC. A graceful winter annual with thin, wiry stems and pale blue or white flowers, native of South Africa from tropical Africa southwards to Namaqualand and Clanwilliam and the Peninsula, growing in sandy soils, flowering in August–November. Stems upright, branching, to 40cm. Leaves narrow, undulate, in a basal rosette. Flowers 1–1.2cm across.
  W. annularis A. DC. is very similar, but has linear, toothed basal leaves, and larger, flatter flowers, 1.5–2cm across, often with more of a streak in the throat.

Wahlenbergia pilosa Buek A dwarf winter annual with lanceolate leaves and pale blue flowers with a white centre, native of South Africa from Namaqualand and Clanwilliam to Piketberg and Ceres, growing in dry, sandy soils, flowering in August–September. Stems minutely hairy, creeping, to 20cm. Leaves to 8mm. Flowers 8–10mm across.

Wahlenbergia prostrata A. DC. A dwarf winter annual with linear leaves and pale blue flowers with a white centre, native of South Africa in the Western Cape from Springbok to the Richtersveld, growing in sandy soils, flowering in August–September. Stems creeping, to 20cm. Leaves to 1.4cm. Flowers around 1.5cm across.

Laurentia species 'Pink Stars'

Lobelia fenestralis in wet fields north of Guadeljara, Mexico

Downingia elegans (Dougl.) Torr. (*Campanulaceae-Lobelioideae*) A winter annual with fleshy stems and small lobelia-like blue flowers with a white spot, native of California from Sierra and Humboldt Cos to Washington, Idaho and Nevada, growing in vernal pools and mud flats, flowering in June–September, as the water dries. Stems 10–40cm, swollen. Leaves 5–25mm, linear. Flowers 6–15mm long. The 12 species of *Downingia* are characteristic plants of vernal pools in California. *D. yina* Appleg. var. *major* McVaugh has dark blue or purplish flowers 7–10mm long, and is found from N California to W Washington. In cold areas, seed may be sown in early spring, and kept well-watered until planting out in early summer.

Lobelia fenestralis Cav. (*Campanulaceae-Lobelioideae*) A tall, upright summer annual or biennial with long spikes of small, purplish-blue flowers, native of W Texas, Arizona and Mexico southwards to Oaxaca, growing in wet meadows at around 1800m, flowering in August–November. Stems to 1m. Leaves mostly in a basal rosette, sharply toothed, the stem leaves amplexicaul. Flowers around 1cm long, sometimes white, with slits in the sides in addition to the dorsal slit, hence the specific name. All the anthers white-bearded. A striking plant, especially when seen in great quantity.

Lobelia tenuior

Lobelia valida at Harry Hay's

Downingia elegans at Harry Hay's

Lobelia bicolor Sims   A delicate, spreading summer annual, with pale blue flowers with a white centre, native of South Africa in the Cape from the Peninsula eastwards to Port Elizabeth, growing in open fields and lower slopes, flowering in September–December. Stems to 40cm, though usually less, sparsely hairy, much branched. Leaves thin, oblanceolate, irregularly toothed, around 5cm long. Flowers around 6mm long. This is an easily grown and attractive plant, self-seeding in the greenhouse. It was illustrated in the *Botanical Magazine* in 1801.

Lobelia tenuior R. Br.   An annual or short-lived perennial with narrow leaves and large flowers with wide, curving lower lobes, native of Western Australia, growing in sandy places, flowering in summer. Stems to 60cm, erect, tufted. Lower leaves oblong-obovate, toothed. Flowers around 2.5cm across. Var. *compacta* is a dwarf variety, probably the same as 'Blue Wings', with stems to 20cm. It is also recommended for growing indoors as a winter-flowering pot plant. The flowers are described as cobalt blue, a colour which often appears too purple in photographs (as here).

Lobelia valida L. Bolus   A stiff, fleshy perennial, usually grown as an annual, with heads of rich blue flowers, native of South Africa in the Bredasdorp and Riversdale districts, growing on hills near the coast, flowering in November–April. Stems 15–60cm. Flowers around 1cm across. Easily grown from seed sown in early spring. Often sold with the name 'African Skies'.

Monopsis debilis (L. fil.) Presl (*Campanulaceae-Lobelioideae*)   A spreading winter annual with almost round, violet-blue flowers, native of South Africa in the Cape from Namaqualand to the Peninsula, and naturalised in Western Australia, growing in wet fields and by streams, flowering in September–November. Stems to 15cm. Leaves elliptic, toothed, to 5cm. Flowers around 1cm across. A very attractive annual for rich, moist soil. *M. lutea* (L.) Urb. is a creeping perennial with deep yellow, 2-lipped flowers. It is illustrated in our *Conservatory and Indoor Plants* vol. 2, p. 205.

Monopsis debilis along a ditch east of Pakhuis Pass towards Wuppertaal above Clanwilliam

Lobelia bicolor in the southern Cape

Monopsis debilis

Lobelia erinus in niches on walls of Edzell Castle, Angus

Lobelia erinus 'Pendula Fountains Lilac'

Lobelia erinus 'Compacta Crystal Palace'

Lobelia erinus L. (*Campanulaceae-Lobelioideae*)   A delicate, straggling summer annual or perennial, with blue, violet, pink or white flowers, native of South Africa from Clanwilliam to the Cape Peninsula and eastwards to Natal, growing on lower mountain slopes, flowering most of the year. Stems 10–80cm, sparsely hairy. Leaves thin, narrowly lanceolate, around 2.5cm long. Flowers around 6mm across.

This is the commonly cultivated annual lobelia, which has been grown in European gardens since 1752. Numerous varieties have been selected since then, from the long, trailing, more-or-less perennial varieties to the dwarf, tufted plants suitable for edging. Flowers colours vary from pinkish-red through purple to blue, pink and white. The seed, which is minute, should be sown as thinly as possible on moist, peaty compost in early spring (February) at 15–20°C. Prick out the young plants as soon as they are large enough to handle. By April, the plants are growing fast, and they can be planted out as soon as the weather becomes warm. Ample water will keep lobelia plants in flower for many months, and the trailing varieties in particular will survive into a second season. A selection of the varieties available is shown here.

'Compacta Crystal Palace'   A dwarf edging variety with deep blue flowers.
'Compacta Rosamonde'   A dwarf edging variety with stems to 15cm and deep pinkish-red flowers with a white eye.
'Pendula Cascade' mixed   A mixture of trailing varieties with stems to 30cm.
'Pendula Fountains Blue'   A trailing variety with stems to 30cm.
'Pendula Fountains Lilac'   A trailing variety with stems to 30cm.

Lobelia richardsonii hort.   A trailing species or variety of *L. erinus*, of unknown origin, sold as a perennial. It has stems to 30cm, and lasts several years if kept rather dry and frost-free through the winter.

Lobelia and *Helichrysum petiolare* 'Limelight' in an old stone tub at Levens Hall

Lobelia richardsonii at Quince House

Lobelia erinus 'Pendula Fountains Blue'

Lobelia erinus 'Pendula Cascade Mixed'

Lobelia erinus wild type at Kew

Lobelia erinus 'Compacta Rosamonde'

Rhodanthe chlorocephala subsp. *rosea*

Bracteantha bracteata

Bracteantha bracteata (Vent.) Anderb. & Haegi, syn. *Helichrysum bracteatum* (Vent.) Andr. (*Compositae-Gnaphalieae*) **Golden Everlasting** An annual, biennial or perennial with yellow flowers surrounded by stiff, papery bracts, native of most of Australia, growing in rocky places, flowering most of the year. Stems to 1m. Leaves linear to oblanceolate, sticky-hairy or woolly. Flowerheads 2–8cm across, in different sizes and colours from yellow to orange, red and pink. All are easily grown from seed, sown indoors at 20–23°C and planted out in early summer. The 'Monstrosum Swiss Giant' series are the traditional tall variety, with stems to 1.2m, and especially good for drying.

Craspedia globosa (Bauer ex Benth.) Benth. (*Compositae-Gnaphalieae*) **Drumsticks** A perennial usually grown as an annual, with globular heads of yellow flowers, native of Australia from Queensland to South Australia, growing in moist, heavy soils, flowering in November–February. Stems to 1m, wiry. Leaves silvery, ribbon-like, to 30cm. Flower heads to 2.5cm across. Sow seed indoors at 15–20°C. The heads are good for drying.

Helichrysum subulifolium F. Muell. (*Compositae-Gnaphalieae*) A winter annual with narrow leaves and yellow flowers, native of Western Australia, growing in sandy soils, flowering in September–December. Stems to 50cm. Leaves 8–12cm long, around 2mm wide. Flower heads 2–4cm across. 'Yellow Star' is a good, selected form. Easily grown and good for drying and for planting in containers.

Helichrysum subulifolium

Rhynchopsidium pumilum near Nieuwoudtville

Craspedia globosa at Suttons Seeds

Schoenia cassiniana 'Tanner's Pride'

Rhodanthe chlorocephala subsp. *rosea* (Hook.) Paul G. Wilson, syn. *Helipterum roseum* (Hook.) Benth. (*Compositae-Gnaphalieae*) A winter annual with narrow, glabrous leaves and pink or white, everlasting flowers, native of Western Australia, growing in sandy soil in open woodland, flowering mainly in June–November (winter–spring). Stems to 70cm. Leaves 1–6cm long, 2–7mm wide. Flowerheads 3–6cm across, with thin papery bracts.

Rhodanthe manglesii Lindl., syn. *Helipterum manglesii* (Lindl.) Benth. **Swan River Everlasting** A winter annual with broad, clasping leaves and pink or white flowers, native of Western Australia, growing in sandy soil in open woodland, flowering mainly in June–November. An easy, quick-growing and very attractive annual for a sunny, well-drained site.

Rhynchopsidium pumilum (L. fil.) DC., syn. *Relhania pumila* (L. fil.) Thunb. (*Compositae-Gnaphalieae*) A mat-forming winter annual with narrow, sticky leaves and small, yellow flowers, native of South Africa, in the Western Cape from Namaqualand to the Little Karoo, growing in sandy places, flowering in August–October. Stems to 20cm. Leaves linear, hairy. Flowers with few, short rays, 1.2–1.5cm across.

Schoenia cassiniana (Gaudich.) Steetz, syn. *Helichrysum cassinianum* Gaudich. (*Compositae-Gnaphalieae*) A branching winter annual with masses of small, pink or white flowers, native of Western Australia, the Northern Territories and South Australia, growing in sandy soil in open woods and scrub, flowering in July–December. Stems to 50cm. Leaves linear-lanceolate, mostly opposite. Flower heads 2–3cm across, in flat-topped clusters of 5–10. 'Rose Beauty' is a pink-flowered form. **'Tanner's Pride'** is pure white. Easily grown from seed, sown in spring.

Helichrysum subulifolium

Rhodanthe manglesii (white)

Schoenia cassiniana

Rhodanthe manglesii (pink)

Specimens from Thompson and Morgan, August 6th, ²⁄₅ life-size

Rhynchopsidium pumilum with other daisies and mesembryanthemums in dry country east of Nieuwoudtville

Callistephus, close to wild type, in China

Ageratum 'Pacific Plus'

Ageratum 'Bavaria'

Bellis perennis 'Habenera'

Ageratum 'Blue Horizon' at Levens Hall

Bellis perennis 'Rose Carpet'

Callistephus chinensis 'Giant Single'

Ageratum houstonianum Mill. (*Compositae-Eupatoreae*) A summer annual or short-lived perennial with fluffy heads of bluish-lilac flowers, native of Mexico and the West Indies, flowering in summer–autumn. Stems to 70cm. Leaves, opposite, ovate, cordate at the base. Flowerheads around 5mm across, the florets with 5 lobes producing the fluffy effect. Many different varieties, in colours from blue to red, pink and white, have been developed. Sow seed in heat of 20–25°C, and plant outdoors only when the weather has warmed up in early summer.

'Bavaria' Flowers with very long, blue filaments from a white centre. Stems to 25cm.

'Blue Horizon' A tall-growing F_1 hybrid with stems to 75cm, and flowers of a good blue. One of the taller varieties, good for general garden use and for cutting.

'Pacific Plus' A very dwarf variety for edging or carpet bedding. Flower heads large, deep violet-blue. Bushy plants to 20cm.

Bellis perennis L. (*Compositae-Astereae*) **Common Daisy** A dwarf perennial with small, white flowers, the cultivars often grown as biennials, growing wild throughout Europe and W Asia from Azerbaijan to Turkey and W Syria, growing in lawns, damp fields and woods, flowering most of the year. Leaves obovate, around 5cm long. Flower stems 1.5–10cm. Flowers 1.5–2cm across, the white rays with pink tips. Seeds without pappus. *B. annua* L., a true annual, is a dwarf with slightly smaller flowers, found around the Mediterranean in damp, shady places.

Most cultivated strains of daisy have double flowers, often with quill-like rays. 'Goliath', not shown, has flowers to 7.5cm across.

'Habenera' Flowers in shades of white, pink or red, and red with white tips, with long, needle-like rays, around 6cm across, on stems 15–20cm tall.

'Rose Carpet' Flowers double, pompom, pink, around 2.5cm across, with quilled rays, on stems 10–15cm tall.

Callistephus chinensis (L.) Nees (*Compositae-Astereae*) **Annual Aster** or **China Aster** An upright summer annual with coarsely toothed leaves and dark purplish-blue flowers with long, often coiled, linear rays, native of China, and cultivated there for 2000 years. Stems to 60cm. Leaves ovate, alternate. Flowers solitary on slightly nodding stalks. Seeds with 2 rows of pappus. Numerous varieties have been grown in the west since the species was first introduced from China in the early 18th century. Shown here are:

'Craw Krallenaster' Flowers large, around 12cm across, with long, narrow petals in a variety of colours, both double and single. Stems around 45cm.

'Duchesse' A series with paeony-like flowers with double, incurving rays. Available in 9 separate colours, including the double shown here.

Experimental variety In this new variety the double flowers have curled rays with a white back. Stems around 20cm.

'Giant Single' Flowers single, in various colours, around 10cm across. Stems to 60cm. The 'Kamo' series from Japan are also single, with stems to 80cm. 'China' mixed is similar. These single varieties have the elegance and form which has been lost in the squat doubles.

'Milady' mixed Flowers double, incurved chrysanthemum-type, of medium size, in a mixture of colours. Stems 20–30cm.

'Starlet' mixed Small flowers around 6cm across, produced in profusion on dwarf, branching stems to 20cm.

'Stripes' Flowers of medium size, with striped rays.

'Stripes'

'Duchesse'

'Giant Single'

'Craw Krallenaster'

'Milady' mixed

'Starlet' mixed

Experimental variety

Specimens from Thompson and Morgan, August 6th, ½ life-size

Brachyscome iberidifolia 'Bravo' series

Brachyscome iberidifolia at Colgrave Seeds

Brachyscome iberidifolia 'Blue Star'

Brachyscome (*Compositae-Astereae*) A genus of around 60 species in Australia and New Zealand, New Guinea and New Caledonia, containing both perennials and small shrubs as well as some annuals. The flowers are usually blue, pink or white; the pappus consists of separate or joined bristles, which may be minute or, rarely, absent altogether.

Brachyscome iberidifolia Benth. **Swan River Daisy** A branching winter annual with divided leaves and white, blue or purple, daisy-like flowers, native of Australia in Western Australia, South Australia and the Northern Territories, growing in Jarrah forest and *Banksia* woodland, flowering in September–February (spring–summer). Stems to 30cm tall and spreading a little more wide. Leaves to 3cm, pinnate with narrow segments. Flowers to 2cm across. Best grown from seed sown in spring, indoors in cold areas, and planted out when all danger of frost is past. In warm climates it can naturalise itself in an attractive way among other plants.

In **'Blue Star'** the rays are rolled to give a starry flower. In most mixtures there is a range of colours and flower shapes. In the **'Bravo'** series the flowers have black centres and are available in separate colours, deep blue, violet and white.

Felicia Of around 80 species of *Felicia* (*Compositae-Astereae*) found in southern Africa, most are perennial and many shrubby. Nearly all have blue, daisy-like flowers.

The genus *Amellus*, with 10 species, is very similar. The familiar perennials *F. amelloides* (L.) Voss and *F. aethiopica* (Burm. fil.) Adamson & Salter, from the Cape, are commonly cultivated and are excellent plants for a cool greenhouse, long-lived and almost continually in flower. They may also be used as summer bedding.

Felicia australis (Alston) E. Phillips A winter annual with rich blue or mauve flowers with 12–25 rays, native of South Africa, in the Western Cape from Namaqualand to the Karoo, Clanwilliam and Franschhoek, growing in sandy or clay flats, flowering in July–September. Stems 5–25cm. Leaves linear, ciliate. Flowerheads 1.5–1.8cm across. A common species in the wild.

Felicia dubia Cass. A delicate winter annual, or sometimes perennial, with rich blue flowers with a yellow centre and around 10 rays, native of South Africa, in the Western Cape from Namaqualand to the Karoo and the Peninsula, growing in sandy or gravelly flats and slopes, flowering in July–October. Stems 5–40cm. Leaves obovate or oblong, hairy and ciliate, to 3cm long. Flowerheads around 2cm across. *F. tenella* (L.) Nees, from much of the Western Cape has similar flowers but linear leaves. *F. bergeriana* (Spreng.) O. Hoffm. has larger flowers to 3cm across.

Felicia elongata (Thunb.) O. Hoffm. A winter annual with white flowers with a maroon band around the centre, native of

South Africa in the Western Cape at Hopefield, growing in sandy places on the coast, flowering in August–October. Stems 15–30cm. Leaves lanceolate, ciliate and with scattered, stiff hairs. Flower heads 1.8–2cm across. An attractive species of unusual colouring.

Felicia heterophylla (Cass.) Grau A winter annual with rich blue flowers with a blue centre, native of South Africa, in the Western Cape from Namaqualand and Clanwilliam to the Peninsula, growing in sandy flats or low hills, flowering in August–October. Stems 15–35cm. Leaves oblanceolate, roughly hairy. Flowerheads around 2.5cm across, sometimes with a reddish or yellow centre, with around 12 rays. 'The Rose' is a pink form. A very good, easily grown species, very quick to flower from seed, sown in autumn or spring, or in cool summer weather to flower in autumn.

Monoptilon bellioides (Gray) Hall (*Compositae-Astereae*) **Desert Star** A dwarf, spreading winter annual with white-hairy leaves and white, daisy-like flowers, native of SE California eastwards to Arizona, S Utah and NW Mexico, growing in sandy and rocky deserts at up to 1000m, flowering in February–May, and often in September. Plant to 25cm across, usually less. Leaves to 2cm long. Flowerheads around 2cm across, with 12–20 rays. *M. bellidiforme* Torr. & Gray, the only other species in the genus, is a smaller and rarer plant, with the pappus reduced to a scarious cup and a single bristle.

Felicia australis and other annuals near Kamieskoom in the Western Cape, in early September

Felicia australis near Kamieskoom

Felicia dubia at Nieuwoudtville

Felicia heterophylla in cultivation

Felicia elongata in the National Botanic garden at Kirstenbosch

Monoptilon bellioides in the Mojave Desert in March

A giant sunflower in Eccleston Square

Helianthus annuus 'Russian Giant'

Helianthus annuus 'Sunspot'

Helianthus annuus 'Moonwalker' at Thompson and Morgan's trial grounds

Sunflowers   There are about 70 species of annual or perennial sunflowers in the genus *Helianthus* (*Compositae-Heliantheae*), all of which are native of the Americas. The species most commonly grown for both commercial and ornamental purposes is ***Helianthus annuus*** L., which is thought to have originated in southwestern North America, where the edible seeds have been used by North American Indians since time immemorial. The exact date of introduction into Europe is unknown, but by 1613 Basilius Besler of Nuremberg was illustrating two examples in *Hortus Eystettensis*, his great *Florilegium*. Sunflowers have long been popular garden plants, partly because of the stupendous size of their flowers, and partly because they are so easy to grow; over the years breeders have produced a wide range of cultivars, some of which are shown here.

Sunflowers are quite hardy in temperate climates, and the large seeds are simply sown outside where they are to flower; as their name suggests, they prefer full sun, but will also grow satisfactorily in partial shade. The richer the soil, the larger they will grow.

'Eversun Deep Yellow'   A tall variety, to 1.8m, with single, yellow flowers producing very little pollen.

'Golden Hedge'   A tall, robust variety, to 1.5m, with golden-yellow flowers.

'Italian White'   This variety grows up to 1.2m tall, and has very attractive cream coloured flowers, with a gold zone and black centre, to 10cm across.

'Moonwalker'   A bushy, branching form, to 1.5 m tall, with large, lemon-yellow flowers with dark brown centres.

'Prado Red'   A free-flowering variety, to 1.5m, which can be encouraged to produce still more blooms if the first bud is pinched out. Good for cutting, as it produces very little pollen.

'Prado Yellow'   As above, but with yellow flowers.

'Russian Giant'   A truly gigantic variety, to 3m or more, and probably the best one for children to grow if they want to win a sunflower competition! Large, yellow flowers.

'Sunspot'   A dwarf variety, to only 60cm high, with golden flowers to 20cm across.

'Teddy Bear'   A recent introduction, this dwarf variety grows to only 60cm. The golden-yellow flowers are fully double, to about 15cm across.

'Velvet Queen'   A tall variety, to 1.5m, with purple stems, dark green leaves, and deep velvety red flowers with brown centres.

'Prado Red'

'Golden Hedge'

'Velvet Queen'

'Prado Yellow'

'Italian White'

'Eversun Deep Yellow'

'Teddy Bear'

'Sunspot'

'Moonwalker'

Specimens from Thompson and Morgan, August 6th, ¼ life-size

Tithonia rotundifolia 'Torch' with *Miscanthus sinensis*

Tithonia rotundifolia 'Goldfinger'

Coreopsis tinctoria

Tithonia rotundifolia 'Early Yellow'

Coreopsis (*Compositae-Heliantheae*)   There are about 80 species of annual or perennial herbs in this genus, native of North and South America, especially Mexico. They flower well over a long period, and are easy to grow from seed sown *in situ* in spring; best on light soils.

Coreopsis tinctoria Nutt.   An annual herb, with bright yellow, daisy-like flowers marked with red, native of North America, from Saskatchewan and Minnesota to Louisiana, Texas and Arizona, flowering from midsummer onwards. Stems erect, branched, to 1m. Leaves to 10cm. Flowers to 4cm across; rays 7–8, yellow, red at base, disc florets dark red.
   Coreopsis tinctoria var. ***atkinsoniana*** (Douglas ex. Lindl.) H.Parker ex E.B.Sm. is a very elegant variant, with curved stem branches and rather more purplish disc florets.

Rudbeckia   There are around 15 species of *Rudbeckia* (*Compositae-Heliantheae*), most of which are perennial, although a few are annuals or biennials. They are native of North America but are also widely naturalised, and as they often flower in the first year, the biennials and some perennials are frequently treated as annuals. Seed is best sown under glass at a temperature of around 15°C in early spring, the resulting seedlings being hardened off before planting out in a sunny place in moist but well-drained soil. Good for cutting.

Rudbeckia hirta L. **Black-eyed Susan** A biennial herb with yellow flowers with black, cone-shaped centres, and narrow leaves, native of North America, as far south as Texas and Florida, flowering in late summer. Stems to 2m, leaves to 10cm, narrowly lanceolate or oblanceolate. Flowers solitary, with yellow rays to 4cm, disc florets purplish-brown.

'Goldilocks'   A compact plant, to about 60cm, with rich yellow, double or semi-double flowers to about 7cm across. The flowers appear early in the season and continue throughout the summer.

'Marmalade'   A good variety for both bedding out and cutting, with large, deep

Coreopsis tinctoria var. *atkinsoniana* at Harry Hay's

Rudbeckia hirta from Ingham County, Michigan

yellow flowers, to around 10cm across. Raised by Hurst.

'Toto' A dwarf cultivar, to only 25cm, with golden-yellow flowers early in the season.

Mexican Sunflower There are around 10 species of annual or perennial herbs or shrubs in the genus *Tithonia* (*Compositae-Heliantheae*), all of them native of Central America and Mexico. Like the true sunflowers, they are usually large, rather coarse plants in the wild, but are desirable because of the late season of their flowers. The seeds are sown under glass in early spring and are normally easy to germinate in gentle heat, around 20°C. The plants will grow well in full sun, in any reasonably fertile soil, provided it is well-drained. Water well in very dry weather.

Tithonia rotundifolia (Mill.) S.F.Blake. A tall annual, with large leaves and orange flowers, native of Central America from Mexico to Panama, flowering in autumn. Stem to 4m, leaves to 30cm long, ovate to triangular-ovate, entire to 3–5 lobed. Flowerhead to 7cm across, with reddish-orange rays to 3.5cm. This is the species that has given rise to most of the garden cultivars available, many of which are considerably shorter than the species.
'Early Yellow' Stems to 75cm. Flowers yellow.
'Goldfinger' A fairly recent introduction, to 75cm, with long, hairy leaves and large, orange flowers to 7cm across.
'Torch' A vigorous, bushy plant, to 1.5m, with large, single, bright reddish-orange flowers to 8cm across.

Rudbeckia 'Marmalade'

Rudbeckia 'Goldilocks'

Rudbeckia 'Toto'

Bidens ferulifolia (Jacq.) DC. (*Compositae-Heliantheae*)   A trailing perennial, often grown as an annual, with fern-like leaves and yellow flowers with few broad rays, native of Mexico, Guatemala and Arizona, growing in the mountains up to 2000m, flowering in August–September. Stems trailing to 1m or more. Leaves 2- or 3-pinnatisect, the lobes linear, to 2mm wide. Flowerheads to 3cm across. A commonly grown and excellent plant for a large urn or hanging basket, also looking good growing in gravel.

The name *Bidens* refers to the 2 (though there are sometimes 3 or 4) teeth on the seed, which in some annual species are barbed and stick into socks. *Bidens cernua* L. and *B. tripartita* L. are especially common on the exposed mud of reservoirs in England in late summer.

Cosmos bipinnatus Cav. (*Compositae-Heliantheae*) **Cosmos**, **Cosmea**   A tall summer annual with finely divided leaves and pink or white flowers, native of Mexico, southwards to Brazil and widely naturalised elsewhere around the world, growing on roadsides and open ground, flowering in late summer and autumn. Stems to 3m. Leaves opposite, 2-pinnatifid, with filiform lobes.

Cosmos bipinnatus 'Purity' with *Lavatera* 'Barnsley' at Cockermouth Castle

Cosmos bipinnatus growing wild north of Guadeljara, Mexico, in late October

Cosmos bipinnatus 'Purity'

Cosmos bipinnatus 'Sea Shells Pied Piper Red'

Cosmos bipinnatus 'Sensation Picotee'

Cosmos bipinnatus 'Psyche'

Flowerheads to 8cm across. Sow seeds at 20–25°C in midsummer for flowering into autumn when other flowers are scarce. There are several good varieties available. Among the more interesting ones not shown are 'Daydream', white shading to a crimson centre, 'Tetra Versailles Dark Rose', a dusky crimson with a dark centre, and 'Sensation Early', a series with single flowers in a range of colours on stems to 1m.

'Psyche' Flowers white, double and semi-double with long, thin rays. Stems to 1m.

'Purity' An excellent pure white, one of the best of all annuals for planting among perennials and shrubs. Stems to 1.2m.

'Sea Shells Pied Piper Red' In this weird variety the rays are conical and tubular. 'Sea Shells' is also available in a mixture of colours.

'Sensation Picotee' Pinks and white with a crimson edge to the rays.

Cosmos sulphureus Cav. A tall summer annual with divided leaves and orange or yellow flowers, native of Mexico, growing on roadsides and open ground, flowering in late summer and autumn. Stems to 2m. Leaves 5–30cm long, opposite, 2- or 3-pinnatifid with flat lanceolate or elliptic lobes. Flowerheads to 4–7cm across. Cultivation is as for *C. bipinnatus*; several varieties are commonly cultivated.

'Ladybird Scarlet' Flowers bright reddish-orange in hot weather, redder in cool conditions. Stems to 30cm.

'Lemon Bird' Flowers soft yellow; stems to 70cm.

'Sunset' Flowers orange, shaded with bronze; stems to 1m.

Cosmos sulphureus wild near Tequila Mountain in central Mexico in late October

Bidens ferulifolia

Cosmos sulphureus 'Ladybird Scarlet'

Cosmos sulphureus 'Sunset'

Cosmos sulphureus 'Lemon Bird'

Dahlia 'Coltness' Hybrids at Suttons Seeds

Dahlia 'Redskin' at Suttons Seeds

Zinnia elegans wild form at Kew

Zinnia angustifolia

Zinnia haageana 'Persian Carpet' mixed

Sanvitalia procumbens

Zinnia elegans 'Envy'

Dahlia This genus (*Compositae-Heliantheae*) is well known to gardeners but, originating as they do in Mexico, dahlias are usually grown as half-hardy perennials from tubers, which are dug up in the winter, kept in a frost-free place, and replanted the following spring. However, they can also be treated as annuals and grown from seed, and used as a bedding plant for late summer and autumn. When growing dahlias from seed it is worth concentrating on the lower-growing varieties, as the taller types produce far fewer flowers, and are better grown from tubers. Dead-heading is essential to keep the plants flowering.

'Coltness' Hybrids Stems to about 50cm; flowers large, single, in a wide range of colours including white, yellow-orange, shades of red, purple and crimson. Raised by Suttons Seeds during the 1980s.

'Redskin' Raised during the 1970s, with unusual, dark red foliage and flowers in a variety of colours, on stems to 50cm.

Sanvitalia procumbens Lam. (*Compositae-Heliantheae*) A slender, spreading annual, with small, bright yellow, black-centred flowers, native of the southwestern USA, Mexico and Guatemala, flowering in summer. Stems branched, to 20cm tall, spreading to 45cm across. Leaves opposite, ovate-lanceolate, to 6cm long. Flowerheads to 2cm across; rays yellow-orange; discs dark brownish-purple. There are a number of cultivars: 'Little Sun' has slender, brownish stems and leaves narrower than the species; 'Irish Eyes' has a green centre. Sanvitalias are low-growing, hardy annuals and perennials, closely related to zinnias. There are around 7 species, but *S. procumbens* is the one most commonly found in cultivation. Seed can be sown outside in spring, and the plants will do well in most soils, but need plenty of sun.

Zinnia There are around 20 species of *Zinnia* (*Compositae-Heliantheae*), some of them low shrubs, the rest annuals or perennials, all of them native of Central America, and especially common in Mexico. The annual species shown here, and cultivars derived from them, do best in well-drained but rich soil, in a warm and sunny position. They are grown from seed sown in spring at around 18°C and do best in single pots rather than trays, as this helps to minimise damping off and disturbance to the roots when potting on and transplanting. Once hardened off and planted out, they become drought-tolerant and almost trouble-free.

Zinnia angustifolia Kunth An upright summer annual with narrow leaves and small orange flowers, native of the southeastern USA and Mexico, flowering in autumn. Stems bristly, to 40cm. Leaves opposite, linear to linear-lanceolate, to 7cm. Rays 7–9, oblong, to 15mm long; disc florets orange, with yellow or black hairs.

Zinnia elegans Jacq. A stout-stemmed, upright summer annual with ovate leaves and small, single flowers, native of Mexico, flowering in summer. Stems bristly, to 1m. Leaves opposite, hairy, ovate or oblong. Rays 8–60, spathulate to obovate, to 2cm long, in shades of white, pinks and orange; disc florets yellow and black. Of the numerous cultivars and seed strains of *Z. elegans* that are avalaible, many have double flowers, and most were raised in North America. Illustrated here are:

'Envy', green and also available double; 'Fantastic Light Pink'; 'Whirligig'; some of the 'Oklahoma' strain; a cactus-flowered type, and a large semi-double pink.

Zinnia haageana Regel, syn. *Z. angustifolia* hort. non Kunth   A slender, upright annual with opposite leaves and small, orange-yellow flowers, native of Mexico, flowering in summer. Stems to 60cm, becoming purple. Leaves opposite, stemless, bristly, lanceolate. Rays 8–9 in the wild type, oblong, to 1.7 cm long; disc florets orange.
'Persian Carpet' mixed   Stems to 45cm, with large, double, flowers in shades of yellow, red, purple, cream, pink and brown.

Zinnia peruviana (L.)L., syn. *Z multiflora* L., *Z. pauciflora* L., *Z. tenuiflora* Jacq. A slender, upright summer annual with opposite leaves and small, red or yellow flowers, native of Arizona and Mexico southwards to Argentina, flowering in autumn. Stems to 90cm. Leaves opposite, lanceolate to ovate. Rays 6–15, linear to almost round, to 2.5cm long. Disc florets yellow or black. A very variable species; the narrow-rayed, red form from Mexico is at present enjoying something of a revival in English gardens.
'Red Spider' is an elegant selection of this, with bright red flowers and purplish-red, slender stems.

Zinnia elegans 'Fantastic Light Pink' at Longwood

Zinnia peruviana wild in Mexico

Zinnia peruviana 'Red Spider' at Suttons Seeds

'Oklahoma Scherlach'

Large-flowered semi-double

'Oklahoma Rosa'

'Whirligig'

Cactus-flowered

'Oklahoma Lax'

'Oklahoma Weiss'

'Oklahoma Gold'

Specimens from Thompson and Morgan, August 6th, ½ life-size

Thymophylla tenuiloba

Trichoptilium incisum in Anza-Borrego Desert

Chaenactis fremontii in the Mojave desert

Gaillardia pulchella

Layia platyglossa in the Chelsea Physic Garden

Tagetes tenuifolia 'Starfire' mixed

Tagetes erecta 'Snowdrift'

Tagetes patula 'Safari Tangerine'

Chaenactis fremontii Gray (*Compositae-Helenieae*) A winter annual with entire or pinnatifid leaves and white or pinkish flowerheads, native of California in the Mojave and Colorado deserts, and eastwards to S Nevada, SW Utah and W Arizona, growing in sandy places, flowering in March–May. Stems 10–40cm, glandular-hairy. Leaves 2–5cm long. Flowerheads around 2.5cm across. A common plant in the S Californian deserts, unusual in that the outer florets are enlarged and lobed, more like scabious flowers than daisies.

Gaillardia pulchella Foug. (*Compositae-Helenieae*) **Blanket Flower, Indian Blanket** A spring annual with flowerheads yellow with a purple base or wholly purple, and a domed disc, native of N Mexico and SE Arizona to Colorado, Nebraska and Louisiana, growing in sandy plains and deserts, especially on roadsides, flowering in June–August. Stems 20–60cm, roughly hairy. Lower leaves 4–8cm long, toothed, upper entire. Flowerheads 2.5–5cm across, double and red-flowered in 'Red Plume'. *G. aristata* Pursh is a much larger perennial from the E Rockies.

Layia platyglossa (Fisch. & Mey.) Gray (*Compositae-Helenieae*) **Tidy Tips** A winter annual with prostrate stems and rich yellow flowers with pale, toothed edges, native of California and Baja California, growing in grassy places near the coast, flowering in May–June. Stems rather succulent, 10–30cm long. Lower leaves jaggedly toothed. Flowerheads around 3.5cm across. Subsp. *campestris* Keck, syn. *L. elegans* Torr. & Gray is more upright, to 50cm and has greyer green leaves; it is found mostly on the coastal plains. *L. glandulosa* (Hook.) Hook. & Arn. is a desert annual with red stems and white flowers fading to pink.

Tagetes erecta L. (*Compositae-Helenieae*) **African Marigold** A stout, upright annual with pinnate leaves and large, yellow to orange flowers, native of Mexico and Central America, growing in open ground, flowering in late summer and autumn. Stems to 1.5m, lower in most cultivars. Leaves with 11–17 lanceolate segments. Flowerheads 5–12cm across.

'Snowdrift' A fine, double-flowered, slightly creamy white. Stems to 30cm. 'Vanilla' is similar, with flowerheads 7.5cm across.

Tagetes patula L. **French Marigold**
A branching annual with pinnate leaves and
large, yellow to orange flowers, native of
Mexico and Central America, growing in
open ground, flowering in late summer and
autumn. Stems to 1.5m, lower in most
cultivars. Flowerheads 5–12cm across. Rays
8–10mm.

'Jolly Jester' Flowers single, red and yellow
striped; stems to 60cm. 'Striped Marvel' is
similar, but has stems to 75cm.

'Safari Tangerine' The 'Safari' series are
dwarf plants to 25cm, and quick to flower
from seed. They are available in separate
shades from scarlet to primrose, as well as
in a mixture.

Tagetes tenuifolia Cav., syn. *T. signata*
Bartling **Signet Marigold** A branching and
spreading summer annual with small, yellow
flowers marked with red, native from Mexico
to Colombia, growing in dry, rocky places,
flowering in October–December. Stems
30–80cm. Leaves with 13–23 linear-lanceolate
segments. Rays 7–8mm.

'Starfire' mixed Flowers similar to the wild
type or unmarked, in various shades of red
and orange; plant more compact, to 20cm.

Thymophylla tenuiloba (DC.) Small, syn.
Dyssodia tenuiloba (DC.) Robinson
(*Compositae-Helenieae*) **Dahlberg Daisy**,
Golden Fleece A bushy summer annual,
biennial or short-lived perennial, with finely
divided leaves and small, yellow flowers, native
of Texas and Mexico, growing in dry, rocky
places, flowering in late summer. Stems
10–15cm. Leaves with filiform segments.
Flowerheads around 2cm across. Easily grown
from plants germinated in warm conditions,
around 20°C.

Trichoptilium incisum (Gray) Gray
(*Compositae-Helenieae*) A much-branched
winter and summer annual with woolly,
toothed leaves and small, yellow, button
flowers, native of California in the Colorado
and Mojave deserts, S Nevada, W Arizona
and Baja California, growing in dry, sandy
flats, flowering in February–May and also in
October–November. Stems 5–20cm.
Flowerheads around 1cm across. This is one of
an interesting group of quick-growing annuals
which germinates both after the winter rains
which come from California and after
summer rains originating in Mexico.

Tagetes tenuifolia growing wild in central Mexico between Guadeljara and Zacatecas in October

French marigold 'Jolly Jester' at Suttons

African Marigolds at The Villa Pallavicino

Ursinia cakilefolia

Ursinia calenduliflora

Cotula barbata at Kamieskroom

Cladanthus arabicus

Chrysanthemum carinatum Schousboe
(*Compositae-Anthemideae*) **Annual
Chrysanthemum** An annual with bright
yellow flowers with red, brown or white bands
of colour around the centre, native of
Morocco, growing in cornfields, flowering in
June–August. Stems to 45cm. All leaves finely
divided into thread-like segments.
Flowerheads 6–8cm across, in a good range
of colours in recent varieties. Double-flowered
forms have been long cultivated. Easily
grown from seed planted outdoors in spring.
'Polar Star' is a lovely white variety with a
dark centre.

Chrysanthemum coronarium L.
An upright annual with pale yellow flowers,
sometimes with darker bands, native of the
Mediterranean area eastwards to NW Iran,
growing in waste ground and grassy places at
up to 300m, flowering in March–June. Stems
15–70cm. Lower leaves 2- or 3-pinnatifid,
upper flat with long, narrow teeth.
Flowerheads 4–7cm across, the rays
7.5–10mm wide. An easily grown annual, long
popular in cottage gardens, and grown as a
vegetable in China, called "chop suey greens".
'Zebra' is a richly coloured variety.

Chrysanthemum segetum L. **Corn
Marigold** An upright annual with bluish,
fleshy leaves and bright yellow flowers, native
of the E Mediterranean area, but an ancient
weed of arable fields, and now found in North
Africa and throughout Europe as far north
and west as Scotland and Ireland. Stems
20–60cm. Lower leaves pinnatifid with

Ursinia cakilefolia, with deep purple *Lapeyrousia,* yellow and white *Nemesia,* mauve *Senecio* and
other annuals on Glenlyon, Nieuwoudtville

toothed lobes, upper leaves almost undivided, amplexicaul. Flowerheads 4–5cm across. An attractive plant, formerly a common weed in W Ireland and Scotland, and on acidic, sandy soils in England.

Cladanthus arabicus (L.) Cass. (*Compositae-Anthemideae*) A spreading, aromatic annual with yellow flowers surrounded by bract-like leaves, native of S Spain and western North Africa, growing in open fields, flowering in April–June. Stems to 30cm, with new branches emerging from just below the flowers. Leaves with linear or trifid lobes. Flowerheads around 4cm across. An attractive and unusual plant, the flowerheads appearing to sit in a mass of narrow leaves.

Cotula barbata DC. (*Compositae-Anthemideae*) A dwarf winter annual with hairy, dissected leaves and white or yellow, rayless flowers, native of South Africa in the Western Cape from Namaqualand to Clanwilliam, growing in dry, bare, sandy and pebbly places, flowering in July–October. Stems slender, wiry to 10cm. Leaves pinnatifid, with thread-like segments. Flowerheads 8–10mm across. Of around 100 species of *Cotula*, about a quarter are found in the Cape region of South Africa. Nearly all are dwarf annuals and a few have short rays.

Ursinia cakilefolia DC. (*Compositae-Anthemideae*) A delicate winter annual with finely divided leaves and orange flowers with a dark, shining disc, native of South Africa from Namaqualand to Clanwilliam, the Piketberg and the W Karoo, growing on sandy plains and hills, flowering in July–October. Stems 6–45cm. Leaves 2-pinnatifid. Flowerheads 2.5–3.5cm across; outer florets with white, papery, petal-like pappus in seed.

Ursinia calenduliflora DC. A winter annual with finely divided leaves and orange flowers with a dark ring at the base, native of South Africa in Namaqualand, growing in sandy places, flowering in July–October. Stems to 36cm. Leaves pinnate, with linear segments. Flowerheads 2–5cm across; outer florets with white, papery, petal-like pappus in seed.

Chrysanthemum coronarium near Algeciras in southwestern Spain, in April

Chrysanthemum carinatum

Chrysanthemum coronarium 'Zebra' at Wisley

Chrysanthemum segetum, wild on Arran

Chrysanthemum coronarium with poppies and *Echium* in southwestern Spain

Dimorphotheca pluvialis 'Glistening White' at Quince House

Dimorphotheca pluvialis in the Karroo Botanic Garden, Worcester

Dimorphotheca sinuata

Tripteris hyoseroides

Calendula officinalis L. (*Compositae-Calenduleae*) **Marigold** An annual or short-lived perennial, with sticky, aromatic leaves and yellow flowers, native of the Mediterranean area but long cultivated, so that its native range is obscured. Stems spreading, to 1m long. Leaves wavy-edged but without teeth. Flowers, in unimproved varieties, 5–6cm across. Outer achenes long, incurved and nail-like. A very attractive plant, flowering almost continually, and good for cutting. The annual *C. arvensis* L. has smaller flowers, 1–2cm across. It is common as a weed in the Mediterranean area.

'Radio' An old cultivar, "new" to Carters Seeds in 1931, but still one of the best, with luminous orange, semi-double flowers 8–9cm across, on thick stems, less sticky and aromatic than the wild type. Rays around 8mm wide, with conspicuously pinked edges. A recent variety 'Golden Princess', not shown, has flowers with black centres.

Dimorphotheca pluvialis (L.) Moench, syn. *Calendula pluvialis* L. (*Compositae-Calenduleae*) **Rain Daisy** A quick-growing annual with narrow leaves and shining white flowers, native of Namibia and South Africa in the Western Cape southwards to Caledon and Riversdale, growing in dry, sandy soils, flowering in August–October. Stems 10–40cm. Leaves obovate to oblanceolate, sinuate-dentate, to 7cm long. Flowerheads 4–7cm across, the rays sometimes with a blue ring, purplish beneath. Fruits of 2 types, narrow, curved and knobbly, or flat and winged. Very beautiful and easily grown in an

open, airy site. In South Africa it germinates quickly after rain, but in wetter climates the flowers rot easily if the summer is rainy.

'Glistening White' With its dark centre, this is probably *D. pluvialis* var. *ringens*. 'Tetra Pole Star' is similar. A double-flowered variety was grown in the 1930s.

Dimorphotheca sinuata DC., syn. *D. aurantiaca* hort. non DC. A spreading winter annual with narrow leaves and shining, orange-yellow flowers, native of Angola, Namibia and South Africa in the Western Cape southwards to Clanwilliam, and naturalised in S California, growing in dry, sandy soils, flowering in August–October. Stems 10–30cm. Leaves obovate to oblanceolate, sinuate-dentate, to 5cm long. Flowerheads 4–5cm across, sometimes pale orange, buff or white, the rays with a dark bluish-black base and brownish beneath. Very beautiful and easily grown in an open, airy site.

Dimorphotheca tragus (Ait.) B. Nord., syn. *Castalis tragus* (Ait.) Norl., *D. aurantiaca* DC. is a perennial with oblanceolate leaves with a few jagged teeth and orange rays. *D. nudicaulis* (L.) B. Nord., is similar, with white rays. Both are found in rocky places in the mountains.

'Salmon Beauty' A variety with pale salmon-orange flowers, cultivated before 1930. Stems to 30cm. Flowers 5–6cm across.

Osteospermum pinnatum (Thunb.) Norlindh. (*Compositae-Calenduleae*) A winter annual with creeping stems, pinnate leaves

Osteospermum pinnatum in sandy semi-desert east of Nieuwoudtville

Calendula officinalis, close to the wild type

Calendula officinalis 'Radio'

Osteospermum pinnatum near Springbok

and shining, buff-orange, yellow or white flowers, native of Namibia and South Africa in the Western Cape southwards to Clanwilliam and Malmesbury, growing in dry, sandy soils, flowering in September–October. Stems 10–40cm long. Leaves with narrow, pointed lobes, to 3cm long. Flowerheads 4–5cm across, the rays with a dark bluish-black base and dark beneath. Fruits with spiny edges. One of the most beautiful species in the spring flora of Namaqualand.

Tripteris hyoseroides DC. syn. *Osteospermum hyoseroides* (DC) Norl. (*Compositae-Calenduleae*) An aromatic, sticky-hairy winter annual with orange-yellow flowers with a dark centre, native of South Africa in Namaqualand and around Calvinia, growing in dry, sandy soils, flowering in August–October. Stems 10–30cm. Leaves oblanceolate, sinuate-dentate, amplexicaul, to 10cm long. Flowerheads 3–5cm across, in loose groups, sometimes yellow to orange, the base of the rays and the disc florets dark bluish-black. Fruits with 3 wings. Sometimes sold with the name 'Gaiety'. The most recent works seem to keep the genus *Tripteris* distinct from *Osteospermum.*

Dimorphotheca sinuata 'Salmon Beauty'

Dimorphotheca sinuata in southern California

Arctotis venusta by the side of the road, near Ladysmith, with leaves of naturalised *Cosmos*

Arctotheca calendula (L.) Levyns (*Compositae-Arctotideae*) **Cape weed**
A sprawling annual or perennial with irregularly divided leaves and pale yellow flowers, native of South Africa from Clanwilliam to the Peninsula and eastwards to Natal, growing in sandy places, especially along the coast, and naturalised in Spain, flowering from early spring to midsummer. Stems to 15cm. Leaves whitish-hairy beneath. Flowerheads to 6cm across, with a ridged stalk, the centre of the rays often darker yellow, and the disc florets black.

Arctotis fastuosa Jacq. (*Compositae-Arctotideae*)   A robust winter annual with woolly buds and orange or white flowers with a dark ring in the centre, native of South Africa from Namaqualand southwards to Clanwilliam, growing in sandy and gravelly places in succulent scrub, flowering in July–September. Stems to 60cm. Leaves deeply lobed and whitish-hairy beneath. Flowerheads 5–7cm across, the outer bracts with short, hairy tails.
A striking and easily grown plant. The white form is sometimes called var. ***alba* 'Zulu Prince'**.

Arctotis fastuosa near Lamberts Bay, South Cape in October

Arctotis × hybrida 'Harlequin Hybrids'

Arctotis fastuosa

Arctotis fastuosa var. *alba* 'Zulu Prince'

Arctotis hirsuta at Kirstenbosch

Arctotis hirsuta (Harv.) Beauv. A hairy winter annual with orange, yellow or white flowers with a yellow ring round the blackish centre, native of South Africa from Malmesbury southwards to the Peninsula growing in sandy places especially near the coast, flowering in August–October. Stems to 45cm. Leaves irregularly divided, stiffly hairy, silvery beneath. Flowerheads around 6cm across.

Arctotis × hybrida hort., syn. × *Venidioarctotis* A group of perennial hybrids, mainly between *A. venusta* and *A. fastuosa*. The plants are sprawling; the leaves are usually greyish, the flowers from red to orange, purple, pink or white. The **'Harlequin Hybrids'** have flowers of muted shades, and some named varieties are propagated by cuttings. Some of the 'Harlequin New Hybrids' have flowers with black rings in the centre.

Arctotis venusta Norl. An annual or short-lived perennial with greyish leaves and white flowers with a blue centre, native of South Africa from E Namaqualand southwards to Bushmanland and the Eastern Cape to Natal, growing in sandy places and roadsides, flowering in August–January. Stems to 75cm. Leaves irregularly divided, softly hairy, silvery beneath. Flowerheads around 5cm across, sometimes pinkish or orange. *A. stoechadifolia* Berg. is similar, but generally creeping and mat-forming.

Gazania lichtensteinii Less. (*Compositae-Arctotideae*) A mat-forming annual with toothed leaves and golden-yellow flowers, with a spot at the base of each ray, native of Namibia and South Africa from Namaqualand to the Karoo, growing in dry, sandy and rocky places, flowering in August–September. Stems to 20cm, with milky sap. Leaves leathery with bristly edges. Flowerheads to 2–3.5cm across. Seed heads with smooth, green, cup-like bracts. This is the most common of the 3 annual gazanias, the larger, more showy species being perennial.

Gazania hybrids Most of the cultivated gazanias are long-lived perennials, which will not tolerate frost and wet. Some of the modern strains are grown as annuals, and will flower in the summer from seed sown in early spring. Good colours may then be overwintered as cuttings. Sow the seed at 15–18°C in early spring, and put out the plants in the hottest and sunniest place in the garden. The **'Daybreak'** series are available in separate colours or as a mixture, both as seed and as young plants. 'Sunshine Mixture' also has well-marked, spectacular flowers.

Gorteria diffusa Thunb. (*Compositae-Arctotideae*) **Beetle Daisy** A mat-forming annual with narrow, rolled leaves and orange flowers, with a beetle-like blotch at the base of some or all the rays, native of Namibia and South Africa from Namaqualand to the Karoo and Swellendam, growing in dry clay and rocky places, flowering in August–October. Stems to 30cm long. Leaves white, felted beneath. Flowerheads to 2–2.5cm across. Seed heads starry, with narrow, pointed bracts. An amazing plant, with flowers looking as if they are being visited by shiny, black beetles.

Gazania 'Daybreak' series

Gazania lichtensteinii

Arctotheca calendula in a semi-desert area of Nieuwoudtville

Gorteria diffusa east of Nieuwoudtville

Gazania lichtensteinii, with *Aloe dichotoma*, north of Nieuwoudtville

Rafinesquia neomexicana

Rafinesquia neomexicana with *Eschscholzia* and *Phacelia minor* above San Andreas Canyon

Malacothrix glabrata in the Mojave Desert

Hispidella hispanica in pine forest above Arenas de San Pedro in the Sierra de Gredos, central Spain

Crepis rubra L. (*Compositae-Lactuceae*) A dandelion-like annual with pink or white flowers, native of SE Europe from S Italy to Greece and Turkey, growing in grassy, rocky places, flowering in April–June. Stems from a rosette of hairy leaves, to 40cm. Flowerheads around 4cm across. An unusual plant for a sunny position. *C. incana* Sibth. & Sm. is rather similar, but is a perennial alpine species confined to S Greece.

Hispidella hispanica Barnades ex Lam. (*Compositae-Lactuceae*) A hairy annual with pale yellow flowers with a dark centre, native of C Spain and N Portugal, growing in sandy and rocky places, flowering in April–July. Stems to 20cm. Leaves entire, linear, linear-oblanceolate or spathulate. Stem thickening below the flower. Flowerheads around 3cm across, the inner florets purple, the outer reddish on the back. Striking with its bicoloured flowers.

Senecio cakilefolius, with *Heliophila*, *Ursinia* and a fascinating array of other annuals at Padstal Farm, Nieuwoudtville

Crepis rubra at the Chelsea Physic Garden

Tolpis barbata

Senecio elegans with *Diascia rigescens* and *Chorisema ilicifolium*

Steirodiscus tagetes at Kirstenbosch

Senecio cakilefolius, near Sutherland

Malacothrix glabrata Gray (*Compositae-Lactuceae*) **Desert Dandelion** A pale yellow annual dandelion native of the deserts of California eastwards to Idaho, Nebraska and Arizona, growing in open, sandy areas, flowering in April–June. Stems branched, 10–40cm. Leaves hairless, pinnatifid, with linear lobes. Flowerheads to 5cm across. This often covers large areas, especially after winters with heavy rain. *M. californica* DC, from the coast of S California up to the desert, is similar, but has leaves woolly when young, and 1 flower per stem.

Rafinesquia neomexicana Nutt. (*Compositae-Lactuceae*) A rather fleshy annual with hollow stems and white, dandelion-like flowers, native of the deserts of California eastwards to Utah and Texas, growing in canyons and dry scrub, flowering in February–May. Stems branched above, 20–150cm. Stem leaves much divided, auriculate, amplexicaul, the upper very small. Flowerheads to 6cm across. *R. californica* Nutt., from W California, has smaller, pure white flowers.

Senecio cakilefolius DC (*Compositae-Senecioneae*) A small, winter annual with branched stems and purplish or magenta flowers, native of Namibia and South Africa in the Western Cape southwards to Clanwilliam, growing in fields and sandy places, flowering in July–October. Stems to 30cm, but usually less. Leaves lobed. Flowers 1.5–1.8cm across, with rather few rays. A very common plant which can colour whole valleys with pinkish-purple.

Senecio elegans L. **Wild Cineraria** A tall, winter annual with branched stems and magenta flowers, native of South Africa in the Cape from Nieuwoudtville southwards to the Peninsula and eastwards to Port Elizabeth, growing in sandy places especially near the coast, flowering in July–March. Stems 30–150cm. Leaves deeply lobed. Flowers 1.5–2.0cm across, with many rays. An easily grown plant like a purple ragwort, good for early flowering in an unheated greenhouse.

Steirodiscus tagetes (L.) Schltr. (*Compositae-Senecioneae*) A delicate annual with yellow flowers, native of South Africa in the Western Cape from the Pikctberg to the Peninsula, growing in sandy places, flowering in August–October. Stems 10–30cm. Leaves deeply dissected, with narrow segments. Flowers 1.5–2cm across, with narrow rays.

Tolpis barbata (L.) Gaertner. (*Compositae-Lactuceae*) A winter annual with pale yellow flowers often with a dark centre, and spreading, starry bracts, native of the Mediterranean area, growing in open woods and sandy fields, flowering in April–July. Stems to 80cm. Lower leaves lobed, upper entire, linear, often toothed. Stems slender, much-branched. Flowerheads around 4cm across, the inner florets purplish, the outer reddish on the back. An attractive annual for a sunny position.

Carlina vulgaris

Carthamus tinctorius

Xeranthemum annuum

Carlina vulgaris above Wastwater, in the Lake District

Carlina vulgaris L. (*Compositae-Cardueae*) **Carline Thistle** A small, spiny biennial with straw-coloured flowers, native of most of Europe eastwards to the Caucasus and NW Iran, growing on dry, grassy slopes and in open woods, flowering in June–September. Stems 20–30cm. Leaves whitish beneath. Flowers 1.5–2.5cm across, with a petal-like ring of stiff, papery, shining phyllaries. The genus *Carlina* consists of around 28 species, mainly perennials, all with the characteristic shining phyllaries.

Carthamus tinctorius L. (*Compositae-Cardueae*) **Safflower** A thistle-like annual with scarlet or orange flowers, long cultivated for its oil and as a red dye, and not known in the wild. Stems shining, white, 25–45cm. Leaves entire or spiny-edged. Flowerheads around 2cm across, produced in July–August. Seeds without pappus. The dried flowes are used as a substitute for, or an adulterant of, saffron (the styles of *Crocus sativus*). The oil from the seeds is used for painting. The wild *C. persicus* Willd. has bright yellow flowers and seeds with pappus, It is found in Turkey, Syria and Iraq.

Cirsium eriophorum (L.) Scop. (*Compositae-Cardueae*) **Woolly Thistle** A huge biennial, with long spines on the leaves, and large, rounded, woolly flowerheads, native of Europe from S England to Spain and eastwards to Poland and Greece, growing in fields and open woods, flowering in June–August. Stems to 2.5m. Heads around 5cm in diameter. Leaves deeply divided. Florets 2.5–4.4cm long. In England this species fo thistle is characteristic of chalk and limestone grassland. Other, closely related species are found as far east as the Himalayas.

Onopordum acanthium L. (*Compositae-Cardueae*) A very tall biennial thistle with greyish-white leaves and purple flowerheads, native of much of S Europe eastwards to European Russia, growing in open ground, flowering in July–September. Stems to 3m, with wide, spiny wings. Leaves shallowly toothed with wavy edges. Heads around 4cm in diameter, with linear bracts. Florets 2–2.5cm long. A very handsome plant, lending style and stature to any border. In cold, wet summers in NW Europe the seed may not ripen, but usually the plant will seed itself in the garden in subsequent years. Shown also on page 124.

Silybum marianum (L.) Gaertn. (*Compositae-Cardueae*) **Milk Thistle** A large, fleshy thistle with white-veined leaves, and long spines native of much of S Europe and naturalised elsewhere in Europe, and commonly in California, growing in open ground, flowering in May–September. Stems to 1.5m, usually glabrous. Leaves toothed, with wavy edges and long, white spines. Heads 2.5–4cm in diameter, with a ring of spiny bracts 2–5cm long around the flowerheads. Florets 2cm long. An attractive plant for u large garden, forming a large, flat rosette of marbled leaves in the first year.

Xeranthemum annuum L. (*Compositae-Cardueae*) A slender, greyish annual with pink, papery flowerheads, native of the Mediterranean region, eastwards to Turkey and N Iran, growing in open ground, on steppe and dunes flowering in June–September. Stems 5–60cm. Leaves linear-elliptic. Flowerheads around 2cm across, with a petal-like ring of stiff phyllaries. A modest, everlasting-type flower, easy to grow in full sun.

Onopordum acanthium with *Phlox* 'Mount Fuji' at Cothay Manor

Cirsium eriophorum near Sherbourne, Gloucestershire

Cirsium eriophorum

Silybum marianum

Silybum marianum with cosmos and *Cleome*

Centaurea depressa

Centaurea pullata in southwest Spain

Centaurea depressa between Isparta and Antayla, Turkey

Amberboa moschata mixed

Centaurea americana 'Aloha Blanca'

Amberboa moschata (L.) DC., syn.
Centaurea moschata L. (*Compositae-Cardueae*)
Sweet Sultan An annual or biennial with
divided upper leaves and large, pale mauve
flowers, native of the Transcaucasus and
NE Turkey, growing on dry hills around
Mount Ararat, at 1000–1060m, flowering in
May–July. Stems 20–60cm. Leaves nearly
glabrous, mostly deeply divided. Flowerheads
around 6cm across. Long cultivated in Turkey
and in N Europe for its soft and scented
flowers. It is now available in a range of
colours from yellow to white, purple and pink.
The 'Imperialis' series have stems around 1m.
The plants are very cold-hardy and can be
sown in autumn in dry, well-drained soil, or in
spring in areas with very wet winters.

Centaurea americana Nutt. **'Aloha Blanca'**
(*Compositae-Cardueae*) A tall, upright annual
with lanceolate leaves and white flowers,
native of the midwest, southwards to Arizona
and Mexico, where it grows on dry plains,
flowering in May–August. Stems to 1.8m.
Leaves to 12.5cm. Flowerheads 5–10cm
across, pink to purple in the wild, and in
'Aloha' and 'Lilac Charm'. Bracts with long,
finely serrate teeth. This should be a fine plant
for a mixed border or for a meadow planting.

Centaurea cyanus L. **Cornflower**
A tall, slender annual with narrow leaves and
bright, deep blue flowers, native probably of
Turkey, where it grows in pine forests and on
rocky slopes, but most common there and
elsewhere as a cornfield weed, flowering in
April (in the south) to August (in the north).
Stems to 80cm. Lower leaves lyrate or
lanceolate, upper linear-lanceolate or filiform.
Flowerheads 2–2.5cm across, with a ring of
tubular, deeply lobed ray florets.

The wild form is an attractive plant;
cultivars have larger flowers, in a variety of
colours, with more numerous ray florets.

Some of the more striking cultivars shown
here include **'Baby Blue'**, dwarf, stems to
30cm; **'Black Ball'**, flowers double, dark
maroon, stems to 1m; **'Blue Diadem'** flowers
double, stems to 1m; **'Frosty' mixed** some
flowers with a white rim on the florets, to
50cm; **'Polka Dot' mixed** stems dwarf and
bushy, to 40cm.

Centaurea depressa M. Bieb. A spreading
and much-branched spring annual with
white-woolly leaves and blue and purple
flowers, native of Turkey eastwards to the
Himalayas and Central Asia, and naturalised
in SE Europe, growing in cornfields and waste
places, flowering in May–August. Stems

Centaurea cyanus 'Black Ball' with
Helichrysum petiolare

Centaurea cyanus and *Matricaria perforata*
growing wild in a cornfield in Spain

Cornflower 'Frosty' mixed

10–60cm. Leaves around 1cm wide. Flowerheads around 2.5cm across, with slightly shorter ray florets than *C. cyanus*. A very attractive plant which I grew for many years in a bulb frame in SE England, before it died out in a series of wet summers.

Centaurea pullata L.   An annual or short-lived perennial with very short stems and bright purple flowers, native of Spain, Portugal and western North Africa, naturalised elsewhere in the Mediterranean area, growing in dry, stony places, flowering in April–June. Stems 5–50cm. Leaves entire or lyrate, the upper surrounding the flower. Flowerheads 3–5cm across. An attractive dwarf for a sunny place.

Matricaria perforata Merat, syn. *Tripleurospermum inodorum* (L.) Schulz Bip. (*Compositae-Anthemideae*) **Scentless Mayweed**   An upright spring or summer annual with finely divided leaves and white, daisy-like flowers, native of most of Europe, eastwards to Central Asia, growing in waste places and cornfields, flowering in May–September. Stems 30–80cm, usually branched, at least in the upper part. Leaf segments very narrow and soft, glabrous. Flowerheads 3–4.5cm across. A common and pretty annual weed, always welcome when it appears in my garden. *M. maritima* L. is a biennial or perennial with spreading stems and larger flowers. It is most common near the sea.

Cornflowers in Eccleston Square

'Baby Blue'

'Polka Dot' mixed

'Frosty' mixed

'Blue Diadem'

Specimens from Eccleston Square July 3rd ⅖ life-size

Panicum miliaceum 'Violaceum' with *Cerinthe major*

Asphodelus fistulosus near Seville in SW Spain

Lagurus ovatus near Santander in NW Spain

Eleusine indica

Aegilops triuncialis L. (*Graminae*)
An annual grass with long, spreading awns, native of S Europe, North Africa, Turkey and the Transcaucasus, growing in dry, stony places, flowering in April–May. Stems to 45cm. Lower leaf sheaths hairy. Spike 3–6cm, gradually narrowed towards the top. Awns of terminal spikelet around 3–6cm, longer than those of the other spikelets. The genus *Aegilops* is striking for its awns. *A. speltoides* Tausch. and *A. squarrosa* L. genomes are included in early and modern wheats (*Triticum* spp.) in the Middle East and elsewhere.

Asphodelus fistulosus L. (*Asphodelaceae*)
A winter annual or short-lived perennial, with hollow leaves and small, white, starry flowers, native of Portugal and the Mediterranean area, growing on dry, rocky hills, flowering in April–May. Stems 15–70cm. Leaves 3–35cm. Flowers 1–2.4cm across. This is one of the few annual members of the petaloid monocotyledons, which include mostly bulbs and perennials with thickened roots or rhizomes.

Briza maxima L. (*Graminae*) **Greater Quaking Grass** An upright grass with few large, hanging spikelets, native of the Mediterranean area, and commonly naturalised in California, growing in dry, rocky places and roadsides, flowering in April–May. Stems 10-60cm. Spikelets 1.4–2.5cm long, often purplish. *B. minor* L., from S and W Europe, has very numerous, small (3–5mm) spikelets in a much-branched inflorescence. Both are good for drying.

Eleusine indica (L.) Gaertner (*Graminae*)
A robust annual with upright, slender spikes, native of the tropics, but widely naturalised elsewhere, flowering in summer. Stems 15–85cm, Spikes 5–12, 3.5–15cm long. Easily grown in rich soil in warm, moist conditions.

Hordeum jubatum L. (*Graminae*)
A perennial barley, often grown as an annual, with long, purplish, silvery awns, native of NE Asia and Alaska to Mexico, and naturalised in Europe and E North America, growing in waste places and alkaline pastures, flowering in May–July. Stems 20–60cm. Leaf sheaths hairy. Spike 3–8cm long, with awns 2–10cm long. A lovely grass, for a position where the sun can shine through it.

Lagurus ovatus L. (*Graminae*) **Hare's Tail**
A tufted winter annual with oval, fluffy heads, native of the Mediterranean area, growing mainly in sandy soils near the sea, flowering in April–June. Stems 8–50cm. Upper sheaths inflated. Spikes 0.5–6cm long. Easily grown and pretty in a mass.

Panicum miliaceum L. **'Violaceum'** (*Graminae*) **Purple Millet** A large summer annual with purple leaves and purple spikelets in nodding heads, native of China and E Asia, but widely naturalised elsewhere, often from bird seed. Stems to 1.2m. Leaves 1–2cm across. Spikelets 4–5.5mm. The normal form is all-green.

Hordeum jubatum, used for summer bedding at Wisley

Aegilops triuncialis near the ruins of Termessos, Antalya

Briza maxima, becoming a weed at Quince House, Devon

Index

INDEX

INDEX